Later Phases of the Family Cycle

The International Union for the Scientific Study of Population Problems was set up in 1928, with Dr Raymond Pearl as President. At that time the Union's main purpose was to promote international scientific co-operation to study the various aspects of population problems, through national committees and through the work of individual members. In 1947 the International Union for the Scientific Study of Population (IUSSP) was reconstituted in its present form. It expanded it activities to:

- stimulate research on population
- develop interest in demographic matters among governments, national and international organizations, scientific bodies, and the general public
- foster relations between people involved in population studies
- disseminate scientific knowledge on population.

The principal ways in which the IUSSP currently achieves its aims are:

- organization of worldwide or regional conferences and operations of scientific committees under the responsibility of the Council
- organization of training courses
- publication of conference proceedings and committee reports.

Demography can be defined by its field of study and its analytical methods. Accordingly, it can be regarded as the scientific study of human populations with respect to their size, their structure, and their development. For reasons which are related to the history of the discipline, the demographic method is essentially inductive: progress results from the improvement of observations, more sophisticated methods of measurement, and the search for regularities and stable factors which lead to the formulation of explanatory models. In summary, the three objectives of demographic analysis are to describe, measure, and analyse.

International Studies in Demography is the outcome of an agreement concluded by the IUSSP and the Oxford University Press. This joint series is expected to reflect the broad range of the Union's activities and, in the first instance, will be based on the seminars organized by the Union. The Editorial Board of the series consists of:

LATER PHASES OF THE FAMILY CYCLE

Demographic Aspects

---

edited by

E. GREBENIK

C. HÖHN

R. MACKENSEN

CLARENDON PRESS · OXFORD

1989

Oxford University Press, Walton Street, Oxford OX2 6DP
Oxford New York Toronto
Delhi Bombay Calcutta Madras Karachi
Petaling Jaya Singapore Hong Kong Tokyo
Nairobi Dar es Salaam Cape Town
Melbourne Auckland
and associated companies in
Berlin Ibadan

Oxford is a trade mark of Oxford University Press

Published in the United States
by Oxford University Press, New York

British Library Cataloguing in Publication Data
Later phases of the family cycle:
demographic aspects—(International
studies in demography).
1. Families. demographic aspects
I. Grebenik, E. II. Höhn, C.
III. Mackensen, R. IV. Series
306.8′5
ISBN 0-19-828657-0

Library of Congress Cataloging in Publication Data
Later phases of the family cycle: demographic aspects
Edited by E. Grebenik, C. Höhn, R. Mackensen.
1. Family demography—Cross-cultural studies. 2. Life cycle, Human—Cross-cultural studies. I. Grebenik, E. II. Höhn, Charlotte. III. Mackensen, Rainer, 1927–
HQ759.98.A38 1989 306.8′5—dc19 88-19622
ISBN 0-19-828657-0

Typeset by Cotswold Typesetting Limited, Gloucester, UK
Printed and bound in Great Britain by
Biddles Limited, Guildford and King's Lynn

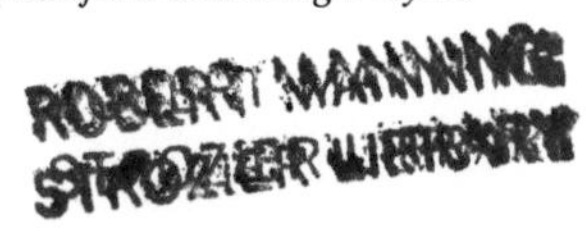

Preface

In 1982 the International Union for the Scientific Study of Population convened a committee with the remit of elaborating the essential aspects of family demography. Its terms of reference included the family life cycle (it was called 'the Committee on Family Demography and the Life Cycle'). When the Committee was founded, the Union may have been under the impression that the study of the life cycle would be one of its easier tasks. This view proved to be mistaken, however, as will become evident from a study of the papers collected in the present volume.

The Committee began its work by asking a number of experts to draft chapters for a textbook on family demography, its concepts and applications. These drafts were discussed at a Workshop held in New York in December 1983, and were subsequently revised and prepared for publication[1]. To follow up this work, the Committee intended to organize two additional seminars which would be devoted respectively to the early and to the later phases of the life cycle. For a number of reasons only the second of these seminars was held, in West Berlin in September 1984. The chapters that follow consist of selected and revised versions of papers discussed at that seminar, and deal with divorce, widowhood, remarriage, the departure of children from the parental home, kinship networks, and the living arrangements of the elderly.

[1] J. Bongaarts, T. Burch, and K. Wachter (eds.), *Family Demography: Concepts and Applications* (Oxford, 1987).

Contents

Contributors

John Bongaarts	The Population Council
D. A. Coleman	Oxford University
Magdola Csernák	Demographic Research Institute, Budapest
Alice T. Day	Australian National University
Charlotte Höhn	Federal German Institute for Population Research, Wiesbaden
Kathleen Kiernan	City University, London
Rainer Mackensen	Technical University of Berlin
Marietta Pongrácz	Demographic Research Institute, Budapest
Michel Poulain	Université Catholique de Louvain
Louis Roussel	Institut National d'Études Démographiques, Paris
Karl Schwarz	Formerly of the Federal German Statistical Office, Wiesbaden
Peter Uhlenberg	University of North Carolina
Karl Ulrich Mayers	Max Planck Institute, Berlin
Richard Wall	Cambridge Group for the History of Population and Social Structure
Christabel M. Young	Australian National University

1 Introduction

CHARLOTTE HÖHN *Federal German Institute for Population Research, Wiesbaden*

and RAINER MACKENSEN *Technical University of Berlin*

Family demography is a relatively new aspect of population studies. In 1979 Hervé Le Bras wrote, in a study of household and family statistics undertaken for OECD: 'Married life punctuated by marriage and divorce, procreative life marked by birth, and life itself ending in death, are three chapters of demography, whereas all these events are experienced in families.'[1] Le Bras's implied criticism is based on the observation that few textbooks on population contain a special chapter on the demography of families. Where such a chapter does exist, it is generally shorter and more superficial than those concerned with fertility, mortility, nuptiality, and migration, or with the dynamics of age structure.

There are good reasons for this neglect of family demography. Traditional demographic analysis of events such as births, marriages, divorces, deaths, and migration has the advantage that numbers of these events can be related to exposure to risk of these events in different age groups, and thus be measured more easily, and the results included in models. The inclusion of other members of the family in such analyses causes difficulties, because they will normally differ in age and sex, and also because they do not generally live together continuously. Family and household size vary with time: a family is founded, grows, contracts, and is dissolved within the lifetime of each member. To cope with these difficulties, much more complex methods and analyses are required. Some of the difficulties can be overcome by using micro-simulation methods, but data, particularly many important sets of transition probabilities between different states, are generally lacking. There is thus a continuing reluctance to include family variables in demographic studies, and such variables tend to be disregarded as potential explanations of demographic developments. But, as Le Bras noted, almost all demographic events occur within a family context, and it seems reasonable to assume that the occurrence and frequency of such events will, at least in part, depend on the structure of the family.

During the last ten years or so, there has been a plethora of formal

[1] H. Le Bras, *Child and Family: Demographic Developments in the OECD Countries* (Paris, 1979), p. 52.

methodological as well as substantive descriptive studies of the family. Two very valuable studies of the present position and problems of family demography have been published.[2] Both stress that the subject forms one of the less developed aspects of demography. This is less true of the concept of the family life cycle, which has been studied for at least 40 years. Paul Glick published his first paper on the 'family cycle', as he called it, as early as 1947. His work was influenced by a number of predecessors, who had, however, generally worked in disciplines other than demography. Glick was the first demographer to concern himself with the concept of the family life cycle, and throughout his life continued to develop and refine this concept.[3] Besides providing aggregate data which could be used for empirical studies, his main contribution lay in the substitution of longitudinal for period analysis in a paper which he published jointly with Parke in 1965. At the time cohort analysis was widely used in demographic studies, and the concept also appealed to sociologists and historians, who had for some time been conducting research into life courses. This was the principal reason which led Glick to apply cohort analysis to the study of the family life cycle.[4] It does not, however, imply general acceptance of the concept of the family life cycle.[5]

In this volume we shall use the term 'demography' in a wide sense, to include both formal and social demography. The reader who expects to find only formal analyses or masses of internationally comparable data is likely to be disappointed. There are several reasons for this: the lack of empirical data, particularly those which can be compared between countries, wariness on the part of a number of authors of an over-ambitious empiricism which lacks a theoretical foundation, and, last but not least, a shortage of researchers who are trained in the formal demography of the family. On the other hand, the volume is not confined to sociological theoretical considerations. It is a compromise between formal and social demography: indeed, the subject of family demography needs both approaches.

An unfortunate example of naïve empiricism is provided by those

[2] J. Bongaarts, 'The Formal Demography of Families and Households: An Overview', *IUSSP Newsletter*, 17 (1983); T. Burch, 'Household and Family Demography: A Bibliographic Essay', *Population Index*, 45 (1979)

[3] P. C. Glick, 'The Family Cycle', *American Sociological Review*, 12(2) (1947); 'The Life Cycle of the Family', *Marriage and Family Living*, 17(1) (1955); *American Families* (New York, 1975); 'Family Statistics', in P. M. Hauser and O. D. Duncan (eds.), *The Study of Population* (Chicago, 1959); 'Demographic Analysis of Family Data', in H. T. Christensen (ed.), *Handbook of Marriage and the Family* (Chicago, 1964); 'Updating the Life Cycle of the Family', *Journal of Marriage and the Family*, 39(1) (1977); P. C. Glick and R. Parke, Jr., 'New Approaches in Studying the Life Cycle of the Family', *Demography*, 2 (1965).

[4] E. M. Duvall, *Family Development* (Philadelphia, 1957); R. Hill and D. Hansen, 'The Identification of Conceptual Frameworks Utilized in Family Study', *Marriage and Family Living*, 22(4) (1960); R. Hill and R. Rodgers, 'The Developmental Approach', in Christensen, op. cit. (n. 3).

[5] C. Höhn, *Der Familienzyklus: Zur Notwendigkeit einer Konzepterweiterung* (Boppard, 1982); 'The Family Life Cycle: Needed Extensions of the Concept', in J. Bongaarts, T. Burch, and K. Wachter (eds.), *Family Demography: Methods and their Applications* (Oxford, 1987).

researchers (not represented in this book) who use data for different countries without looking carefully at their definitions. This is particularly dangerous where family and household statistics are concerned. Though the international agencies involved in the collection and dissemination of data make every effort to ensure that the information they produce is comparable, definitions of family and household remain highly divergent.[6] The family may be regarded as the basic reproductive unit, and kinship as a network of families, including single persons related to a family. Households may be larger or smaller than families, and are normally defined by the criterion of co-residence or commensality.[7] Demographers have often been forced to accept these definitions because they are used in the collection and tabulation of statistical data which form the basis of their work. But if we are to be clear about the basic concepts, it will be necessary to distinguish between the concepts themselves and the indicators which we are forced to use in the absence of better data. Burch has reported discussions on this point.[8] Laslett has regarded the household as a unit which includes the family,[9] but Wheaton has hesitated to differentiate at all between the household and the family.[10]

We shall find it useful to begin by disregarding the concept of the household altogether, until we have achieved a more precise definition of the family. Only then will it be profitable to ask whether the concept 'household' adds to our understanding of the family, and to consider whether the definition of either needs to be modified. Bongaarts has criticized both the delimitation of the family by an all-embracing household concept[11] and the use of marriage as a defining factor. He pleads for a more differentiated study of marriage (including cohabitation), marital disruption, and remarriage, and of relations between kin which do not depend on membership of the same household. He suggests a sequence of concepts which could be used in differentiating the different units:

- the *conjugal couple*, not necessarily constituted by a formal marriage, but who live in conjugal union, with formal marriage as an additional characteristic;
- the *nuclear family* as defined by the United Nations, consisting of a conjugal couple or a single parent, together with their unmarried children, but who do not necessarily live in the same household (which is violating the UN criterion of co-residence);

[6] A comprehensive analysis of discrepancies in such definitions is provided by Le Bras, op. cit. (n. 1).

[7] United Nations, *Principles and Recommendations for Population and Housing Censuses* (New York, 1980).

[8] Op. cit. (n. 2).

[9] P. Laslett and R. Wall (eds.), *Household and Family in Past Time* (Cambridge, 1972).

[10] R. Wheaton, 'Family and Kinship in Western Europe: The Problem of the Joint Family Household', *Journal of Interdisciplinary History*, 5(4) (1974–5)

[11] Bongaarts, op. cit. (n. 2).

- the *family*, consisting of members of a household related by blood, marriage, or adoption (i.e. the UN definition), including any unmarried children who have left the parental household but are still financially dependent on their parents;
- the *household*, a residential and economic unit, which can contain a family or families (e.g. a three-generation family, just one nuclear family, or a family of two sisters) and which might then be called a 'family household', or no family at all (e.g. one-person households, or a childless conjugal couple);
- the *kin group*, a concept which Bongaarts leaves undefined, though he obviously means to refer to the 'extended family', i.e. the family as defined above, together with members of the families of origin of both spouses, and their descendants, irrespective of co-residence.

Even if this classification were to be used consistently, a number of problems would remain. Does the household form part of the definition of the family, or is it a separate category, which may or may not overlap with the family? If the latter view were accepted, some difficulties—particularly those associated with the existence of formal marriage—could be overcome. If formal marriage were to be regarded as an additional characteristic of the conjugal couple, there is no reason why the couple should be defined in terms of co-residence or commensality. Some couples in conjugal unions today live in separate dwellings, and a small proportion of those who share a dwelling budget separately. This new life-style has already been studied under the title 'living apart together'. From a demographic point of view, the legal status of the couple, co-residence, or joint budgeting could be regarded as an additional modifying characteristic of the family, rather than forming part of its formal definition.

We shall also need to decide whether an inclusive series of concepts or one which follows a sequential logic is to be preferred. Provided that the 'household' is regarded as one characteristic which may define a family, Bongaarts's scheme is inclusive: each unit contains those which precede it in the list. But it is also based on a developmental sequence in the life of the family. The conjugal couple may be regarded as preceding the nuclear family in many cases, and the family and the kin group could develop from the nuclear family. But once again the concept of the household, or more specifically of co-residence, raises difficulties. As long as there is no general agreement on what constitutes a family or a household, it will be necessary to specify the definitions used in any particular study.

The central problem in using the concept of the family life cycle is that it refers only to the nuclear family: the married couple with children and without co-resident kin. The period between marriage and the dissolution of the nuclear family is divided into six phases, with seven transitions to mark the beginning and the end of each phase (Table 1.1). Elegant and illuminating though this classical concept may be, it is subject to some methodological difficulties.[12] Only the determination of the ages of parties at first marriage and the ages of the parents at the birth of their first child is relatively straightforward. The date of birth of the last child, the dates of the children's eventual marriage, and the date when they leave the parental home must normally be estimated, and such estimates require a number of assumptions. Nor is it simple to calculate the date of death of the first or that of the surviving spouse.

Table 1.1 The classical family life cycle

Phases	Transitions characterizing	
	Beginning	End
1. Formation	Marriage	Birth of first child
2. Extension	Birth of first child	Birth of last child
3. Completed extension	Birth of last child	First child leaves
4. Contraction	First child leaves	Last child leaves
5. Completed contraction	Last child leaves	First spouse dies
6. Dissolution	First spouse dies	Other spouse dies

Note: Phase 5 is called the 'empty-nest phase', or, preferably, the 'post-parental phase'.

These problems could be overcome by using biographical or longitudinal information; but there is another, which has so far hardly been given sufficient recognition. Glick's concept of the family life cycle is based on the explicit assumption that all members of a cohort marry, and that none of the marriages end by divorce or by death before the wife has reached the end of her reproductive period. This elimination of the possibility of early widowhood or divorce is not modified in the classical model by the possibility of remarriage. At first sight this appears logical: it is impossible to re-enter a marriage cohort by remarrying, for remarriage leads to membership of a new marriage cohort. Glick overcame this difficulty by confining his analysis in the models which he published in 1977 to first marriages. Although this made the population studied more homogeneous, it also narrowed the scope of his study. In some countries a large proportion of families are excluded if neither divorce nor remarriage is taken into account. The exclusion seems even more peculiar because later widowhood is always considered in the analysis of the family life cycle and is, indeed, regarded as important.

Childless marriages pose another difficulty for the stage-model of the family life cycle, particularly since they are by definition no family at all. Trost, who has been a severe critic of this concept, pours scorn on the 24-stage model constructed by Rodgers:

[12] Cf. n. 5.

However, Rodgers's scheme does not solve the problem of the couple who never have children. According to Rodgers's pattern, that couple begins in the first category and then has to jump over to the next-to-last category. There are some curious aspects in this solution, one of them being that the couple will never be anything but young or old . . . a family might be a beginning family until their fiftieth year of marriage; after that they jump to the next-to-last category, i.e. the aging couple.[13]

Childless 'families', therefore, stay in the 'empty-nest' stage throughout their lives. Glick 'solved' this problem by excluding childless families from his study in 1977. Even if the awkward phrase 'empty nest' is replaced by 'post-parental stage', childless couples remain logically excluded, because they never become parents.

However, the term 'post-parental stage' is to be preferred to 'empty-nest' for describing the period a married couple spend between the time when their last child has left the parental home and the death of the first spouse. Though 'empty nest' means nothing more than that the parents live in a separate household, it suggests that the parents have no relations with their children or grandchildren, but live entirely alone. The classical concept of the family life cycle gives the impression, at least, of portraying the isolated nuclear family in Parsons's sense, and of excluding relationships and contacts with other members of the family such as parents, grandparents, aunts, uncles, cousins, nephews or nieces. It is the reverse of helpful to suggest that no relationships with other family members exist, not even with adult children who have formed their own households. This lack of concern with family relations can only be remedied by the analysis of kin and other informal networks. To live on one's own does not imply complete isolation. Studies of kin networks must, therefore, form one of the most important aspects of the later stages of the family life cycle. This is particularly important, not only in the post-parental stage, but also when the surviving spouse must himself—or more often herself—decide on his or her place of residence, life-style, and relations with other members of the family.

Children, too, are neglected in the classical concept of the family life cycle. It is uncommon to consider the number of children in studies of the family life cycle. Generally, the dates of birth of the first and last child are known, though it is often more difficult to determine the latter date. But there are considerable difficulties when it comes to determining the age of the children at the time when they leave the parental home. Another unsolved problem relates to the number, duration, and position of single-parent families. Trost is explicit on this point:

The one-parent families are excluded, since they do not fit the existing family life cycles. All three types of one-parent families are non-fits: those resulting from divorce, those resulting from the death of one or the other spouse, and those that never have been

[13] J. Trost, 'The Family Life Cycle: A Problematic Approach', in J. Cusenier (ed.), *Le Cycle de la vie familiale dans les sociétés européennes* (Paris, 1977), pp. 468–9.

knitted into a marriage group (the unmarried mother or father with children). The first two of these families have belonged to the family life cycle, but have been removed from it at the time of dissolution.[14]

It will be generally agreed that such incomplete families should be included in any study of the family life cycle, especially because the post-parental stage in such families may occur earlier or later in their lives than in complete families, and may prove to be a more traumatic event for the single surviving parent than for the married couple.

To summarize: the principal objections to the classical concept of the family life cycle are the absence of consideration of divorce, early widowhood, remarriage, or incomplete families, and of matters relating to the post-parental stage—living conditions after the death of the first spouse, or in incomplete families after the children have achieved independence. All these topics need to be considered in a book devoted to the later stages of the life cycle. However, matters are not quite so simple, as Norman Ryder points out:

By definition, the individual is brought into being as a member of the junior generation of a nuclear family, called in the sociological literature his or her family of orientation. The first phase of life is exposure to the competing risks of death or passage. Subsequently, although the typical sequence involves early movement into what is called the individual's family of procreation, many individuals remain solo, and others (many) move back and forth between solo and familial residence throughout their lives.[15]

The concept of the family life cycle and its stages as put forward by Glick can lead to no further progress in either methodological or substantive studies. The most promising approach would seem to be to consider, not the 'family life cycle', but a set of life courses which would include the family life cycle. This concept is hardly innovative. A large number of models have been proposed, so that one obtains the impression of an almost uncontrolled proliferation. We do not mean to imply that these models are normally competing or even mutually exclusive, but that there are too many plausible models:

An individual's life course is multidimensional, since movements through successive life stages entail the concurrent assumption of multiple roles, from those of son or daughter, age-mate, and student during years of dependency to adult lines of activity in major institutional domains of society. One's life history is thus the product of multiple histories, each defined by a particular time-table and event sequence—histories of education and work-life, marriage and parenthood, residence and civic involvement.[16]

Many of the applications of this concept are beyond the scope of demography; demographers will, however, be interested in accounts of

[14] Ibid., p. 469.

[15] N. Ryder, 'Methods in measuring the family life cycle', *International Population Conference, Mexico, 1977*, vol. iv (Liège, 1978), p. 223.

[16] G. H. Elder, Jr., 'Family History and the Life Course', in T. Hareven (ed.), *Transitions: The Family and the Life Course in Historical Perspective* (New York, 1978), p. 26.

individuals' educational and work histories as well as in changes of residence. But the first task is to make proper use of demographic events in life histories. In this respect, too, the concept of the life course seems promising.

> In applying the life-course perspective to marriage and the family unit, we begin with the interdependent life histories of their members . . . A life-course framework views the family unit in terms of mutually contingent careers, their differentiating characteristics and problems of management. It facilitates study of divergent or non-conventional family patterns, as well as the conventional, by working with the life histories of individuals.[17]

If we translate this into demographic terms, it means that a chronology of demographic events may be used to study, not only the life cycle of a stable first marriage, but also the important stages of incomplete families, of families which have been reconstituted by remarriage, including those with the parent's own children and with children who have been brought into the second marriage, and even the life courses of childless single persons.

The suggestions that retrospective surveys or histories of demographic events might be used to construct a series of different life courses and even to provide a typology of such life courses has had a mixed reception: 'It seems unlikely that the way out of the impasse is the development of a family of family life cycles, given the plethora of exigencies, which produce non-comparability.'[18] Ryder's pessimism would seem to be excessive, as may be seen in a study published by Norton in 1983,[19] in which a large number of biographies collected by the US Bureau of the Census were used. Such a project is bound to be costly: the sample consists of more than 50,000 biographies of women, grouped into different birth cohorts. Norton distinguished the following types of family (see Table 1.2): women married once only and remaining married (i.e. stable first marriages), divorced mothers (i.e. incomplete families), women who had been married twice and whose first marriage had ended in divorce (i.e. remarriages), women who had been divorced more than once and were still divorced (i.e. a new variant of incomplete families), and women who had been divorced more than once but who were married (i.e. remarriages of a higher order).

The incidence of certain family type-related life courses is different in different cohorts, thus providing an illustration of social change. For each of these family types constructed from life courses a number of indicators of events and transitions (e.g. age at (re)marriage, birth of children, divorce) are provided— relating however only to the early phases of the family life cycle. In further tables Norton distinguished members of his sample by ethnic origin, income and women's educational level. As regards the value of such studies he

[17] Ibid., p. 26.

[18] N. Ryder, 'Recent Developments in the Formal Demography of the Family', *Proceedings of the International Population Conference, Florence, 1985*, vol. iii (Liège, 1985).

[19] A. J. Norton, 'Family Life Cycle, 1980', *Journal of Marriage and the Family*, 45(2) (1983).

Table 1.2. Ever-married US women by family type and birth cohort (000)

Women in/after	Birth cohort of women					
	1910–59	1910–19	1920–9	1930–9	1940–9[a]	1059–9[a]
Stable first marriage	37,727 (78.9)[c]	5,911 (86.3)	7,769 (81.0)	7,585 (76.7)	9,391 (74.5)	7,071 (79.3)
First divorce[b]	3,596 (7.5)	309 (4.5)	547 (5.7)	758 (7.7)	1,162 (9.2)	820 (9.2)
Second marriage	4,989 (10.4)	433 (6.3)	928 (9.7)	1,136 (11.5)	1,610 (12.8)	882 (9.9)
Second divorce[b]	843 (1.8)	113 (1.6)	197 (2.1)	219 (2.2)	226 (1.8)	88 (1.0)
Third marriage	686 (1.4)	85 (1.2)	151 (1.6)	186 (1.9)	213 (1.7)	51 (0.6)
TOTAL	47,841 (100)	6,851 (100)	9,592 (100)	9,884 (100)	12,602 (100)	8,912 (100)

[a] Truncated results.
[b] Including incomplete families.
[c] Figures in brackets indicate percentages.

wrote: 'Practical programmatic application of knowledge gained from life cycle studies is one aspect of the utility of such information. Another is the contribution to the existing knowledge of family development and dynamics. The family life cycle measures presented here are essentially descriptive and broad-based and have limited explanatory power.'[20] It seems hardly likely, however, that a reliable explanation can be achieved without a solid quantitative base. We therefore believe that Norton is too modest in his claims, and that his work is very promising and points the way to further progress. It shows that large-scale analyses of life courses are feasible. As Tamara Hareven has pointed out,[21] the life course approach is the interaction between 'individual time', 'family time', and 'historical time'.[22] Accordingly, the life course encompasses 'pathways' by which individuals move through their lives, fulfilling different roles sequentially or simultaneously.[23]

While the life course approach incorporates the family life cycle, it differs from it both conceptually and methodologically in that it measures the pace, sequencing, and coincidence of transitions, rather than strictly stages of family life. When using a life-course perspective, one is concerned not merely with the duration of a stage in the family life cycle but rather with the process by which individuals make their transitions from one stage to the next. Analytically, the

[20] Ibid., p. 274.

[21] In the following we make direct use of the paper 'The Life Course and the Family in the Later Years of Life' which Tamara Hareven kindly put at our disposal.

[22] T. Hareven, *Family Time and Industrial Time* (Cambridge, 1982).

[23] G. H. Elder, 'Family History and the Life Course', in T. Hareven (ed.), *Transitions: The Family and the Life Course in Historical Perspective* (New York, 1978).

life-course perspective examines the *transitions*—such as leaving home, getting married, setting up a separate household, becoming parents, or, in the later years of life, transitions to the post-parental stage—rather than these stages themselves. The family life-cycle approach is limited by the fact that it does not take account of earlier life history and is not concerned with the process of transition into and out of various stages, or with the variability and spread of such transitions. The family life-cycle approach measures stages of the family only (to be precise, it measures stages of parenthood).

Unlike the family life-cycle model, which is based on a sequence of a priori stages in the family unit's progression from marriage to widowhood, the life-course approach is concerned with the synchronization, conjunction, and sequencing of individual with family transitions. For example, children's departure from the parental home involves the age not merely of the parents at the time but also that of the children themselves; it also affects the configuration of their family of orientation, especially their parents' status. If the children's departure from the home is followed by marriage, it results in the formation of a new household and of new kinship ties with the spouse's family. What might appear, therefore, to be an individual transition such as leaving home is actually a *family* transition which, in certain population groups, might result in an empty nest. The connection between earlier and later transitions during the life course is particularly important in the study of old age. It is not sufficient to study each phase of the life course independently; rather it is necessary to examine the ways in which the career paths of family members interlock and influence the timing of transitions at different points of the life course.

Historically, in the USA and Western Europe, earlier life transitions of the young generation were closely intertwined with the later transitions of the older generation, especially when economic need and familial values dictated interdependence within the family. Even life transitions that today seem to be strictly individual or couple-based—leaving home or getting married, for example—were timed in relation to the status and needs of one's family or orientation. Thus, a son's or a daughter's departure from home or his or her marriage had to be synchronized with the needs of ageing parents; in an agricultural society it could depend on whether there were other siblings remaining at home, or whether they, too, intended to marry or leave. If, in a modern industrial society, such life transitions appear to be independent of the family of orientation (and in the vast majority of cases they are), they nevertheless remain connected with earlier transitions. A very low age at marriage implies a higher risk of divòrce, as does a pre-nuptial conception. Individual or couple-based decisions or events still determine the later transitions. What might appear, therefore, to be simple demographic variables, such as age at marriage, were and are still subject to complex interactions.

Lastly we are concerned with determining the nature of the later stages of the family life cycle. There has not as yet been a satisfactory solution to the problem of determining when these later stages begin and which phases and transitions should be included.

The definition of the early and the later stages of the family life cycle was also discussed by the IUSSP's Committee during the preparation of this seminar, when decisions were made about the topics to be covered. If the classic concept, which, however, only applies to stable first marriages, were used, the answer would be easy. The later stages of the family life cycle begin when the last child leaves the parental home and they end with the death of the second of the spouses. However, this concept cannot be used to answer a number of interesting questions. The Committee agreed that it would be neither sensible nor desirable to limit the discussion to stable first marriages. Events which are not found in such marriages, such as divorce, early widowhood, and remarriage of widowed or divorced persons, would have to be included. After these topics had been discussed, other events, such as the departure of children from their parental home, kin networks, and the economic, housing, and family conditions of elderly married or widowed persons, should also be considered. This basic sequence of events was used to structure the seminar, and consequently this volume. However, this procedure raises two problems. In the first place, the distinction between the early and the later stages of the life cycle becomes less clear-cut, and, secondly, a division of the life cycle into different stages makes it difficult to maintain a life-course perspective throughout.

As regards the first problem, marriages may end by divorce or death of one spouse at any stage. However, most divorces occur relatively early in marriage when the parties are young. In such cases, the later stages of the family life cycle would begin at a time when continuing marriages are still in their early stages. If marriages which are ended by death are divided into those which end when the woman is still capable of bearing children (early widowhoods) and others (late widowhoods), the problem for early widowhoods is essentially the same as for divorces. But as early widowhood is much rarer than early divorce, at least in modern Western societies, it seemed reasonable not to discuss early widowhood as such. This should not be taken to mean that a study of early widowhood, and of the conditions of widows and widowers who are left with young children, is unimportant. However, very little work has been done on this topic and there are few internationally comparable data. Late widowhood is also dealt with in the chapters which describe kin networks and the economic status and living conditions of older persons. A relatively large amount of space is given to the study of the process by which children leave the parental home: this seems justified in view of the dearth of empirical studies on this topic.

Only a few authors use the concept of the life course. But if the Committee's instructions had confined them to dealing with typical forms of life courses only, it would have been difficult to find a sufficient number of authors with access to appropriate empirical data, and the seminar might have had to be abandoned. It is true that the division of the life course into stages, which is the way in which some of the authors have treated their topic, tends to give the impression of a fragmentation of the life course. It is also true that only partial aspects of the life course can be treated by the different methods employed in these papers. However, these treatments can be used as building blocks for a more comprehensive structure, and the Committee and the editors will be satisfied if they thus stimulate further research.

These remarks on basic concepts such as family demography, definitions of family and household, family life cycle, and life course will be included with a brief introduction to the individual chapters in the book. In each case, we have tried to stress observations which relate to the life course, and to assess the relative contributions made to formal and to substantive demography.

The first two contributions are concerned with divorce. Louis Roussel begins by providing a typology of marriage, and explains the rise in the number of divorces in terms of attitudinal changes to marriage. Fewer couples take the traditional Western view of marriage as a lifelong and indissoluble union, and a relatively larger proportion regard it as a contract which can be broken, if the partners fail to achieve satisfaction. It is not, therefore, surprising that the number of divorces has increased almost everywhere. Roussel's types of marriage are defined in sociological terms, and it is not easy to obtain empirical information about the prevalence of different types in different countries. It is, of course, also possible for individuals to change their views about marriage during the course of their lives. From the life-course perspective it is important to assess the effect of different types of first marriage on the chances of remarriage when the first marriage has been ended by divorce. The effects of divorce on changes in attitude can have important repercussions on an individual's life course.

Marietta Pongrácz and Magdolna Czernák provide a case-study of divorces in Hungary, which they analyse in relation to a number of social and economic variables. Pre-marital pregnancy increases the risks of a marriage ending in divorce, and inebriety on the part of the husband is frequently cited by wives as a reason for marriage breakdown. The authors attempt to relate changes in the frequency of divorce in Hungary to changes in socio-economic conditions, and point to the increase in one-parent families which has been one of the results of the increased number of divorces.

In Chapter 4, John Bongaarts discusses widowhood. At first sight it would seem that this chapter would be of interest mainly to the formal demographer. Bongaarts uses life-table methods applied to different periods in the USA, i.e. a cross-sectional analysis. The innovative part of his chapter consists of studying not only the transition from the married to the widowed or the divorced state but also the transition from the divorced to the remarried and from the widowed to the remarried state. He also considers probabilities of remarriage for persons who were divorced, but had previously been widowed, as well as for persons who had been widowed more than once. The material he uses is impressive. However, Bongaarts's chapter also has implications for a study of the life course. His analysis is concerned with the effect of previous demographic events in the life course on later events. For instance, he looks at the effect of age at marriage and of age differences between the spouses on the frequency and duration of widowhood. His contribution is a good example of the application of an appropriate method of cross-sectional analysis to problems which are highly relevant to the life course.

Early widowhood is an important topic in the study of the situation of widowed persons of either sex who have young children to care for. It will influence their chances of remarriage, their value in the labour and marriage markets, and their general position in society. The effects of early widowhood on household structure and the help given by other relatives to widows and widowers with young children should also be considered. The chances of remarriage for those who are widowed relatively late in their lives are small, though much higher for widowers than for widows. However, it was pointed out in the discussion that widows are likely to be less affected by loneliness than elderly divorced women, and even than some older married or single women. Widows tend to live in peer groups, or near their relatives from whom they can obtain and to whom they can render informal assistance.

The subject of remarriage is treated in greater depth in Chapters 5 and 6. Peter Uhlenberg explores 'the effects of one's location (position in the life course, social structure and historical setting) on each step of the remarriage process'. After pointing out the obvious fact that a marriage which is dissolved by widowhood releases only one marriageable person onto the marriage market, whereas a marriage which is dissolved by divorce releases two, he considers the different probabilities of remarriage following widowhood and divorce respectively. He takes account of such factors as age, sex, ethnic group, educational level, presence or absence of dependent children, and recourse to social security, as well as the historical period. The last factor is particularly important because it influences the meaning and function of marriage and also the possible alternatives available: to remain alone, to remarry, or to live in a consensual union. In his references to the possibility of consensual unions he considers a topic on which very little empirical information is available and which it is difficult to treat statistically. Indeed, it is the very existence of consensual unions which provides an additional reason for the view that classical family demography, which to a large degree is based on official statistics and transition probabilities derived from such statistics, is an inadequate representation of reality. Uhlenberg also shows that, in Western societies, women 'are less vulnerable than men to kin disruption by marital status transitions'. Remarriages of widowed persons create less kin ambiguity than those of the divorced, where the presence of an ex-spouse may create additional complications. In this connection, Burch has pointed to the paradoxical situation in which, whilst the small family system has led to a reduction in the number of kin, the increased incidence of remarriage has tended to increase it.

Uhlenberg's discussion of remarriage is largely theoretical, and he makes only limited use of statistics, though he does use the concept of the life course to point out the social variables which affect the chance of a marriage being dissolved and of an eventual remarriage. David Coleman, on the other hand, provides a rich statistical case-study of remarriage in England and Wales (Chapter 6). The information he provides will be particularly valuable to formal demographers, in spite of the lack of data to which Coleman draws attention. In particular, there is no information about the interval between the dissolution of a marriage through death or divorce and an eventual remarriage. The absence of information on this topic makes the measurement of the propensity to remarry very difficult. Most calculations of the total remarriage rates of divorced persons have been based on a system of weights devised in France, because it was in that country (and more recently in Switzerland and Hungary as well) that statistics about the interval between remarriage and the dissolution of the previous marriage are available.

Chapters 7, 8, and 9 are devoted to problems associated with the departure of children from the parental home. Whilst Chapters 8 and 9 consist of case studies of this process on which only limited statistical information has been available, Kathleen Kiernan, in Chapter 7, lists some of the problems which have yet to be solved and comments on the dearth of available statistics. She points out that the launching-stage of the life cycle applies not only to nuclear families but also to one-parent families and to those which have been reconstituted by remarriage. But past empirical studies of the ages of the parents or of the children at the time when the latter leave the parental home have generally been confined to complete nuclear families. This is true also of the case-studies in Chapters 8 and 9 by Karl Ulrich Mayer and Karl Schwarz and by Christabel Young respectively. Kiernan attempts to use family and household statistics to throw light on the age distributions of members of single-person households in Denmark, Great Britain, and the USA, as well as in a number of other European countries, to estimate the ages at which young people leave the parental home. The strength of ties to the parental family will depend on the educational level achieved by its members as well as on conditions in the housing market. These conditions differ in different countries, and Kiernan's contribution is a warning against a crude empirical approach to the problem and premature generalizations. She points out that in present circumstances women whose children have left home may have elderly relatives to care for, and may not, therefore, experience an 'empty-nest' stage in which they share their life only with their spouse. She concludes: 'Research on the overlapping phases of the life courses of parents and children and the interactions between parents and grown-up children over their life span is still in its infancy. During recent years, there has been a growth of interest in this area across the spectrum of the social sciences, but the demographic under-pinnings to such studies still remain elusive. Therein lies our challenge.'

Suggestions on how to meet this challenge are contained in the two following chapters, which present case-studies from the Federal Republic of Germany (Mayer and Schwarz) and Australia (Young), derived from sources in which different methods have been used—from retrospective surveys and from current data.

Karl Ulrich Mayer and Karl Schwarz demonstrate that, where detailed statistics are available, current data, if properly used and if the data are collected at frequent intervals, can provide information about the time when children leave the parental home. From information provided in the German micro-census, an annual sample of 1 per cent of the population, it is possible to study the behaviour of quasi-cohorts. Mayer and Schwarz conclude that the process of contraction of the parental household takes much longer than has commonly been thought, particularly when the family consists of several children. An analysis of statistics from different sources shows that demographic and other changes in behaviour are both cohort- and period-specific, and that 'declining nuptiality and an increased desire for independence have both affected the process of emancipation. Because the first tendency was stronger than the second, the proportion of men and women between the ages of 20 and 30 who remained in their parents' household has increased slightly.' But the proportions who lived in consensual unions and one-person households also increased. Surprisingly, the median age at which children of either sex left home increased in the younger cohorts and the dispersion was reduced, indicating a more homogeneous pattern of behaviour. Mayer and Schwarz cite survey results which show the reasons that prompted children to leave home; among them marriage remains the most important. Important and valuable information about the distance separating the filial and parental households is also provided. This question whether the 'empty nest' is really empty provides a link between the chapters which deal with children leaving home (Chapters 7–9) and those which deal with family networks (Chapters 10 and 11).

Family demographers interested in the process of children leaving home have for long quoted the important work of Christabel Young. For a long time, hers were the only reliable published data describing this process, first in Melbourne and later for the whole of Australia. Her contribution was, in a sense, surprising, as is evident from the title: 'The Effect of Children Returning Home on the Precision of the Timing of the Leaving-Home Stage'. In one sense, Young stands the problem on its head, because until now interest has centred on the process of children leaving rather than returning to their parental home. However, she shows that the process of separation between parents and children is much more complex than others had thought (or hoped). It may consist of several stages. The smooth classical concept of the family life cycle, which we have already criticized earlier, is given its final burial by Young's latest researches. It is quite wrong to assume (for heuristic reasons) that children leave the parental home at the age of 18, as do Herberger (with some qualifications) and Kwong for some countries of east Asia.[24] Nor does it seem right to do as Glick did and take the mean age at marriage as equivalent to the mean age when the younger generation leave the parental home. Glick adds, however: 'During more recent times an increasing proportion of young adults have been leaving home before they marry, but a long series of statistics to demonstrate this well-recognized fact is not available.'[25] Young shows that more than one-half of young adults in Australia leave their parents' home before they marry, but that about half of these return home before leaving finally.

Kiernan's warning that results obtained in one country cannot be applied to another are very pertinent in this respect. The results for West Germany and Australia are surprisingly different. However, this warning applies only to the mean age at leaving home, the distribution of reasons for leaving home, behaviour relating to a return to the parental home, and the type of independent household that members of the younger generation form. The fact that marriage is no longer the sole reason for leaving the parental home applies in most Western societies. It will not in future be possible, therefore, to study the family life cycle without undertaking either longitudinal or retrospective inquiries, and these inquiries will have to be specific to a particular country. It is only in this way that it will become possible to obtain information on the different forms that the process of leaving the parental home takes, and to gain a deeper understanding of the process.

Formal demographers who look for data relating to the ages of children (and perhaps of parents) at the time when the former leave the parental home, perhaps because they wish to use these data for micro-simulation, find the situation less than satisfactory. Empirical work shows that the launching phase has become more complex. But even the research worker, whose main interest is to obtain substantive results relating to the life cycle, will find a number of problems for which there is as yet no solution. Young's study consists of interviews with young respondents who are under 35 years old. For this reason, she has no information on the interesting question whether children who have been divorced, and who have young children themselves, return to live with their parents, thus filling the 'empty nest' once again. Nor does she answer the question whether parents ultimately move in with their independent children, when they reach the stage when they need care from them. These questions are dealt with in the next two chapters which are concerned with kin networks.

[24] L. Herberger, 'The Population Census as Source for Family Life Cycle Data' and P. C. Kwong, 'Patterns of Family and Household Composition and the Family Life Cycle in East Asia, 1950–1970', in WHO, *Health and the Family Life Cycle* (Geneva, 1982).

[25] Cf. Glick, op. cit. (n. 3).

Alice Day in Chapter 10 deals with kinship networks and informal support in the later years, and criticizes formal demographers who are satisfied with studies that are limited to ascertaining the number of available kin. From the point of view of social policy it is important to obtain information about the actual situation relating to kin. Formal demographic studies are often limited to kin related by blood. However, reciprocal help is given by relatives through marriage, as well as by persons who are not related at all. Social scientists and those responsible for framing social policy must know both the number of persons who are, in theory, available to give help, as well as the number of those who actually do give help, and need to consider how the discrepancy between these two figures can be reduced. More recent demographic developments, such as divorce and remarriage, complicate the study of kin networks, in theory and in reality. We do not know yet to what extent relatives who are lost through divorce, or those who are gained by remarriage, are respectively absolved from and recruited to giving emotional and financial assistance.

The life-course perspective is particularly important in this context. Early events will determine the availability of relatives and friends. Experience in childhood, adolescence, and the family stage will affect the behaviour relating to kin networks of members of different cohorts. History tells us that in the past, help given by relatives was supplemented by the Church, village, or guild. Purely demographic studies of this topic need to be complemented by qualitative research, so that a fruitful collaboration between associated disciplines becomes possible. Too narrow a definition of the family, such as is used in the classical analysis of the family life cycle, must be avoided. Such a definition tends to give the impression that the nuclear family is isolated, that relations between the partners during the post-parental stage are eroded and new orientations are necessary, and that widows and widowers who live on their own are inevitably isolated.

In Chapter 11, Michel Poulain points to the importance of the concept of co-residence in the analysis of both family and other social networks. He defines a family life space, which has a geographical dimension, and within which relations between members of the family occur. He describes a number of studies, mainly conducted in France, which makes it possible to define such a life space. Such studies range from micro-simulation of the number of kin theoretically available for reciprocal help to studies which describe actual relations between older and younger members of the family. Poulain shows that a high proportion (more than half) of married children live less than 20 km. away from their parents, although only a very small proportion of them share a household with them. (Alice Day also agrees that too close a proximity between members of different generations is not considered desirable under modern conditions.) In the second half of his chapter, Poulain points to some results which he regards as important for the projection of the number of households headed by older persons. This, however, is only an exploratory study, which would have to be repeated with a larger sample for the results to be useful, though Poulain shows that it is in principle possible to obtain this information. Men and women tend to move more frequently as they grow older and lose the life space to which they have been accustomed. Though this study is too small to be statistically valid, and contains no information on the destinations to which the oldest widowers and widows move, it suggests a promising field for further research.

In Chapter 12, Richard Wall considers the difficult problem of comparing the structures of households of older persons. Statistics relating to households and families are generally not comparable: the definitions of the household and the family differ, as do those of the head of household and the reference person. However, the tables relating to older persons who live in institutions (mainly old people's homes) suggest that informal and family networks are much stronger than is generally believed, as only a small proportion of the old live in institutions.

The principal conclusion is, inevitably, the need for further research and improved data. The obvious gaps which have been shown in the analysis of the later phases of the life cycle make these demands more than routine. Better household and family statistics are particularly important. They should be drawn up on the same principles in different countries, and information is particularly desirable on consensual unions and the numbers and ages of relatives. Far too little is known about the duration of widowhood, and about the interval that elapses between the end of a marriage (through divorce or death) and eventual remarriage. Biographies of demographic events, which can only be obtained retrospectively, are particularly important for the study of the family life cycle. Retrospective questions should be asked in official statistical inquiries. Only in this way will it be possible to produce mass data which can be used for the analysis of the many different aspects of the life course and of different types of family. Smaller samples, such as are used by academic researchers, can never produce statistically valid transition probabilities. However, they can—and this is their principal value—enlarge our theoretical knowledge and conceptual framework. Without such a framework no convincing analysis of life courses, formal or substantive, is possible. Because such life courses have become more complex, present research methods cannot provide more than is contained in this volume: a first approach to the demography of the later phases of the family life cycle.

2 Types of Marriage and Frequency of Divorce

LOUIS ROUSSEL
Institut National d'Études Démographiques, Paris, and Université Paris V

The word 'divorce' has meant different things in different civilizations. Its significance in a matrilineal society differs from that in a society which was patrilineal or bilateral. Its meanings and consequences in a Christian culture differ from those in a Muslim country. But is it possible to extend this argument and claim that there exist different forms of divorce within the same country?

It is easy to classify divorces by certain obvious characteristics, such as duration of marriage, sex of petitioner, and sometimes (as in France) by legal type. These characteristics make it possible to describe the frequency of different groups of divorces; but it is not possible, by considering these characteristics alone, to aver that different types of divorce coexist in the same country. When we use the word 'type', we imply that there is an internal logic which governs behaviour and which gives a specific meaning to a 'type of divorce'. It would not be possible to construct a proper typology of divorces from a distribution of the number of divorces by duration of marriage, even though it might appear that certain classes of divorce could be distinguished by such an analysis.

The principal object of this chapter is to show that the recent upturn in the number of divorces has coincided with a differentiation of types of divorce, and that it is impossible to understand this increase without taking this diversity into account.

The Sudden Increase in the Frequency of Divorce

The size of the increase becomes apparent when we look at Table 2.1, showing the number of divorces granted since 1950. This table also shows that the rate of increase accelerated in about 1965, at least in the industrialized countries of the West.[1]

At the beginning of the 1950s the after-effects of the Second World War were

[1] In Eastern Europe attempts have been made to control the rise in the number of divorces by policy measures. Romania is a typical example, but attitudes towards divorce have also changed in the Soviet Union. See H. Yvert-Jalu, 'L'Histoire du divorce en Russie soviétique: Ses rapports avec la politique familiale et les réalités sociales', *Population*, 1981 (1).

still being felt. For example, in the two Germanies there was a recession between 1950 and 1960, following the recovery of the immediate post-war period. During that time the number of divorces remained constant, or grew very little. But, between 1965 and 1980 there was a very large increase. In Western countries numbers of divorces often doubled; in Australia, Canada, the Netherlands, and the Soviet Union the increases were even larger.

Table 2.1 Number of divorces in some industrialized countries, 1950–1980 (000)

	1950	1960	1965	1970	1980
Canada	5.4	7.0	9.0	29.1	62.0
USA	385.0	393.0	479.0	715.0	1182.0
Japan	83.9	69.4	77.2	95.9	141.7
German Democratic Republic	42.4	21.6	23.0	27.4	44.8
Federal Republic of Germany	74.6	44.4	52.9	76.5	96.2
England and Wales	17.9	23.4	37.1	57.4	148.3
Austria	10.3	8.0	8.4	10.4	13.3
Denmark	6.9	6.6	6.5	9.5	13.6
France	35.4	27.8	34.9	40.0	83.0
Hungary	11.3	16.6	20.3	22.8	27.8
Netherlands	6.2	9.7	6.2	10.3	25.7
Romania	—	36.9	36.9	7.9[a]	34.1
Sweden	8.0	8.9	9.6	12.9	20.7
Switzerland	4.2	4.6	5.0	6.5	10.9
Czechoslovakia	13.1	15.3	18.7	24.9	33.9[b]
USSR	67.4	270.2	360.4	636.2	929.6[c]
Australia	7.3	6.6	8.5	12.2	37.9

[a] This very steep but temporary decline was due to a reform in the law in 1966.
[b] Estimated no. in 1979.
[c] *Source:* UN *Demographic Yearbook*.

Crude numbers of divorces are not adequate for constructing a satisfactory period measure of divorce frequency. The main difficulty is to find a denominator to which the number of divorces could be related. The most commonly used measure, which is also published in the UN *Demographic Yearbook*, relates the total number of divorces to the total population of a country. This rate will of course be affected by changes in the age distribution of the population in the country concerned. A more satisfactory index relates the number of divorces to the total number of married women, but changes in the age distribution of married women which may have resulted from changes in nuptiality will affect movements of this rate.

Some demographers have constructed a measure which is analogous to the total of period fertility rates: the synthetic index of divorce. Divorce rates specific by duration of marriage in a given year are summed, and the resulting index measures the number of divorces per 100 marriages that would occur if duration-specific divorce rates were to remain constant. The major defect of this measure is its sensitivity to timing,[2] but in spite of this the index may be preferred to the other two, because it abstracts from the growth in the total population and from the age structure of the married population. In Table 2.2 we show the movement of this index for a number of countries since 1965.[3]

Table 2.2 Synthetic index of divorce (mean number of divorces per 100 marriages)

	1965	1970	1975	1977	1978	1979	1980	1981
Federal Republic of Germany[a]	—	—	22.3	16.6	6.8	17.2	21.3	24.7
Austria	14.5	18.2	20.0	22.6	23.8	25.4	26.1	26.6
Belgium	8.2	9.6	16.0	18.4	19.3	18.7	20.0	22.6
Denmark	18.2	25.1	36.7	37.8	36.6	37.8	39.8	42.5
Finland	13.7	17.1	25.8	28.2	29.2	28.9	27.4	27.9
France	10.7	12.0	17.2	20.4	22.6	24.3	24.7	—
Norway	10.2	13.4	20.7	22.7	23.3	24.8	25.1	27.2
Netherlands	7.2	11.0	19.8	21.2	21.8	23.5	25.5	28.6
England and Wales	10.7	16.2	32.1	33.8	37.9	36.7	39.4	38.8
Scotland	5.9	10.3	18.7	21.2	21.8	23.5	25.5	28.6
Sweden	17.8	23.4	50.8	41.3	41.7	42.5	42.7	43.4
Switzerland	12.7	15.5	20.9	25.2	25.7	27.4	27.4	28.2
German Democratic Republic	—	—	28.8	28.9	29.9	32.3	—	—
Bulgaria	10.3	14.8	15.4	18.1	17.7	16.8	18.5	18.8
Hungary	22.7	25.0	27.7	28.6	29.7	28.9	29.4	29.3
Poland	—	14.6	15.4	15.5	12.3	13.8	13.6	13.4
Romania	20.4	4.8	20.2	15.1	19.5	20.9	—	—
Czechoslovakia	16.8	21.8	27.3	25.0	26.2	25.3	26.6	—
USSR[b]	14.9	26.1	29.8	32.7	—	—	—	—
USSR[c]	—	—	—	37.7	37.9	38.8	37.4	—

[a] Divorces at durations of marriage less than 25 yrs.
[b] Divorces at durations of marriage not exceeding 20 yrs.
[c] All durations of marriage.

The figures in Table 2.2 confirm the increase in the frequency of divorce which has occurred since 1965. It shows that if the trend were to continue (and duration-specific divorce rates were to remain constant), about 40 per cent of all marriages would end in divorce in Denmark, Sweden, and the Soviet Union, whereas in 1965 the proportion in the majority of countries was between 10 and 15 per cent. The size of the increase suggests that some qualitative changes must have occurred in attitudes to marriage, as an event which was previously regarded as exceptional is now experienced by one

[2] A summary of period measures of divorce will be found in Josianne Duchêne and G. Wunsch, 'Les Mesures de la fréquence du divorce', *Population*, special issue, 1977. Cf. also L. Henry, *Démographie: Analyse et modèles* (Paris, 1972).

[3] This table has been taken from the annual accounts by A. Monnier, which are published in *Population*, 1983 (4–5).

couple in every three or four. Demographers and sociologists need to find a reason for this change.

Searching for an Explanation

One hypothesis would attribute a large part of the increase in the divorce rate to changes in timing. The frequency of divorce may have increased a little, but it now occurs sooner after marriage. As divorces occur at ever earlier durations of marriage, the period divorce rate increases. Once this readjustment in timing has been completed, it is suggested that the divorce rate will return to a level similar to that recorded in 1965.

It is not necessary to spend much time in dismissing this hypothesis. Changes in timing have indeed contributed to an increase in the period divorce rate, and are likely to continue to do so. However, a detailed analysis of these rates shows that the frequency of divorce has increased at all durations of marriage. It can hardly be suggested that it was a change in timing, which has now extended over two decades, that led to a doubling or trebling of the number of divorces.

There can be little doubt that there has been a real increase in the frequency of divorce. A number of 'reasons' have been put forward to account for this: lower age at first marriage, increased numbers of pre-nuptial conceptions, increases in women's labour force participation rates, liberalization of the divorce laws, etc. These factors, even if taken together, do not however provide an adequate explanation. Consider, in the first place, changes in the law relating to divorce. Their impact is evident: in England and Wales, the Netherlands, and Sweden, changes in the law relating to divorce were followed by a large increase in the number of divorces. However, the increase began before the law was changed, and this is not surprising as changes in the law generally follow changes in behaviour. Moreover, the large increase in the number of divorces following a change in the law lasted only a short time; some two or three years after the change the number of divorces returned to its previous trend. This narrow peak tends to confirm that, as Festy has shown, the immediate effect of changes in the divorce law is limited to a rapid reduction in the number of couples who wished to divorce for reasons which were not admissible before the change was enacted.[4]

The rapid growth in women's labour force participation rates may be more directly linked with the rise in divorces. There are very many women (nearly two million in France alone) who achieved a much greater degree of economic independence during the years after 1970. This will have led to a change in the situation of many wives who refrained from petitioning for divorce because they were frightened of the economic consequences. The obstacle put in their

[4] P. Festy, 'L'Évolution récente du nombre des divorces en Europe occidentale', in J. Cammaille and P. Festy (eds.), *Le Divorce en Europe occidentale: La loi et le nombre* (Paris, 1981).

way—the prospect of a sudden reduction in their standard of living following divorce—was removed or became less threatening in a number of cases. It is not, therefore, surprising that the number of wives' petitions for divorce increased. The available statistics confirm the existence of a very considerable difference between the divorce rates of economically active and economically inactive women. (For the situation in France, see Table 2.3.)

Table 2.3 Number of petitions for divorce per 100 married women (France)

	All women	Economically inactive women
1975	6.2	4.1
1976–7	6.7	4.2

Source: Le Divorce en France (Paris, 1981), vol. i; p. 67.

The statistics can only be regarded as approximate, because some women will not have stated their occupation on their petitions. Even so, the difference is likely to have been appreciable, and it must be admitted that there is a correlation between women's labour force participation rates and divorce rates. It is not easy, however, to know how to interpret this correlation. It is possible that the increased frequency of divorce has resulted in more women taking employment outside the home in order to safeguard their standard of living if their marriage were to break down. In other words, higher women's labour force participation rates may be a consequence, rather than a cause, of the higher frequency of divorce.

It is also possible that economically active women may differ from those who are not economically active in other respects. Their conception of the nature of marriage and of women's roles may be different. They may be better educated, more engaged politically, and less influenced by religion. It is generally thought that 'economic activity' on the part of a woman represents a specific and definite characteristic, but it may in reality be a cluster of diverse characteristics which we discover when we relate them to this single concept.

The other two factors which have been mentioned, a reduction in the age at first marriage and an increase in the number of pre-nuptial conceptions, could well be invoked as an explanation during the 1960s. But during the 1970s, the period when the number of divorces increased more rapidly, the effect of these factors became much less important. Indeed, if the hypothesis were true, numbers of divorces would have been expected to decline.[5] However, we shall find a consideration of pre-nuptial conceptions instructive. Christiansen has shown that the importance of this factor varies considerably between

[5] For a more detailed discussion see L. Roussel 'Développements récents dans l'analyse de la nuptialité et de la formation et dissolution des familles', *Proceedings of the International Population Conference, Mexico, 1977*, (Liège, 1977), vol. iii, pp. 333–51.

societies with different degrees of tolerance of pre-marital sexual relations; in societies in which strict moral codes apply, pre-nuptial conceptions are often followed by divorce; where there is greater permissiveness—in Denmark, for example—there is practically no correlation.[6] It is not therefore the number of pre-nuptial conceptions in itself which is important, but the social attitude towards such conceptions.

The same remarks apply to the other 'explanatory factors'. Neither separately nor together is there an intrinsic relation between them and the frequency of divorce. It is the norms of a society that designate them as incompatible with the idea of a 'good marriage', and in doing so make marriages with these characteristics more likely to end in divorce. Christiansen shows that the probability of divorce is linked, not to any specific characteristic of marriages, but to the relation between this characteristic and the dominant 'model' of marriage in the society. The more the characteristic differs from this dominant model—for instance, the greater the degree of heterogamy—the greater the probability that the marriage will end in divorce. But this does not explain the sudden rise in the number of divorces. Social mores have, in fact, become more tolerant: 'differences' are accepted more easily, and there are diverse 'models' of divorce.

We look for an explanation of our phenomenon in this very variety of models. For a long time, a single model of marriage prevailed in society—one which did not admit the possibility of divorce, or at best only admitted it with a small probability. We shall argue that as new 'models' of marriage have become diffused in society, their logic has led to a greater fragility of marriage. The increase in divorce is a simple function of the greater diffusion of these models and a progressive weakening of the model which implied stability.[7] It is the basis of the conjugal link which measures the probability of divorce and defines its type.

We use the term 'model' in the Weberian sense as an ideal type. Society does not contain different classes of married persons whose marriages are characterized by distinct and exclusive characteristics. Our models are a type of limit, as a square or a circle is in geometry. Each actual marriage is a complex mix of these ideal types, and the mix itself may be unstable. But it remains true that at any moment in time, each couple has a preference for one or other type, either provisionally or permanently. The definitions of different types are to some extent arbitrary and depend on the type of problem that is being considered. This should be borne in mind when considering the very rough typology outlined here.

[6] H. T. Christiansen, 'Timing of First Pregnancy as a Factor in Divorce: A Cross-cultural Analysis', *Eugenics Quarterly* (Sept. 1963).

[7] Family sociologists are to a great extent agreed on the existence of diverse models of marriage, even though they may disagree about individual definitions. Cf. e.g. J. Kellerhals *et al.*, *Mariages au quotidien* (Lausanne, 1983); L. Roussel *Le Mariage dans la société française contemporaine* (Paris, 1975); G. Menahem, 'Une famille, deux logiques, trois modes d'organisation', *Dialogue*, 2nd trimester (1983).

We begin by recalling briefly the characteristics of a 'traditional' marriage. This was a union where the spouses' expectations were relatively modest: to survive, to maintain their property, and to ensure security in old age through the procreation of children. The family defined by this type of marriage was also the unit of production, and health and work were its major preoccupations. Moreover, the roles of the two spouses were complementary, so that any deliberate breaking of the conjugal bond, or any attempt to live in isolation, led to problems which were nearly insoluble. The spouses' roles were defined by the institution of marriage which was itself legitimated by the culture. Marriage, therefore, was a destiny: there could be no question of breaking it; miracles were not expected, nor were changes in the institution itself.

Consider next the industralized societies of the West during the nineteenth century. Here, another type of marriage was dominant, at least among the bourgeoisie: it was based on the solidarity of the couple through affection which was expected in marriage, and which would result in the mutual happiness of the spouses. This state of affairs was regarded as natural, and implied a permanence of the conjugal bond.

This type of marriage continues today. But it is increasingly in competition with another type, where the institution of marriage itself is secondary, and where the union is founded on the search for solidarity through affection. In this type the ceremony of marriage itself is reduced to a formality which happens to be socially convenient. The couple regard their marriage as nothing less than salvation, a type of rebirth in which each partner sees his or her identity recognized, approved, and comforted. Expectations are unlimited, but there is no possibility of these expectations being permanently fulfilled. The fragility of this type of marriage is the result of the unrealistic nature of the spouses' expectations.[8]

Lastly, another type of marriage has appeared during the last decade, though it constitutes a minority as yet: the contractual type. In this type, the partners fear the storms of romance.[9] They need a guarantee against the torments of a false passion and the spells of love. Instead, a new type of marriage is desired, based on reason, in which each partner draws up a balance sheet, as it were. Everything will depend on the benefits that each spouse will derive from the marriage. The institution here is nothing more than a façade.

Are marriages of this type more likely to end in divorce? It is impossible to give a definite answer to this question. On one hand, the smaller degree of emotional investment in the marriage may impose less constraint on the spouses' behaviour. However, the opposition of one of the spouses to an

[8] On this point see the argument of J. Kellerhals and P. Y. Troutot, on 'divorce as a normative expression of an exaggerated model of marriage' in their paper, 'Quelques lignes de relation entre divorce et modèles matrimoniaux', *19ème séminaire international du Comité de recherche sur la famille de l'ISA* (Louvain, Sept. 1981).

[9] On occasions, romantic love is feared more by the partners the more they are fascinated by the characteristics of such marriages.

eventual divorce is not taken into account, because, explicitly or implicitly, the permanent availability of divorce is part of the contract. All we can say is that this type of marriage appears more precarious than that which is based on the presumed harmony between nature, law, and happiness. It seems to us that the most pertinent answer to the question why divorce rates have doubled or even trebled during the last 15 years is connected with the fact that the proportion of those types of marriage which are more likely to end in divorce has increased in the total of marriages.

To be consistent, we should classify marriage breakdowns into different types just as we have done with marriages, for to every type of marriage there corresponds a type of divorce. The divorce which ends the marriage of the institutional type is, logically enough, presented both in the law and in real life as a sanction against the party which has committed a matrimonial offence. In marriages which are based on romantic love, the breakdown occurs when affection between the partners ceases. If both spouses become disenchanted with one another simultaneously, there will be divorce by mutual consent; if this does not happen the divorce may be difficult and acrimonious. Divorces of this type may be regarded as breaking an 'oath of love' and it is this, rather than their secondary characteristics, which gives such divorces their meaning, and their often dramatic character. The divorce which ends a marriage of the companionship type can often be the result of a unilateral decision. In principle, it should be easier to break the conjugal bond in such marriages, and the divorce may be more serene because its possibility had been envisaged from the very start of the marriage.

As the nature of divorce is determined by the nature of the marriage which it dissolves, it follows that the models of divorce put forward, just like those of marriages, are ideal types. It therefore seems useless to suggest that divorces can be classified by type, and different types enumerated exactly.[10] This conclusion is reinforced by other considerations. A couple may contract a marriage of a particular type, but as it progresses its nature may change. Some couples continue their marriages, as it were at the limit: the bonds of affection which united the spouses have disappeared in practice, and the marriage is maintained apparently only because of its social convenience. Lastly, there are a minority of spouses, though their number is growing, who separate and form new unions, but who believe that the legal termination of their first marriage is a useless formality.[11]

[10] The legal characteristics of a divorce do not explain this distribution either. In the first place, in most countries there is only one procedure for obtaining divorce. Secondly, where there are different procedures there is not necessarily a concordance between the type of marriage and the procedure which is used. However, it is worth noting that in France a large number of divorces are obtained by mutual consent.

[11] In France, this applies particularly to couples whose children have grown up and have left the parental home. 'Desertions' appear more frequent in certain parts of the USA: they were twice as frequent as divorces in Philadelphia, and the total number during the 1950s was estimated to be between 100,000 and 400,000. Cf. W. M. Kephart and T. P. Monahem, 'Divorce and Desertion in Philadelphia', *American Sociological Review*, 17 (1952).

This is obviously a very summary account of the true situation. Its main advantage lies in offering a general explanation of the growth in the frequency of divorce by relating this growth to changes which have occurred in the institution of marriage, and in integrating all the factors which have been put forward previously in explanation. For instance, the increase in women's labour force participation rates is seen as a consequence of the attitude which makes women wish to maintain their economic independence. The decline in the number of pre-nuptial conceptions indicates the desire of unmarried couples to avoid being trapped into marriage because of an unwanted pregnancy. Cohabitation among young people marks a refusal on their part to acknowledge the legitimacy of marriage as an institution, and to assert the spouses' individual sovereignty in shaping their own destiny. Current low fertility rates illustrate the wish only to have children who are wanted, and at the time when they are wanted. If, in the future, it were to become possible for the couple to determine the sex of their unborn child, their degree of choice would be still further extended. All these factors bear witness to a radical change in the nature of the marriage bond, and to a lower valuation of marriage as an institution and of the privileged position of married people, and which leaves all decisions, including the decision to divorce, to the spouses themselves.

However, this is not a complete explanation of the situation. It is also necessary to explain why the frequency of divorce has increased simultaneously in Western Europe and North America. Why was there a turn in the divorce curve in about 1965? Carlson claims to have answered this question for the United States.[12] He believes that the large increase in divorce rates coincided with the period when the large birth cohorts of the 'baby boom' years during the immediate post-war period were growing up. These cohorts were, in the author's words, 'unusually large'. Their parents were 'engulfed' by a flood of babies. They reacted to this phenomenon by substituting a more distant type of education for the process of socialization in which the parents played a leading role. Children often lived separate lives from their parents. This attitude meant that a large proportion of these children spent their childhood and adolescence in a world of their own, where there were fewer constraints of reality. They acquired a utopian view of life in general, and of marriage in particular. Their excessive expectations of marriage were the result of a demographic pressure and a secondary type of socialization. They themselves avoided such pressure by limiting the numbers of their own children in order to achieve a greater degree of togetherness with them. In turn, this meant that their children obtained a more realistic view of the nature of married life. Carlson thinks that, as a consequence, the divorce rate in these new and smaller cohorts will decline. His explanation of the movement in

[12] E. Carlson, 'Divorce Rate Fluctuation as a Cohort Phenomenon', *Population Studies*, 33(3) (1979).

divorce rates is analogous to that which Easterlin has provided for fertility rates.

Although this theory appears attractive at first sight, it is not in our view altogether convincing. There was, indeed, a rise in fertility after 1945, but it was of modest proportions. Is it really justified to say that parents were 'engulfed' by babies? Moreover, when age-specific divorce rates were analysed it is seen that between 1967 and 1969, for example, they rose not only for couples between the ages of 20 and 24, but also for couples in the age groups 25–9 and 30–4. The rise in divorce rates which has occurred since 1965 cannot be reduced to a cohort phenomenon. It was a period phenomenon which applied to all adults.[13]

There may still have been a cohort influence; but we interpret this differently from Carlson. A large proportion of members of cohorts who had their children during the immediate post-war period had lost confidence in the values which underlay and legitimated social institutions in general, and marriage in particular. In Europe, the violence and terrorism of totalitarian regimes resulted in a wider diffusion of the ideas that certain intellectuals first put forward towards the end of the First World War: ideas which questioned the values underlying our culture. The legitimacy of all social institutions was increasingly questioned. Parents tended to transmit these doubts to their children. They themselves often retained a nostalgia for the culture in which they had been brought up, and continued to respect institutions which they recognized as necessary. Their children, however, having been brought up in a more sceptical frame of mind, adopted a more radical view and rejected the traditional norms which applied to their sexual and family lives. These children were of the generation which reached the age of twenty between 1965 and 1970.

Such an hypothesis would lead to conclusions very different from those of Carlson. Whereas he regards the movement in divorce rates as an increase which will soon have reached its maximum and will thereafter decline, we are inclined to think that the increase is more fundamental and is likely to continue. We shall now discuss whether the most recent data relating to divorce are sufficient to enable us to make a choice between the two hypotheses.

Some Data

Statistics for recent years seem at first sight to confirm Carlson's hypothesis. There appears to have been some stabilization in numbers of divorces since 1977 (see Table 2.4), and in a number of countries there appears to have been

[13] For a discussion of Carlson's thesis see L. Roussel, 'A propos de la divortialité aux États-Unis: Un article de Carlson', *Population*, 1980 (4–5). This paper was followed by a reply from Carlson.

an actual decline. Clearly there has been a change compared with the period 1970–80. However, the large increase during that decade occurred mainly during the first seven years. This is true for the USSR and the German Democratic Republic, as well as for England and Wales, Sweden, and Switzerland. At first sight the statistics would seem to indicate a movement such as Carlson had predicted.

Table 2.4 Annual number of divorces (000s) in some countries since 1977

	1977	1978	1979	1980	1981	1982	1983
Canada	55	57	59	62	70	—	—
USA	1,091	1,130	1,181	1,182	1,219	1,180	1,179
German Democratic Republic	43	43	45	45	49	50	50
England and Wales	128	143	137	148	145	147	—
Denmark	13	13	13	14	14	15	15
Finland	10	10	10	9	9	—	—
Italy	12	12	12	12	13	13	13
Sweden	20	20	20	20	20	21	20
Switzerland	10	10	10	11	11	12	12
USSR	898	911	951	930	931	903	946

However, this reduction does not apply everywhere: in some countires, e.g. in France and Japan, the number of divorces has increased steeply since 1977. It would, however, be reasonable to assume that there will be a constancy, or possibly even a decline, in the number of divorces. This movement is clearly linked to the change in the number of marriages, with a certain time-lag. This decline will be reinforced by the reduction in the number of persons at risk of marrying, following the fall in fertility which has occurred since the 1960s. If the force of nuptiality were to decrease more steeply in some countries, we would expect an appreciable fall in the number of divorces. However, it is not necessarily the case that the *divorce rate* will fall. It is possible to envisage a situation where the proportion of marriages that are unstable will increase. This would happen if there were a progressive decline in the number of those marriages in which the spouses attach importance to the institutional aspects of marriage. However, it may be felt that among the smaller proportion of the population who continue to marry, there will be a larger fraction who are attached to marriage as an institution. If this were so, the divorce rate might cease to grow. The number of divorces in the near future is therefore likely to decrease, and divorce rates may stabilize. Paradoxically, in the medium term the likely decline in the divorce rate will not necessarily lead to a strengthening of the institution of marriage: the number of divorces will have been stabilized because the number of *de facto* unions will have increased. Marriage will become rarer, and those who contract it will attach more importance to it as an institution.

What effect will a prolongation of the economic recession have on the divorce rate? This question cannot be satisfactorily answered, for there are contradictory a priori considerations, all of which seem equally well founded. Economic insecurity may strengthen the bond between spouses who regard marriage as an insurance against insecurity. On the other hand, difficult economic conditions may lead to marital conflict and tensions: unemployment may result in a more frequent breakdown of marriage rather than its consolidation. There is considerable uncertainty: it is impossible to forecast how the economic recession will develop, and we cannot assess its impact on the stability of the marriage bond. We believe, however, that the impact of economic difficulties on divorce will be limited. It could prevent some divorces and postpone others, but it will not change couples' attitudes to marriage. It is increasingly true that a marriage's solidarity depends on the satisfactions that it provides for the spouses. As long as this idea prevails, marriage will remain fundamentally precarious in our society, irrespective of economic conditions.

The fragility of marriage has important consequences: an increase in the number of households consisting of one-parent families, to which sociologists and those responsible for the framing of social policy have given considerable attention. Some figures are given in Table 2.5. There are other statistics which illustrate this tendency but which, in spite of their general interest, often remain unpublished.

Table 2.5 Number of households with a divorced head, by sex of head (000)

	First date		Second date	
	Men	Women	Men	Women
USA, 1974, 1982[a]	290	1,836	681	3,478
Federal Republic of Germany, 1970, 1981[b]	30	232	48	340
France, 1975, 1981[c]	43	221	65	350
Switzerland, 1970, 1980[d]	12	69	15	94

[a] *Marital Status and Living Arrangements*, Mar. 1974, Mar. 1982 (Washington, DC), table 6.

[b] K. Schwarz, 'Les Ménages en République fédérale d'Allemagne', *Population*, 1983 (3).

[c] Recensement 1975 and Enquête Emploi 1981 (data provided by M. Villac).

[d] Unpublished data from the Censuses of 1970 and 1980, provided by J. E. Neury.

The increase in the number of such households is generally larger in the USA than in Europe. This is caused neither by a greater number of divorces nor by a more rapid decline in remarriage rates in the USA compared with the situation in Europe.[14] In Europe, at least in the countries cited, a relatively

[14] L. Roussel, 'Le Remariage des divorcés', *Population*, 1981 (4–5).

larger proportion of one-parent households are rapidly transformed into free unions. However, this is at best only a working hypothesis. It is not surprising that the number of one-parent households with a male head is relatively low. The explanation lies in the judicial practice of generally awarding the guardianship of children to the mother. Moreover, during the last 20 years the social situation of a divorced woman who is head of a family has changed considerably. In the past she was stigmatized by society and was often dependent on payments of alimony which were irregular; her general situation changed rapidly for the worse after divorce.[15] Today the position has improved, mainly because many more younger women are economically active.

Another type of household which has increased considerably in numbers in the recent past is the one-person household. Divorced persons have contributed to this increase. However, the proportion of divorced persons among one-person households is lower than that of unmarried or widowed persons, particularly widows. Since 1965 the largest *increase* in the number of such households occurred among divorced persons. For instance, between 1970 and 1980 the proportion of divorced men among one-person households in the USA has increased two and a half times. Even so, the proportion only amounts to 27 per cent.

Thus, whether one-person households or one-parent households are considered, the rise in divorce has contributed to an increase in the numbers of small demographic units (see Table 2.6). This development has economic consequences, and in countries such as the United States industrialists have reacted to this situation.[16] The stock of dwellings has been adapted to take account of the new situation and manufacturers of household equipment and the leisure industries have also taken account of this development. The impact of these statistics is considerably weakened, however, when it is remembered that one-person and one-parent households often represent a transitory situation. Divorced persons remain on their own or with their children for a few years only; thereafter, they most frequently remarry or enter into free unions. A divorced woman with children, and even more frequently a divorced man, often begins a new life with a new partner outside marriage. Thus, whereas period analysis suggests that the distribution of households has become more heterogeneous, longitudinal analysis shows a more fundamental change, a greater degree of movement between different marital statuses in an individual's lifetime.

Divorce makes it possible for some individuals who have been disappointed in their first marriage to contract a marriage with another partner. But this function is becoming less and less important. The most significant change brought about by divorce is not the increase in its frequency, but the lower

[15] W. J. Goode, *After Divorce* (Glencoe, Ill., 1956).

[16] See e.g. G. Masnick and M. J. Bane, *The Nation's Families 1960–1990* (Cambridge, Mass., 1980).

Table 2.6 Number of one-person households (000s) consisting of a divorced person living alone, and as a proportion of all one-person households by sex

	First date No.	%	Second date No.	%
Men:				
Federal Republic of Germany 1972, 1981	218.4	12	334.9	14
Denmark, 1981	—	—	39.9	17
France, 1975, 1981	138.9	11	217.5	14
Hungary, 1980	—	—	59.5	24
Netherlands,[a] 1960, 1978	9.0	8	25.1	9
Switzerland, 1970, 1980	17.1	14	41.7	15
USA, 1970, 1980	688.0	19	1,726.0	27
Canada, 1971, 1976	22.7	7	46.6	10
Women				
Federal Republic of Germany, 1972, 1981	345.9	8	479.4	9
Denmark, 1981	—	—	49.5	14
France, 1975, 1981	194.0	8	278.9	6
Hungary, 1980	—	—	66.7	14
Netherlands, 1960, 1978	15.0	6	35.1	6
Switzerland, 1970, 1980	29.3	11	52.0	12
USA, 1970, 1980	789.0	11	1,651.0	15
Canada, 1971, 1976	22.4	5	47.4	7
Both sexes				
Federal Republic of Germany, 1972, 1982	564.3	11	814.3	11
Denmark, 1981	—	—	89.4	15
France, 1975, 1981	332.9	8	496.4	10
Hungary, 1980	—	—	126.2	18
Netherlands, 1960, 1978	24.0	6	60.2	7
Switzerland, 1970, 1980	46.4	12	93.7	13
USA, 1970, 1980	1,477.0	14	3,377.0	19
Canada, 1971, 1976	45.1	6	94.1	8

[a] We have used 1960, rather than 1971, for the Netherlands, because the definition of a divorced person in 1971 differed from that of 1960 and 1978.

probability of remarriage and the increase in the number of *de facto* unions among divorced persons. It is not therefore justified to conclude a discussion of divorce, as some authors have done,[17] by the statement that the high frequency of remarriage testifies to the vigour of marriage as an institution, as those who have been disappointed in a previous marriage to do not delay entering on a second one.

Divorce affects not only the spouses: the situation of children of a marriage, too, is altered. In this chapter we shall not discuss the psychological consequences of a divorce between its parents for the child. This discussion has on occasions been heated, and the right questions have not always been asked. Little account has been taken of the conflicts, tensions, and violence which

[17] See e.g. P. Berger, *Affrontés à la modernité* (Paris, 1980), p. 43.

precede the breakdown of a marriage, and their effects on children. We shall be concerned here only with the demographic aspects.

The first question to be asked is whether the recent increase in the divorce rate has played a part in the reduction of fertility. It is true that the number of divorces has risen and fertility has fallen at roughly the same time. But this in itself is not sufficient evidence to establish a causal association. Such an association seems more probable when we consider that the rise in divorce has led to a reduction in the period of exposure to risk of conception, particularly among women under 30 years old. But this argument only becomes important if women were to desire three or more children. When a woman wishes to have no more than two children, an interruption of the period of exposure to risk of conception lasting for only two or three years would not make the realization of her objective impossible: it will only affect the timing of births. Moreover, even if there were occasional cases where divorce averts an additional conception, this deficiency would be compensated for by those cases in which women remarry and attempt to mark their new union by having children of their own. Lastly, in some countries with very high divorce rates the total of period fertility rates is higher in Sweden (1.63) than in Germany (1.43), and higher in the USA (1.87) than in Italy (1.56).[18]

It should be noted that the total number of children affected by divorce continues to increase.[19] Bumpass and Rindfuss have used data from the Family Growth Survey of 1973 to show that 26.2 per cent of American children born between 1956 and 1958 experienced the divorce of their parents before they had reached their 16th birthday. This proportion was as high as 51 per cent among black children. An extrapolation of divorce rates of 1970–3 would yield a proportion of 35 per cent for the USA and the figure would be even larger, if the rates of 1980–2 had been used. Haskey has used indices for 1980 in England and Wales to show that 20 per cent of children in that country experience the divorce of their parents before their 16th birthday.[20]

Most of the children of divorced parents are cared for by their mother, only a few by their father. The guardian parent may or may not remarry. Where he or she does, the child will enter into a more or less complex relationship with adults who may or may not be its parents, and with children who may be full sibs, half-sibs, or children of its guardian parent's new spouse. The network of relationships may be even more complex where there is a free union rather than a remarriage. This diversity of possible situations explains the recent desire to define some independent rights of children which do not depend on the wishes of their parents. For example, children who have reached a certain age may, under certain conditions, be given the choice of which parent they wish to live with.

[18] A. Monnier, 'L'Europe et les pays développés d'outre-mer', *Population*, 1983 (4–5).

[19] L. Bumpass and R. Rindfuss, 'Children's Experience of Marital Disruption', paper presented to the annual meeting of the Population Association of America (1978).

[20] J. Haskey, 'Children of Divorcing Parents', *Population Trends*, 31 (1983).

Whether we are concerned with the spouses themselves or with their children, there has been a complete transformation of the nature of marital breakdown following the increase in the number of divorces and of common-law unions of divorced persons, as well as attitudinal and legal changes. This has led to an extension of the objectives of demographic research. The analysis of divorce frequency has never been a straightforward problem in demography. But in the past it was possible to hold that it was not important, because it only affected a small section of the population. This is clearly no longer the case. Demographers can no longer afford to be uninterested in a phenomenon which occurs increasingly often and which, in the majority of European countries, affects at least one-fifth of all couples.[21]

Taking account of the points made above, the following improvements in statistics or methods of study seem desirable:

(i) Statistics relating to the living arrangements of divorced persons should be improved, and at least four different categories should be distinguished for each sex: (*a*) those who live on their own; (*b*) those who live apart from their previous spouse, but have at least one child; (*c*) those who live with their spouses but have no children; and (*d*) those who live with their spouse and children. In Table 2.7 we show data of this type which have been published in France and are based on information given in the census of 1975.

(ii) Longitudinal analyses similar to those which Leete described in his paper entitled 'New Directions in Family Life'[22] should be developed.

(iii) Simulation studies based on recent statistics should be carried out. These would provide a picture of the life cycles of divorced persons on the assumption that present conditions would continue. A more complete model would make it possible to obtain the probable life histories of children of such couples between birth and their 16th birthday.

Overview

Is it possible to state that divorce is one of the 'regulators' of the institution of marriage? If we take this to mean that some of the population who marry have their decision to marry, consciously or unconsciously, influenced by the availability of divorce, and therefore find marriage more acceptable, the answer will be in the affirmative. This will also be the case if we suggest that marriage makes it possible for those whose first marriage has foundered to normalize their status. But if it were suggested that divorce enabled the institution of marriage to retain the same characteristics that it had in our grandparents' days, then the term 'regulator' would become meaningless.

We have tried to show that the rise in the number of divorces has coincided

[21] On the basis of period measures.
[22] *Population Trends*, 15 (1979).

Table 2.7 Position of divorced persons in households by type of household, France, 1975

Type of household in which divorced person lives	Position of divorced person: Head of household			Spouse of head			Child of head			Others			Total		
	M	F	Total	M	F	Total	M	F	Total	M	F	Total	M	F	Total
One-person household	146	192	338	—	—	—	—	—	—	—	—	—	146	192	338
Couple without children aged below 25 years[a]	39	20	59	24	36	60	10	5	15	2	11	13	75	72	147
Couple with children below 25 years	31	18	49	13	27	40	3	8	11	10	9	19	57	62	119
Parent with children below 25 years	20	157	177	—	—	—	2	6	8	3	7	10	25	170	195
Household consisting of several persons but not containing a family	12	36	48	—	—	—	15	12	27	15	14	29	42	62	104
Multi-family household	2	2	4	1	1	2	1	9	10	2	2	4	6	14	20
TOTAL	250	425	675	38	64	102	31	40	71	32	43	75	351	572	923

[a] This and the following types of household sometimes contain 'isolated' persons: 75 divorced persons are members of households in which they are neither the head, nor the spouse, nor children of the head.

Source: Population, 2 (1981).

with a change in the significance of divorce and in its social consequences. Whereas in the past divorce carried a certain social stigma, it is acceptable today. In the past divorce was regarded as a remedy for the innocent partner whose spouse had committed a matrimonial offence; today it takes place with the mutual consent of the parties, and sometimes even following a single unilateral decision. In the past divorce was frequently followed by remarriage; today it is more likely to be followed by a consensual union. In the past divorce was regarded as an unfortunate accident in matrimony; today it is regarded by many people as a normal situation for a couple to find themselves in, and even for the institution of marriage as a whole. And this does not take into account those cases where the spouses separate without even bothering to mark the breakdown of their marriage by the formality of divorce. In most post-industrial societies couples appear to have gained the right to some fluidity in their status, and they exercise these rights increasingly. This attitude not only modifies the traditional concept of a divorce, it changes the meaning of marriage. We may be going, as Toffler has suggested in *Future Shock*, towards an 'ephemeral' civilization.

Our analysis of divorce and its sequelae highlights another development in our modern matrimonial system: a greater tolerance for *de facto* situations. It is true that their frequency differs in different countries, and between different sub-populations within the same country. Moreover, it is clear (though exact figures are not available) that remarriages are increasingly preceded by a period of cohabitation. It has therefore become less uncommon for cohabitation after divorce to continue as a permanent consensual union. There have thus been considerable changes. Quantitatively, divorces have become more frequent; qualitatively, more diverse types of divorce have arisen. We cannot, however, give an exact weight to any particular type.

The progressive disappearance of the type of marriage in which the probability of divorce is low, therefore, leads us to the belief that the increase in divorce has not yet run its course, and that the trend will continue during the coming decades. However, the progressive devaluation of institutional procedures, which applies both to marriage and to divorce, makes this forecast somewhat hazardous in the medium term. It is by no means impossible that the frequency and number of divorces may decrease, because the number of free unions and *de facto* breakdowns of marriage will increase.

In this chapter we have tried to show that changes in divorce can only be properly understood provided they are related to changes in marriage. The frequency of divorces depends on the relative frequency of marriages of different types, and is related basically to a growing indifference towards the institutional aspects of the foundation and breakdown of unions.

3 Divorce in Hungary

MARIETTA PONGRÁCZ and MAGDOLNA CSERNÁK
Demographic Research Institute, Central Statistical Office, Budapest

Introduction

During the 40 years since the end of the Second World War, social, economic, political, and cultural conditions in Hungary have changed radically. Such changes are characteristic of development in modern societies, and include industrialization, urbanization, changes in the system of traditional social obligations, rising educational and cultural levels, and more widespread rationalist attitudes. They have occurred within specific historical circumstances, and changes in power and property relationships, the socialist reorganization of agriculture, and the rise in the proportion of women gainfully employed outside the home have all been achieved within a reasonably short period of time. They have affected many areas of people's private and personal lives, including relationships within the family. Both the structure of family and its functions have been affected.

Employment outside the home has become general in Hungary, and the traditional multi-generation family has been replaced by the nuclear family consisting of a couple and their children. At the same time, the number of planned births has fallen sharply. The mean size of completed families is now below replacement level: it fell from 2.11 children per family in 1949 to 1.69 in 1980.[1] However, the proportion of all children born within marriage has remained high, at between 91 and 92 per cent.

Practically no function of the family, with the exception of reproduction, has remained unaffected by these changes. Families are no longer units of production. Their importance in the socialization of children has been reduced by the provision of State services for child care—crèches, kindergartens, and schools—but emotional and affective relations between parents and children have become stronger. Ties with more distant kin have become weaker, norms and behaviour have changed, as has the traditional division of functions between the sexes. All this has resulted in a greater frequency of conflict within the family and a reduction of its inner unity and stability, and the results of these changes manifest themselves by an increase in the number of marriages that end in divorce. This phenomenon is not confined to Hungary; it is found in other countries at similar stages of development. A significant proportion of

[1] *1980. évi Népszámlálás*, 23, *Háztartás és család*, i, (1980 *Census*, vol. 23, *Household and Families*, pt. i) (Budapest, *1980*).

families face functional difficulties today, because they have not been able to adjust to the new demands which are a consequence of these social changes.

The Frequency of Divorce in Hungary

In 1984 a total of 28,711 marriages were dissolved by divorce in Hungary: a rate of 2.7 divorces per 1,000 population and of 10.5 divorces per 1,000 existing marriages (Table 3.1). Both the number of divorces and the divorce rate have increased practically continuously over the last 100 years. The increases were particularly pronounced at times when there were changes in the power, economic, and social structure of the country, and after wars and conflicts (the beginning of the 1920s, the second half of the 1940s, and the later 1950s).

Table 3.1 Number of divorces and divorce rates, 1880–1984

Year	No. of divorces	Divorce rates per 1,000		
		Existing marriages	Population	Marriages during the year
1880	484	0.4	0.1	10.1
1890	457	0.4	0.1	9.3
1900	1,075	0.8	0.2	17.5
1910	2,890	1.9	0.4	44.3
1921	6,188	3.8	0.8	66.3
1930–1	4,926	2.6	0.6	63.9
1938	5,754	2.8	0.6	77.5
1948	11,058	5.3	1.2	113.2
1960	16,590	6.5	1.7	187.3
1970	22,841	8.4	2.2	236.4
1975	25,997	9.3	2.5	250.5
1976	27,075	9.6	2.6	269.5
1977	27,167	9.6	2.6	280.0
1978	28,407	10.1	2.7	307.3
1979	27,606	9.8	2.6	316.7
1980	27,797	9.9	2.6	346.0
1981	27,426	9.8	2.6	355.6
1982	28,500	10.3	2.7	377.2
1983	29,337	10.7	2.7	386.2
1984	28,711	10.5	2.7	383.1

Source: Demográfiai Évkönyv, 1984 (*Demographic Yearbook, 1984*) (Budapest, 1984).

The continuous increase in the numbers of divorces and in divorce rates is particularly noteworthy because, during the earlier years of this period, a divorce could only be granted for reasons specified in the Marriage Act of 1894. This law was based on the doctrine of the matrimonial offence and restricted the right to petition for divorce to the innocent party, who was required to prove some grave dereliction of marital duties by the respondent (such derelictions being specified in the Act). The principle of the matrimonial offence was abolished in 1952, when divorce became available provided the marriage had irretrievably broken down. The law did not lay down specific grounds for a divorce: it was left to the court's discretion to determine whether or not there had been an irretrievable breakdown. In 1974 the law was further liberalized, and divorce by mutual consent of the spouses was permitted. The figures in Table 3.2 show that the greater instability of marriage was not confined to Hungary, but could be found throughout Europe.

Table 3.2 Crude divorce rates in different countries, 1960–1981

Country	Divorces per 1,000 population		
	1960	1970	1981
Austria	1.13	1.40	1.79
Belgium	0.50	0.68	1.55
Bulgaria	0.90	1.16	1.48[b]
Czechoslovakia	1.12	1.72	2.26
Denmark	1.46	1.93	2.83
England and Wales	0.51	1.17	3.01
Finland	0.82	1.29	1.98[b]
France	0.66	0.76[a]	1.59[c]
German Democratic Republic	1.34	1.61	2.90
Federal Republic of Germany	0.83	1.24	1.56
Hungary	1.66	2.22	2.59
Italy	—	—	0.19[a]
Netherlands	0.49	0.79	1.96
Norway	0.66	0.88	1.62[b]
Poland	0.50	1.06	1.11
Romania	2.01	0.38	1.54[b]
Sweden	1.20	1.61	2.42
Switzerland	0.87	0.96[a]	1.65[b]
Yugoslavia	1.20	1.02	1.00
USSR	1.30	2.62	3.48
Japan	0.74	0.94	1.31
USA	2.18	3.51	5.30

[a] 1969.
[b] 1980.
[c] 1979.
Source: Demographic Yearbook of the United Nations (New York, 1981).

By international standards the numbers and rates of divorce in Hungary are high, and have been so in the past, even before the First World War. Hungary's predominant position in this league has continued in spite of the fact that the divorce rates in other European countries have also increased. During the last 20 years, only the divorce rates of Romania in 1960 and the

USSR in 1970 exceeded those of Hungary for the same year. By 1981, the situation had changed slightly: Hungary now occupied fifth place, being preceded by the USSR, England and Wales, the German Democratic Republic, and Denmark.

Neither local nor international trends in the divorce rates give a true picture of the extent of divorce. Crude divorce rates are affected by the age distribution of the population and by its composition according to marital status, and international comparability is made difficult by differences between the legal systems and the socio-economic structure of different countries. To obtain a true measure of the instability of marriage we would need to know how many of the marriages contracted during a given calendar year were terminated by divorce at different durations. Provided statistics are available to show the number of marriages entered into each year, as well as the number of divorces granted each year classified by duration of marriage, it would be possible to calculate an index of divorce unaffected by distortions caused by the changing size of marriage cohorts.[2] Such an index would give slightly too low a value because, in time, the size of a marriage cohort is reduced by mortality as well as by divorce. In a cross-sectional study disturbances may also be introduced by the timing of divorces. However, the sum of duration-specific divorce rates provides a relatively good indicator of the proportion of marriages that are terminated by divorce. If statistics are available for a sufficiently long period, both cohort and period indices of divorce frequency can be calculated and compared to show the proportion of marriages in a given year that are terminated by divorce.

Such indices for different European countries are compared in Table 3.3. The figures in the table show that there was an increase in divorce frequency after the Second World War in all European countries, irrespective of their social or political systems. The only exception is provided by Romania, a country in which divorce became much more difficult to obtain when the law was changed in 1966. The instability of marriage increased more in the countries of eastern Europe, where changes in the law relating to families came into effect after the end of the war. From the 1960s onwards, however, marriages in western Europe, too, became noticeably less stable, irrespective of whether or not the laws relating to divorce were liberalized. Even before the law reforms of the late 1960s and early 1970s in England and Wales, Finland, Norway, and Sweden, the number of divorces in these countries increased considerably, and the same is true of countries in which the divorce laws remained unchanged. The impact of these changes became manifest in the tendency for divorces to occur at even earlier durations of marriage in successive marriage cohorts.[3]

[2] L. Henry, 'Mesure de la fréquence des divorces', *Population*, 2 (1952).

[3] J. Cammaille, P. Festy *et al.*, *Le Divorce en Europe occidentale: La loi et le nombre* (Paris, 1983), p. 242.

Table 3.3 Percentage of marriages terminating in divorce in different European countries, 1955–1980

Country	1955	1960	1965	1970	1975	1980
Eastern Europe[a]						
Bulgaria	6	10	10	15	—	—
Czechoslovakia	11	13	17	22	—	—
Hungary	18	18	23	25	28	29
Romania	19	20	20	5	—	—
USSR	—	14	30	30	—	—
Western Europe[b]						
Austria	15	14	15	18	20	26
Belgium	7	7	8	10	16	21
Denmark	19	19	18	24	37	39
England and Wales	7	—	11	16	32	39
Finland	11	11	14	17	26	27
France	10	10	11	12	17	25
Federal Republic of Germany	—	10	12	16	21	—
Netherlands	7	7	7	11	20	26
Norway	8	9	10	13	21	25
Sweden	16	17	18	23	50	42
Switzerland	13	13	13	16	21	27

Sources:
[a] P. Festy and F. Prioux, 'Le Divorce en Europe depuis 1950', *Population*, 6 (1975).
[b] Commaille *et al.*, op. cit. (n. 3).

The apparent diminution in the number of divorces in the Federal Republic of Germany after the law relating to divorce was changed in 1977 does not constitute a real exception to this trend. The decrease was only temporary, and did not indicate any change in the attitude to marriage: it resulted mainly from a change in legal procedures. The trends over the last 20 years in the Federal Republic of Germany are in line with those in other European countries. The rates for 1975 imply that almost one marriage in four (24 per cent) will be terminated by divorce, and the upward trend is likely to continue.[4]

The large differences between the divorce rates of different European countries are due to the fact that the recent rises began from very different initial levels. The statistics for 1980 demonstrate that marriage and divorce behaviour has changed throughout Europe. More than one-quarter of all marriages now end in divorce, and this figure goes to show that divorce has nowadays become institutionalized, and forms an integral part of the European family system.

Statistics from Hungarian cohort studies confirm the conclusions drawn

[4] C. Höhn, 'Rechtliche und demographische Einflüsse auf die Entwicklung der Ehescheidungen seit 1946', *Zeitschrift für Bevölkerungswissenschaft*, 3–4 [1980].

from the cross-sectional data (see Table 3.4).[5] Table 3.5 shows information relating to divorces by duration of marriage. The sum of the duration-specific divorce rates comes to 2,766 per 10,000 marriages in 1975 and to 3,211 in 1984, an increase of 16 per cent within ten years. Although more recent marriages appear to have been slightly more stable, it could well be that the proportion of marriages ending in divorce at longer durations will increase, and that if the trends of the 1970s and 1980s were to persist, the proportion of all marriages that end in divorce could reach 40 per cent during the 1990s.

Table 3.4 Proportion of marriages ending in divorce, 1962–1977

Marriage cohort	Proportion of marriages ending in divorce after	
	6 yrs.	10 yrs.
1962	11	14
1967	12	16
1972	13	17
1977	14	—

Table 3.5. Divorces by duration of marriage, 1970–1984

Duration of marriage (yrs.)	No. of divorces				% of divorces				Duration-specific rates			
	1970	1975	1980	1984	1970	1975	1980	1984	1970	1975	1980	1984
0	642		852	671	2.8		3.1	2.3	66	72	106	90
1	1,798		2,127	1,808	7.9		7.6	6.3	188	208	244	238
2	2,014		2,358	1,911	8.8		8.5	6.7	211	219	255	253
3	1,936		2,305	1,914	8.5		8.3	6.7	201	217	238	248
4	1,748		2,184	1,865	7.7		7.9	6.5	187	198	217	232
5	1,561		1,908	1,835	6.8		6.9	6.4	174	181	184	211
6	1,310		1,611	1,723	5.7		5.8	6.0	150	164	161	186
7	1,121		1,449	1,672	4.9		5.2	5.8	133	141	143	172
8	929		1,252	1,563	4.1		4.5	5.4	114	124	128	156
9	840		1,131	1,533	3.7		4.1	5.3	101	118	120	148
10–14	3,519		4,448	5,303	15.4		16.0	18.5	380	430	465	541
15–19	2,519		2,541	3,407	11.0		9.1	11.9	250	290	300	362
20+	2,904		3,631	3,506	12.7		13.0	12.2	345	404	375	374
TOTAL	22,841		27,797	28,711	100.0		100.0	100.0	2,500	2,766	2,936	3,211

Source: *Demográfiai Evkönyv* (*Statistical Yearbook*), 1970, 1980, 1984 (Budapest). Duration-specific rates were calculated from the statistics given in this publication.

[5] J. Csernák, 'A házasságkötési mozgalom és várható alakulása a következő *évtizedekben: házasodási és válási hipotézisek*' ('*Movements in Nuptiality and Expected Changes therein during the Coming Decades: Hypothesis on Marriage and Divorce*'), in *Társadalmi-demográfiai prognózisok: A Népességtudományi Kutató Intézet Kutatási Jelentései* (*Socio-demographic Forecasts: Reports on Researches of the Demographic Research Institute*), 17(3) (1984).

Any assessment of the social and demographic consequences of the greater instability of marriage must take account of the ages of divorced persons as well as of the duration of the dissolved marriages. Age-specific divorce rates vary considerably. For men, they are highest in the age groups 20–4 and 25–9 (Table 3.6). In 1984 divorce rates in these two age groups reached 21 and 22 per 1,000 respectively. Age-specific rates for men decline gradually after the age of 30, but are not negligible even among men aged 60 and over. Nine hundred and twenty-five men of these ages were divorced in Hungary in 1984. Women's age-specific divorce rates reach a maximum in the age group 20–4 (23 per 1,000). Rates for the age group 25–9 are slightly lower, and they continue to fall at an increasing rate for older woman. Age at divorce will of course depend on age at marriage and duration of marriage. In 1984, duration-specific divorce rates were highest for marriages which had lasted three years. Seven per cent of all divorces occurred during the third year of marriage. Allowing for year-to-year fluctuations, it would be justified to say that the frequency of divorce is at a maximum for marriages which have lasted between two and four years. Similar results have been obtained from a cohort analysis.[6]

Table 3.6 Age-specific divorce rates in Hungary, 1970 and 1984 (per 1,000)

Age	1970		1984	
	Men	Women	Men	Women
–19	8.9	12.9	12.4	18.6
20–4	18.6	18.8	21.2	22.7
25–9	17.9	16.1	22.1	20.5
30–4	14.1	11.1	19.2	16.9
35–9	10.8	8.9	15.7	13.4
40–9	7.9	6.3	10.3	7.8
50–9	4.3	3.3	4.2	3.1
60+	1.7	1.4	1.5	1.2
TOTAL	8.4	18.4	10.5	10.5

Source: Demográfiai Évkönyv (*Demographic Yearbook of Hungary*) 1970 and 1984 (Budapest).

It is generally believed that the probability of a marriage ending in divorce is negatively correlated with age at marriage. However, the results of recent studies in western Europe, where ages at marriage have recently increased, suggest that the relationship is not as systematic as had been thought.[7] But in Hungary, where, in common with other eastern European countries, people tend to marry young, there does appear to be a negative correlation. In a

[6] *Demográfiai Évkönyv* (*Demographic Yearbook*), 1984 (Budapest).

[7] P. Festy and F. Prioux, 'Le Divorce en Europe depuis 1950', *Population*, 1975 (6).

cohort study of marriages of 1966 and 1974, it has been shown that the marriages of women who marry in their teens are less stable than those of older brides. Thus, among women married in their teens in 1966, 8 per cent were divorced within three years of their marriage, while the corresponding proportion for women married between the ages of 20 and 24 was 4 per cent. For women married in 1974, the figures were 6 and 4 per cent respectively.[8]

In a study of marriages which had ended in divorce and in which there were minor children of the marriage, it has been shown that there is a close relationship between early marriage and the propensity to divorce. The mean age at marriage of grooms whose marriages ended in divorce was 22 years, between two and two and a half years lower than the mean age at marriage of all men in any one of the last 15 years. The age difference for brides was slightly smaller, but in the same direction. The average age at marriage of women whose marriages ended in divorce was 20 years, between one and one and a half years lower than the mean age at marriage of spinsters in the recent past.[9]

Unfortunately there are no statistics which make it possible to calculate divorce rates for different social groups. All that we can do is to relate the number of divorces to the total number of workers in different occupations or occupational groups (Table 3.7). The highest divorce rates are found among professional workers, followed by manual workers employed outside industry or agriculture (i.e. in transport, commerce, etc.). Divorce rates are significantly lower among workers employed in agriculture than among either non-manual or other manual workers. However, the proportion of older workers in the agricultural labour force is higher than in other occupational groups, and as divorce rates among older persons tend to be lower, this may account for the discrepancy. This is also the reason for the low proportion of women in the 'shopkeepers and small independent producers' group.

The social incidence of divorce in Hungary is similar to that found in other countries. Although international comparability is made difficult by the existence of different social classifications, it is generally found that divorce rates are low among agricultural workers and that they are also lower in the higher social strata. Divorce rates of non-manual workers exceeded those of manual workers in Austria, England and Wales, and Hungary. However, in Belgium, Finland, the Federal Republic of Germany, and Norway, divorce

[8] F. Kamarás and Z. Oroszi, *Házasság és család az* 1970-*es években* (*Marriage and Family in the 1970s*) (Budapest, 1983).

[9] *A válás következtében felbomlott, kiskorú gyermekes családok életkörülmény vizsgálatának táblái* (*Statistics Relating to the Circumstances of Families which have been Dissolved by Divorce and which have Minor Children*) (Budapest, 1983), p. 145. This enquiry was based on a representative sample taken in 1980 by the Institute for Sociological Research of the Hungarian Academy of Sciences and the Demographic Statistics Division of the Hungarian Statistical Office. The sample consisted of couples divorced in 1978, and contained 1.8% of all divorces granted in Budapest and 3.2% of those granted in the rest of the country. It was stratified to reflect differences by area, socio-demographic characteristics, and numbers of minor children.

Table 3.7 Number of divorces per 1,000 workers in different occupations, 1981

Occupational group	Men	Women
Manual workers		
Industry	9.6	12.8
Agriculture	5.5	8.3
Other	10.7	13.2
Foremen	7.0	11.6
Agricultural labourers	6.7	6.0
All manual workers	9.7	12.8
Non-manual workers		
Managers and Directors	6.8	9.8
Professional workers	13.4	13.8
Administrative workers	5.0	11.2
All non-manual workers	10.4	12.4
Shopkeepers, small independent producers, etc.	11.9	4.5

Source: 1980. évi Népszámlálás, 22, *Foglalkozási adatok*, I (*Census of 1980*, vol. 22, *Occupations*), (Budapest), *Demográfiai Évkönyv* (*Demographic Yearbook*), 1981 (Budapest).

rates were highest among manual workers, and in some cases particularly high among unskilled labourers.[10] It has been shown that differences in incomes, working conditions, and life-styles all affect divorce rates. There is no evidence for the proposition that divorce occurs most frequently in the higher social groups, and that its frequency is reduced as one descends the social scale.[11]

Statistics are available showing the educational level achieved by persons who are divorced, but there is no information about the educational level of the population by marital status. By using as a denominator the population aged 20–59 of different educational status, but without distinction of marital status, a rough estimate of the divorce rate by educational status can be obtained (Table 3.8). Divorce rates for each sex are highest amongst those who have received no more than an elementary education, and fall as the level of education achieved increases. The relatively low divorce rate among people in the lowest educational group is probably accounted for by the fact that this group contains a disproportionately high humber of older people, among whom divorce rates are low.

The Causes of Divorce

In countries where divorces are granted on the grounds of a matrimonial offence it is, in theory, possible to describe the causes of divorce by tabulating the offences which lead to a divorce. But the reasons adduced in a court of law

[10] R. Chester, *Divorce in Europe* (Leiden, 1977), p. 316.

[11] L. Cseh-Szombathy, *Családszociológiai problémák és módszerek* (*Problems and Methods of Family Sociology*) (Budapest, 1979), p. 402.

Table 3.8 Estimated divorce rates per 1,000 persons aged 20–59 by level of education, 1981

Level of education	Men	Women
Lower than eighth grade primary school	5.2	3.8
Eighth grade, primary school	17.5	13.2
Secondary school, grades 9–12	10.2	11.4
College or university	9.9	10.2

Sources: 1980. évi Népszámlálás, 21, *Demográfiai adatok* (*Census of 1980*, vol. 21, *Demographic Data* (Budapest); *Demográfiai Évkönyv* (*Demographic Yearbook*), 1981) (Budapest).

are not necessarily the true reasons for the breakdown of the marriage. In present-day Hungary, a divorce can only be granted on the grounds of irretrievable breakdown of marriage, and the court files do not contain any particulars relating to the reasons for the breakdown.

An alternative method for studying the causes of divorce would be by survey. However, this method is not altogether satisfactory either, because respondents may not be prepared to reveal to an interviewer all the circumstances which resulted in the breakdown of their marriage, or they may attach disproportionate importance to some specific causes. At best, interview studies can only give subjective interpretations for the reasons which have resulted in breakdown. However, in spite of these reservations some interest attaches to the results of an enquiry undertaken jointly by the Institute of Sociological Research of the Hungarian Academy of Sciences and the Central Statistical Office in 1980.[12] In this survey, living conditions of broken families in which there were minor children were studied in 1980, two years after the marriage had ended. Respondents were asked for the causes which, in their view, had resulted in the breakdown of the marriage. The answers are of some interest (Table 3.9). As two years had elapsed between the date when the divorce was granted and the survey, it may be assumed that respondents had had sufficient time to re-evaluate their former marriages and the circumstances which led to their breakdown with some degree of objectivity.

One-third of both men and women believed that the causes which had resulted in the breakdown of their marriage had already been present at the time when the marriage took place. The most frequent reason stated by respondents was pre-marital sexual relations (29 per cent). There are two reasons for the frequency of this reply. Greater sexual permissiveness has resulted in pre-marital sexual relations occurring much more frequently than formerly, particularly between engaged couples, and this has resulted in an increase in the number of 'forced marriages', in which the bride was already pregnant at marriage. Respondents were also asked for the reasons that had

[12] Op. cit. (n. 9).

Table 3.9 Principal reasons stated by respondents as reasons for divorce as given by respondents (%)

	Men	Women	Total
Reasons present at the time of the marriage			
Pre-marital sexual relations	29.5	27.6	28.5
Influence of parent(s) or other relative(s)	2.8	2.3	2.5
Financial or other reasons	—	0.4	0.2
Too young when married	0.5	0.7	0.7
Other	2.1	1.3	1.5
Total	34.9	32.3	33.4
Reasons arising during the marriage			
Alienation from partner by reason of			
Character differences	6.6	6.2	6.4
Jealousy	3.0	1.3	2.1
Illness	0.5	0.4	0.4
Other	6.6	6.4	6.5
All alienation	*16.7*	*14.3*	*15.4*
Sexual incompatibility	3.0	2.5	2.7
Drunkenness	4.8	15.9	11.1
Ill-treatment	1.0	3.4	2.4
Spends free time away from home	0.8	2.5	1.7
Love-affairs at workplace	1.0	1.1	1.1
Love-affairs elsewhere	10.6	9.3	9.8
Differences caused by children	0.8	0.8	0.8
Crime	0.5	0.6	0.6
Living with in-laws	4.1	1.7	2.7
Employment far from home	0.5	—	0.2
Chronic neglect of family	0.8	2.6	1.8
Housing problems	2.5	2.3	2.4
Financial arguments	3.0	2.6	2.8
Mutual lack of understanding	8.4	3.4	3.7
Other	4.0	3.3	3.7
Total	62.5	66.3	64.7
No answer/unknown	2.6	1.4	1.9
GRAND TOTAL	100.0	100.0	100.0

led to conflict in their marriages. Thirty-six per cent of the respondents blamed a pre-marital pregnancy for the deterioration in their relationship, though it should be emphasized that the reasons for conflict given by the respondents often differed from the main reasons which led to a divorce.

Two-thirds of the reasons given for the breakdown of marriages related to events which had emerged during the course of the marriage. The most important of them were drinking habits—particularly those of men—and emotional alienation. The results of several Hungarian studies on the causes of divorce show the increasing importance of drunkenness as a cause. The proportion of marriages in which this is given as a reason for dissolution has increased by 30 per cent since 1960. Although alcohol abuse can be found in all social groups, its effects differ in different social strata and at different levels of education. The proportion of divorces in which drunkenness is given as the reason is highest among manual workers and among those who have not completed their primary school education (in this group the proportion is between 32 and 38 per cent).[13]

Divorce is an indication that the personal, conjugal, and family conflicts of the spouses cannot be resolved in any other way. However, if we are to understand the reasons for the increased frequency of divorce, it is also necessary to look at the larger society, as some of the conflicts between spouses can be related to that area.[14]

Socio-economic Conditions in Hungary and their Effect on Marriage and Divorce

Levinger has stated that divorce rates will be affected by the inhibitions and attitudes which surround and protect the institution of marriage, as well as by the alternative life-styles that are available to divorced persons, and that these variables must be investigated, as well as the deterioration of the relationship between the spouses. Where inhibitions relating to marriage are strong and few alternatives are available, a marriage may remain in existence in spite of tension or differences between the partners. On the other hand, if the inhibitions can easily be broken, and divorced persons are able to reorganize their personal and economic lives reasonably easily, even minor frustrations may lead to a breakdown of the marriage.[15]

We shall use Levinger's findings to consider the part played by socio-economic changes in Hungary in raising the frequency of divorce.

The Transformation from Private to Social Ownership

The predominance of social ownership is a basic characteristic of Hungary's present socio-economic order. For the individual family this means that its livelihood depends on the work performed by its members for institutions which are socially owned, or for government, education, or the health services which work for society as a whole.

Property relationships and the organization of production changed in Hungary as a result of the social upheavals which occurred between 1945 and the mid-1960s, and these changes had a profound effect on family life. Private ownership of the means of production was abolished to a very large extent,

[13] A. Klinger (ed.), *A válás, a válás okai* (*Divorce and Grounds for Divorce*) (Budapest, 1975) summarizes the judicial statistics for 1975, as well as women's replies to interviews.

[14] L. Cseh-Szombathy, *A házastársi konfliktusok szociológiája* (*Sociology of Marital Conflict*) (Budapest, 1985), p. 188.

[15] G. Levinger, 'Marital Cohesiveness and Dissolution: An Integrative Review', *Journal of Marriage and the Family*, 1 (1965).

and large-scale organizations became more important. By 1960, four-fifths of the working population were employed in the nationalized or co-operative sector of the economy, and only one-fifth in the private sector. Between 1952 and 1961, the proportion of land held by state farms and co-operatives increased from 15 to 93 per cent, and farming based on the private ownership of land was virtually abolished.[16]

The socialist reorganization of agriculture and the retreat from the traditional system of peasant farming removed some of the limitations which had surrounded the dissolution of marriages and restrained divorce. Under a system of private ownership family members were forced to stay together, because their property formed the basis of their livelihood. In the socialist system of farming, an individual's livelihood will depend on his or her input of personal work. Where there is a difference between spouses' income, continued cohabitation does not compensate the spouse with the lower income sufficiently to make him or her put up with the negative aspects of the marriage. Each spouse would continue to have a secure livelihood even if their marriage were to end.

Full Employment of Women

Among the socio-economic changes of the last few decades, unquestionably the one which had the largest effect on divorce was the increase in the gainful employment of women. Today, nearly all women in Hungary are gainfully employed. This has resulted in changes in the structure of families, and has made a continuation of the traditional way of life almost impossible; as the family has become much more open to outside influences, the roles of the spouses needed to be modified (Table 3.10). Conflicts between husbands and wives were caused because women who were gainfully employed outside the home could no longer discharge the traditional household obligations which were regarded as appropriate for them. The majority of men had grown up at a time when the woman's role as a wife and mother was considered to be the most important. But today women are increasingly trained, both in school and in society, to enter the same occupations and have the same career ambitions as men.

The dual role of the wife remains possible as long as there are no children of the marriage. At the beginning of a marriage most men are prepared to accept an egalitarian view of the family and are prepared to undertake some domestic tasks. But the situation changes with the birth of the first child, when motherhood forces the wife to remain at home, at least for a time. The egalitarian structure of the family then tends to shift back into the traditional direction. If the wife leaves her employment for a period of several years, this

[16] *1960 évi Népszámlálás. Demográfiai adatok* (*Census of Demographic Data* 1960) (Budapest, 1960).

Table 3.10 Distribution of women of working age by economic activity, 1960–1980: percentages of women aged 15–54

	1960	1970	1980
Economically active	49.9	68.5	80.2
Pensioners	0.7	1.3	3.0
Dependants	49.4	30.2	16.8
TOTAL	100.0	100.0	100.0

Source: 1980. évi Népszámlálás, 22, *Foglalkozási adatok*, I (*Census of 1980*, vol. 22, *Occupations*) (Budapest).

shift tends to become permanent, and many women are unable to accept this. At the time of the Census of 1980, 29 per cent of women between the ages of 20 and 24, and 23 per cent of those between the ages of 25 and 29 were caring for children at home. It is not surprising that divorces tend to peak in these age groups, and between the third and fifth years of marriage, when the majority of first births tend to occur and couples find themselves unable to solve the conflicts which arise as a result. Mass employment of women has also changed the boundaries of the family. Meetings with the opposite sex at the workplace may lead to relationships which result in the breakdown of marriages.

Housing

Housing conditions form an important part of a family's standard of living and can affect the stability of a marriage. During the early stages of marriage, a couple's housing situation may be the single most important factor which affects the development of their relationship. The cohort study of marriages contracted in 1966 shows that two-thirds of married couples began their married lives in the homes of parents, relatives, or friends, where they lived as part of another family. One-fifth began their marriage in an independent home of their own, just over 10 per cent in lodgings, and between 4 and 5 per cent had to live apart, even after their marriage.[17] The housing shortage means that many married couples may have to wait for between six and seven years after their marriage before being able to set up on their own. Seventy per cent of those who have been married for six years and 90 per cent of those who have been married for 14 years have homes of their own. Thus, many married couples will have had to take account of other people's convenience at a time when they need to adjust to their life together. Where a couple have to live with the family of one of the spouses, it is difficult for the new family to develop its own identity, as the strength of the filial tie may lead to role conflicts for one or other of the spouses.[18]

The acquisition of an independent apartment normally entails sacrifices for

[17] Op. cit. (n. 14).
[18] Op. cit. (n. 8).

the spouses: longer working hours, a reduction of consumption levels, and self-denial. Divorces often tend to occur when the strain of obtaining independent accommodation is over: tensions between husband and wife can no longer be explained away, and the couple must face the basic reasons for their incompatibility.

Social Mobility

Even though the degree of social mobility in Hungary has decreased during recent years, many economically active persons belong to a social stratum that differs from that of their parents. This high degree of social mobility is due to the structural changes which occurred in Hungarian society after the Second World War (Table 3.11). Industrialization and the socialist reorganization of agriculture resulted in substantial inter-generational mobility. For instance, in 1973, 70 per cent of the men and more than 50 per cent of the women whose parents were peasants now belonged to a different social group. But even those who have not themselves been socially mobile are likely to have changed their way of life. Those who have entered a different social group will wish to adopt the norms and behaviour of their new group which may well differ from those of their group of origin. Social mobility reduces the cohesiveness of the family and weakens its traditions. In Hungary, it was the rural population which was mainly affected by this change, and it was in that section of the population that the tradition of indissoluble marriage had been strongest in the past. The characteristics that a socially mobile person looks for in his or her spouse will also change, and he or she may find a more suitable partner in the new environment.

Table 3.11 Changes in the social structure, 1949–1980: composition of population by social status (per cent)

	1949	1960	1970	1980
Manual workers, foremen	41.2	56.3	57.4	58.2
Co-operative farmers	0.3	12.1	20.3	15.8
Non-manual workers	8.7	14.8	19.5	23.3
Small independent producers	48.1	16.7	2.8	2.6
Capitalists, landlords	1.7	0.1	—	—
TOTAL	100.0	100.0	100.0	100.0

Source: Statisztikai Évkönyv (*Statistical Yearbook*), 1975; *1980. évi Népszámlálás*, 22, *Foglalkozási adatok*, II (*Census of 1980*, vol. 22, *Occupations*).

Urbanization

The divorce rate per 1,000 existing marriages in 1981 was 13.1 in Budapest, 12.2 in other towns, and only 6.6 in the villages. Even today divorce is mainly an urban phenomenon, and marriages tend to be considerably more stable in the villages. One of the principal causes of social change in the past was the mass migration to the towns, and as a result the distribution of the population by area of residence has changed considerably. The figures in Table 3.12 show that the process is still not complete. The increase in the proportion of married couples living in towns could result in a rise of the national divorce rate. Even at the present time, behaviour in villages is subject to greater restraints imposed by the local community, and the traditional norms result in a greater tolerance of conflict between the spouses. In the towns, informal community restraints are negligible and the determining factors are contacts at the workplace or other friendships, which often result in a weakening of the conjugal bond.

Table 3.12 Proportion of married couples by area of residence (per cent)

	1960	1980
Budapest	19.0	18.6
Other towns	29.2	33.2
Villages	51.8	48.2
TOTAL	100.0	100.0

Source: 1980. évi Népszámlálás, 21, *Demográfiai adatok* (*Census of 1980*, vol. 21, *Demographic Data*).

The Consequences of Divorce

In present circumstances, when divorce is relatively frequent, it no longer carries a social stigma. Divorced persons find it less difficult than formerly to find a place in society. The study of divorces carried out in 1980 showed that more than one-quarter of divorced men and one-fifth of divorced women had achieved promotion in their employment. The proportion who reported that their divorce had had unfavourable effects in their workplace amounted to only 6 per cent of men and 2 per cent of women. During the two years following divorce, the financial circumstances of 50 per cent of the women and 40 per cent of the men improved. Sixty per cent of the women, but rather fewer than one-half of the men, reported that their standard of living had risen.[19] These changes were the result of a combination of factors, such as the advantages gained through an eventual remarriage, the situation of the parent who kept care and control of any children of the marriage, and the possibility of retaining the marital home.

However, there were other consequences of divorce that were far from

[19] Op. cit. (n. 14).

positive. Divorce often inflicts serious emotional damage on the individual. Forty per cent of divorced men and 23 per cent of divorced women experienced disappointment or depression when the divorce was made final. In the enquiry of 1980 it was found that 32 per cent of the men and 39 per cent of the women had not been successful in finding a new spouse or partner within two years of their divorce. In the past, a very high proportion of divorced persons remarried. According to the marriage rates of the 1960s, three-quarters of the divorced men and nearly two-thirds of the divorced women could expect to find a new marriage partner. However, both the number and the rates of remarriage are declining. If the rates of 1980 were to continue, approximately half of all divorced persons could expect to contract a new marriage during the remainder of their lives.[20] However, the decline must not be interpreted as meaning that those who do not remarry have failed to find a new partner. The Census results for 1980 showed that 15 per cent of divorced men and 9 per cent of divorced women were living in consensual unions. The proportion for men was highest in the age group 40–9 (17 per cent), and for women in the age group 30–9 (12 per cent). As extra-marital relationships are regarded with a much greater degree of tolerance today, it can be expected that the proportion living in consensual unions will continue to increase.[21]

These changes have altered the composition of the population by marital status. The proportion of divorced persons in the population has increased: in 1980 it amounted to 6 per cent of men and 8 per cent of women between the ages of 35 and 39. Preliminary estimates suggest that this figure may reach 9 per cent for men and 10 per cent for women by the end of the century.[22] Another consequence is an increase in the proportion of single persons and of one-parent families. In 1980, 11 per cent of families were single-parent families, and in the majority of these cases (84 per cent), it was the mother who was living with one or more of the children.

The fertility of marriages which end in divorce is low (1.05 children per marriage in 1984), but there has been a gradual increase in the proportion of marriages ending in divorce which contained children. Before 1945 the majority of marriages which ended in divorce were childless; today 70 per cent of such marriages contain children. In 1984 a total of 29,932 minor children were affected by their parents' divorce. If current divorce rates were to continue, some 18 per cent of all children will experience a divorce in their family.[23] All children of broken marriages are likely to suffer emotionally by their parents' divorce. However, it has been shown that for the majority the negative effects appear to be temporary, and that they apparently regain their emotional equilibrium within a period of two years following the divorce.

[20] Op. cit. (n. 9).
[21] Op. cit. (n. 5).
[22] Op. cit. (n. 1).
[23] J. Csernák and K. Szabó, *A családok és háztartások előreszámítá, 1981–2001* (*Families and Households: Forecast, 1981–2001*) (Budapest, 1985).

Explanations which attempt to trace later problems of maladjustment to the effects of a parental divorce are, therefore, open to question.[24]

Divorce presents a significant social problem in Hungary today. The increase in the instability of marriages has led to the demand that the State should take steps to encourage family stability by direct or indirect measures. At the same time there is pressure for the difficulties and frictions of divorce to be reduced as far as possible, where a marriage has irretrievably broken down, so that divorced persons and their children can adjust to their new situation. The provision of services for this group of people is one of the most important objects of contemporary Hungarian family policy.

[24] Op. cit. (n. 6).

4 The Demographic Determinants of the Duration and Incidence of Widowhood

JOHN BONGAARTS
The Population Council

In studying the family life cycle, demographers have in the past given more attention to its early phases, particularly formation and expansion, than to the last phase of dissolution. The interval that concludes the family life cycle is usually referred to as the widowhood phase, because it equals the time between the deaths of the two spouses (if the possibility of remarriage and divorce is ignored). The relative neglect of the widowhood process appears to be due to several factors. First, statistics on the demographic characteristics of individuals who are widowed are scarce, because they are not routinely collected in most countries. Secondly, as will be demonstrated in the next section, procedures for estimating widowhood variables are complex, and the simple formulae that give reasonable approximations for the durations of early phases of the life cycle cannot be used to estimate the duration of widowhood. Finally, only a relatively small proportion of most populations is widowed. This is especially true of populations with a rapid rate of natural growth over several decades, because this growth has led to a young age structure.

The recent rise in interest in widowhood is probably in large part due to the rapid changes that are occurring in the age structure of the populations in much of the developed world. A considerable reduction in the level of fertility during the past two decades, combined with continued declines in mortality, have resulted in substantial increases in the proportion of the population that is elderly. Projections of future population generally indicate that this trend will continue for several more decades. Fortunately, demographers are now in a position to respond to the growing need for a better understanding of demographic processes among the elderly, because new analytical tools, such as multiple increment–decrement marital-status life-tables, have recently been developed. It is the object of this chapter to use this new method to investigate the demographic determinants of the incidence and duration of widowhood. Synthetic marital-status life-tables are constructed from period data for the USA in 1800, 1900, and 1980, to study trends in widowhood variables by using a comparative static approach.

Method

It is appropriate to start this brief discussion of methods for measuring variables associated with widowhood by mentioning a simple but incorrect procedure that has been and is still being used to estimate the average duration of widowhood. In this procedure the average is obtained by subtracting the life expectancy of the husband at the time of marriage from the corresponding figure for the wife. That this estimate cannot be accurate is obvious, if one considers the case in which life expectancy at marriage of husband and wife are the same. The mean duration of widowhood would then, of course, not be zero. In fact, if both spouses were subject to the same risks of mortality throughout their married life, exactly half the husbands and half the wives would be widowed. The average period which the survivors would spend in the widowed state would obviously be positive.

Myers[1] was the first to propose a more accurate formula by estimating the duration of widowhood as the mean expectancy of life of the survivor at the death of the spouse. Myers also provided equations to calculate the proportions of husbands and wives who lose a spouse through death, and the mean age when this event occurs. Elaborations of this approach can be found in studies by Feichtinger.[2] Although the work of Myers and Feichtinger provided very valuable insights and constituted a major improvement in method, it still had a significant drawback. To make their analytical equations manageable, it was necessary to assume that there was neither remarriage nor divorce. Since the remarriage of widowers and, to a lesser extent, of widows is common in most societies, and since divorce has become increasingly frequent in contemporary developed countries, remarriage and divorce cannot realistically be ignored in the analysis of widowhood.

To arrive at more accurate estimates of widowhood variables, it is necessary to use the more complex method of the multiple increment–decrement marital-status life-table. In the standard form of the marital-status life-table a cohort of individuals is followed from their birth until the last member has died. (Marital-status life-tables can be calculated for real or for synthetic cohorts. In this study only synthetic cohorts are used.) During their lives, individuals are continuously at risk of dying and of changing their marital status by marriage, divorce, death of spouse, or remarriage. The simplest marital-status life-tables typically divide the cohort into four categories: single, married, divorced, and widowed. Throughout life, the marital-status life-table shows the number of individuals in each marital-status group and the number of transitions between states during

[1] R. J. Myers, 'Statistical Measures in the Marital Life Cycle of Men and Women', *Proceedings of the International Population Conference, Vienna, 1959* (Paris, 1962).

[2] G. Feichtinger, 'The Impact of Mortality on the Life-cycle of the Family in Austria', *Zeitschrift für Bevölkerungswissenschaft*, 4 (1977); 'The Statistical Measurement of the Family Life-cycle', in J. Bongaarts, K. Wachter, and T. Burch (eds.), *Family Demography: Methods and Their Application* (Oxford, 1987).

each age interval. From these 'stock' and 'flow' data, a variety of summary measures, such as the mean number of years spent in each state, can be calculated. An extensive literature on marital-status life-tables now exists,[3] but a review of these studies falls outside the scope of this report.

The analysis of the demographic determinants of widowhood presented in the next sections is based on an extended version of the marital-status life-table proposed by Schoen.[4] Instead of distinguishing between only four different marital-status groups, six will be used (see Fig. 4.1). This more detailed life-table permits the separate identification of individuals who have been widowed once, and of those widowed more than once. With these additional categories it is possible to estimate the proportion of the cohort who ever lose a spouse through death (this cannot be done with the simpler marital-status life-table). The present analysis differs further from Schoen's, in that marriage rather than birth cohorts will be studied. This seemed more appropriate because only married persons can be widowed.

In order to calculate a marital-status life-table, it is necessary to provide as inputs the rates of transition between different states in the table; that is, mortality, widowhood, divorce, and remarriage rates specific by age and marital status are needed for each population or point in time for which a marital-status life-table is constructed. In the applications to be discussed next, marital-status life-table results are calculated from status transition rates estimated to have prevailed in the USA in 1800, 1900, and 1980. Period rather than cohort data were used, because they were more readily available. The procedures and sources used to calculate the various input variables are summarized in the appendix to this chapter. In Table 4.1 we present life expectancies at birth for men and women in 1800, 1900, and 1980, as well as the ages at marriage of the first marriage cohorts whose widowhood experience will now be analysed in more detail.

[3] See R. Schoen and V. E. Nelson, 'Marriage, Divorce and Mortality: A Life Table Analysis', *Demography*, 11 (1974); R. Schoen, 'Constructing Increment–Decrement Life Tables', *Demography*, 12 (1975); R. Schoen and K. C. Land, 'A General Algorithm for Estimating a Markov-generated Increment–Decrement Life Table with Applications to Marital Status Patterns', *Journal of the American Statistical Association*, 74 (1979); T. J. Espenshade and R. E. Braun, 'Life Course Analysis and Multistate Demography: An Application to Marriage, Divorce and Remarriage', *Journal of Marriage and the Family*, 44 (1982); F. I. Willekens *et al.*, 'Multi-state Analysis of Marital Status Life Tables', *Population Studies*, 36 (1982); F. I. Willekens, 'Multidimensional Analysis of Marriage and Family', in Bongaarts *et al.*, op. cit. (n. 2).

[4] Schoen provides equations for calculating a marital-status life table with four statuses: single, married, divorced, and widowed. The marital-status life table cited here, with six marital statuses, as summarized in Fig. 4.1, consists of a combination of two revised versions of Schoen's basic table. The revision consists of dropping the single state, so only three states are left in the basic table. In the first of the revised basic tables, stocks and flows are calculated for the married, divorced, or widowed states before remarriage following widowhood. The second basic table consists of the same calculations for the three remaining states in Fig. 4.1: the married, divorced, and widowed after remarriage following the first widowhood. All individuals enter the marital-status life table in the married state at the minimum age of first marriage. The transition risks between states are functions of age and marital status as described in the appendix to this chapter.

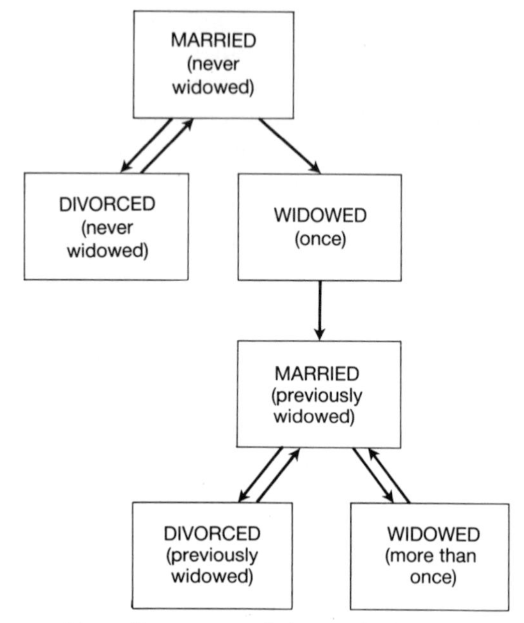

Fig. 4.1 State transition diagram used in marital-status life-table analysis of widowhood process.

Table 4.1 Life expectancies at birth and age at marriage of first marriage cohorts used in the marital-status life-table calculation of widowhood variables

	1800	1900	1980
Life expectancy at birth			
Women	37	48	78
Men	35	46	70
Age at marriage of first marriage cohorts			
Women	20	23	23
Men	24	26	25

Source: S. J. Watkins, J. Menken, and J. Bongaarts, 'Composition and Change in the American Family', paper presented at the Annual Meeting of the American Psychiatric Association, Los Angeles, May 1984.

The Incidence and Duration of Widowhood of First-marriage Cohorts

Although the marital-status life-table can provide an extremely detailed and varied description of the transitions from one marital-status group to another in marriage cohorts, we will for simplicity focus on just two variables relating to widowhood: (i) the proportions of husbands and wives who are widowed at least once during their lives, and (ii) the mean duration of widowhood. In Fig. 4.2 we plot the life-table estimate of the proportions of men and women widowed in the USA at rates prevailing in 1800, 1900, and 1980 (all results are for first-marriage cohorts with ages at marriage as given in Table 4.1). At each point in time, substantially higher proportions of women than of men lose their spouse through death. This is to be expected because men's mortality rates exceed those of women, and husbands are on average older than their wives. The proportion widowed is relatively constant, with values near 0.58 at each point. For men, this proportion was 41 per cent in 1800 and 1900, but declined to 29 per cent in 1980. Fig. 4.2 also gives the estimated average duration of widowhood in 1800, 1900, and 1980. This variable reached maximum values of 13.3 years for women and 7.5 years for men in 1900. The minimum values are 12.3 for women in 1800 and 6.3 years for men in 1980.

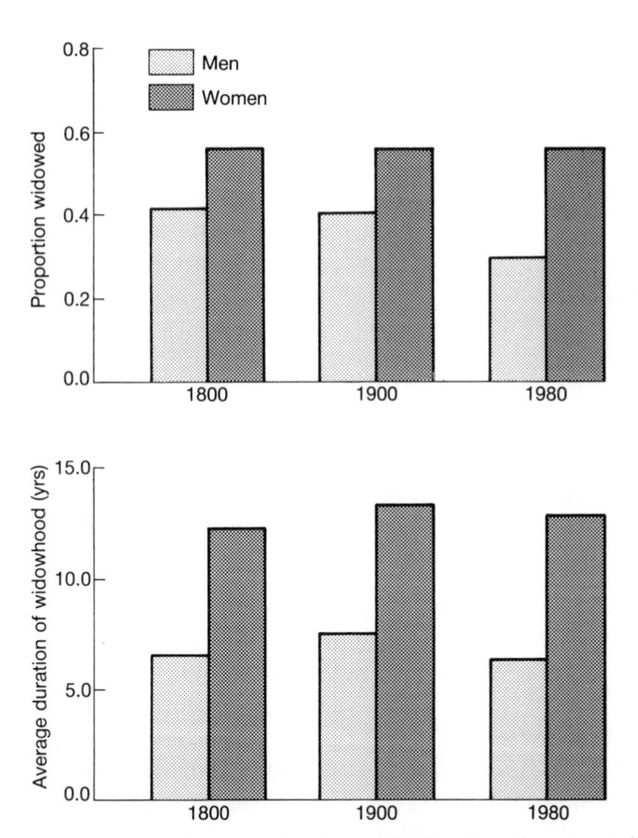

Fig. 4.2 Estimated proportion experiencing widowhood and average duration of widowhood, by sex, for USA first-marriage cohorts in 1800, 1900, and 1980.

Considering the large decline in overall mortality that occurred between 1800 and 1980, it is somewhat surprising to find so little variation in the duration of widowhood. On the other hand, duration of widowhood is, as expected, longer for women than for men because men's mortality rates are higher and a higher proportion of men remarry, the two events that terminate widowhood. The relative constancy of the duration of widowhood for both sexes is probably in large part explained by the compensating effects of increasing life expectancy at all ages and the lengthening duration of marriage before being widowed between 1800 and 1980. Other things being equal, duration of widowhood for an individual who is widowed, at say age 60, would be shorter in 1800 than in 1980 because life expectancy at age 60 has increased between these dates. However, the longer survival of marriages compensates for this, so that widowhood, on average, occurred at an earlier age in 1800 than in 1980.

Fig. 4.3 provides additional insights into the processes that yield the results discussed thus far. In it are plotted the proportion of the first marriage cohorts among *surviving* men and women that were ever widowed at different durations of marriage. There is a very significant trend over time in this proportion: at all durations of first marriage the proportion ever widowed declines between 1800 and 1980. This is, of course, a consequence of the substantial decline in age-specific risks of widowhood over time. The results in Fig. 4.3 are readily reconciled with those in Fig. 4.2, if it is remembered that the overall proportion widowed at each point in time given in Fig. 4.2 equals the weighted average of the duration-specific results in Fig. 4.3. In 1800, the proportion widowed among survivors at a given duration of marriage was higher than in 1980, but fewer survived to the longer durations of marriage, so that the overall proportion widowed for each marriage cohort did not change greatly over the period considered. In other words, the higher mortality in 1800 compared with 1980 produced a higher risk of death for both spouses, with compensating effects on the overall proportions of each sex who are widowed.

The Determinants of the Incidence and Duration of Widowhood

The levels and trends in the widowhood variables estimated to have prevailed between 1800 and 1980 in the USA are determined by a set of demographic factors that include mortality, age at marriage, divorce, and remarriage. A change in any of these factors influences the incidence and duration of widowhood, but their effects differ. To ascertain which of these demographic determinants are most important in affecting widowhood, we will use the marital-status life-table to carry out a sensitivity analysis, by starting with the standard marital-status life-table results given in Fig. 4.2 and varying one input variable at a time (while leaving the others constant) to isolate the effect of each demographic determinant.

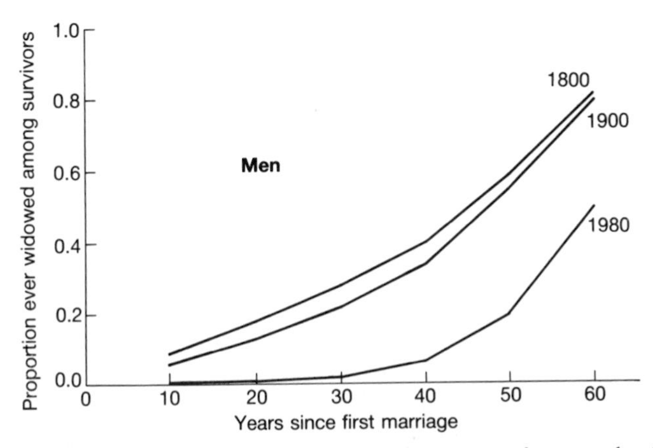

Fig. 4.3 Proportion ever widowed among surviving men and women by duration of first marriage, USA, 1800, 1900, 1980.

Age at Marriage

Changes in the ages at marriage of the first marriage cohorts have remarkably little effect on the proportions widowed in each cohort. For example, increasing or decreasing ages at marriage of both men and women by five years changed the proportion becoming widowed by less than 0.1 per cent, and the duration of widowhood by less than 0.1 years. Clearly, age at marriage is not an important determinant of widowhood variables.

In contrast, the difference between spouses' age at marriage is a crucial factor, as is shown in Fig. 4.4. The two left panels of this figure show that both the proportion widowed and the mean duration of widowhood increased very substantially as age differences between the spouses change from zero to ten years. The increase in the proportion widowed ranged from 12 per cent in 1800 to 18 per cent in 1980, and the rise in the mean duration of widowhood ranged from 0.9 years in 1800 to 3.2 in 1980. The two right-hand panels show the corresponding effects for the marriage cohorts of men. In this case the impact of a ten-year change in the age difference between spouses was also substantial for the proportion widowed, but the average duration of widowhood changed little.

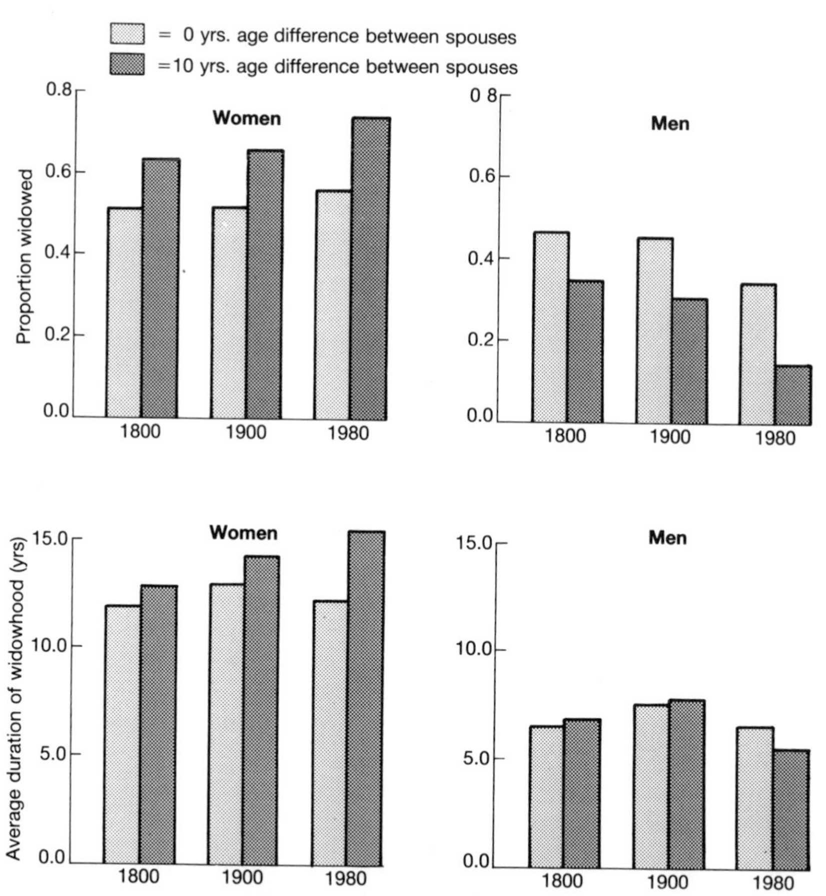

Fig. 4.4 Estimated proportion widowed and average duration of widowhood, by sex and by age difference between spouses, for USA first-marriage cohorts in 1800, 1900, and 1980.

Mortality

Using the marital-status life-table for 1800 as a reference point, an estimate of the effects of mortality on widowhood was obtained by changing the level of life expectancy at birth of both men and women, while leaving all other life-table input variables the same. Increasing the life expectancy of both sexes to the levels prevailing in 1980 (i.e. from 37 to 78 years for women and from 35 to 70 years for men) resulted in an increase of 16 per cent in the proportion of women widowed and a decline of 14 per cent of the proportion of men becoming widowers. The mean duration of widowhood rose from 12.3 to 14.6 years for women, and from 6.5 to 7.6 years for men. These rather substantial changes are due in part to the absolute increases in life expectancies of both sexes, and in part to the rise in the difference between life expectancies from two years in 1800 (37 compared with 35 years) to eight years (78 compared with 70 years).

Divorce

To evaluate the significance of divorce as a determinant of widowhood, a series of marital-status life-tables were calculated in which the probability of divorce was set equal to zero. In Fig. 4.5 the estimated widowhood variables without divorce (dashed lines) are compared with the standard values (solid lines, as in Fig. 4.2). As would be expected from the low levels of divorce in 1800 and 1900, reducing the risk of divorce to zero has virtually no effect at those dates. In 1980, the risk of widowhood is increased by 9 per cent when divorce is removed, but all other variables showed little change.

Remarriage

Removing the possibility of remarriage from the marital-status life-tables produces very different effects on the two widowhood variables studied here. As expected, the level of remarriage does not affect the proportion who lose a spouse, because remarriage takes place after a marriage has ended (the divorce risk is also set equal to zero). However, as is clear from the two bottom panels in Fig. 4.5, eliminating remarriage dramatically lengthens the mean duration of widowhood. For example, in 1800 more than five years are added to the mean duration of widowhood and its value more than doubles from 6.5 to 13.5 years. Between 1900 and 1980 the duration of widowhood in the absence of remarriage shows a clear downward trend which is not evident in the presence of remarriage.

Conclusion

The preceding marital-status life-table analysis of the proportion widowed and the mean duration of widowhood in the USA in 1800, 1900, and 1980 indicates that these variables have remained fairly constant over time. The only exception to this generalization was a decline between 1900 and 1980 in the proportion of men that were widowed. The variables examined did not show a substantial trend over time despite the fact that demographic conditions, in particular the level of mortality, had changed drastically between 1800 and 1980. The probable explanation of this finding is

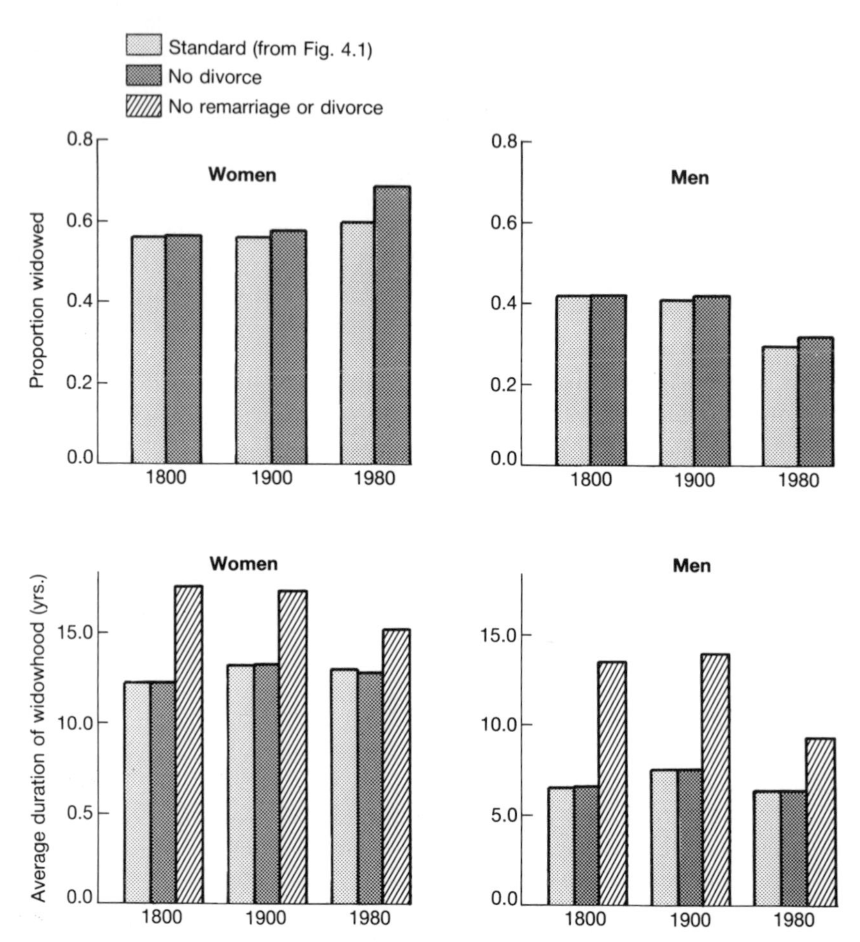

Fig. 4.5 Estimated effects of divorce and remarriage on proportion experiencing widowhood, and average duration of widowhood, by sex, for USA first-marriage cohorts in 1800, 1900, and 1980.

that different determinants had compensating effects on widowhood.

In the previous section of this chapter the effects of changes in mortality and of age at marriage, divorce, and remarriage on widowhood were examined separately. We concluded that widowhood variables are quite sensitive to the level of mortality, differences between mortality of the two sexes, the age difference between spouses, and the level of remarriage. The latter finding clearly indicates that erroneous estimates of levels and trends in the duration of widowhood are obtained if the possibility of remarriage is ignored. Results from analyses of widowhood that do not rely on the marital-status life-table for taking into account the impact of remarriage and divorce must, therefore, be used with caution.

Appendix

The calculation of a marital-status life-table requires that the transition rates between different marital-status groups given in Fig. 4.1 are specified as inputs. These include mortality rates specific by age, sex, and marital status, divorce, widowhood, and remarriage rates. The task of specifying input data is simplified here by introducing model schedules which can be identified with a limited set of input parameters (this procedure is similar to the one outlined by Bongaarts).[5]

Remarriage and divorce. Age-specific remarriage rates for widowed and divorced women and age-specific divorce rates for married women are derived from standard schedules. Two standards are used, equal to the US 1975 and 1910 patterns respectively, as estimated by Schoen.[6] The actual remarriage and divorce rates used in marital-status life-tables are calculated from these standards by multiplying by an 'index' which is assumed to have the same value for all age groups. Specifying remarriage and divorce rates, therefore, requires the selection of the standard either of 1975 or of 1910, and the specification of three parameters: the index of remarriage for divorced women, the index of remarriage for widowed women, and the index of divorce. The following indices were used in the preparation of the illustrations in this chapter:

	1800	1900	1980
Standard schedule	1910	1910	1975
Index of divorce	0.2	1.0	1.1
Index of remarriage (widowed)	1.0	1.0	1.0
Index of remarriage (divorced)	1.0	1.0	1.0

Mortality. Average age-specific mortality rates for men and women are taken from Coale and Demeny's model life-tables,[7] using interpolation as required. Input parameters are the life expectancies for men and women at birth. To make mortality rates marital-status-specific, the average rates are inflated or deflated by proportions equal to those found in Schoen's marital-status-specific marital-status life-tables for 1910 or 1975.[8] For the USA in 1800 and 1900 the relative levels in Schoen's tables for 1910 are used, while in the tables for 1980 the relative marital-status-specific mortality rates for 1975 were employed.

Widowhood. The age-specific rate of widowhood is set equal to the mortality rate of the male spouse whose age is a predetermined number of years higher (or lower) than that of their female spouses. This age difference is an input parameter equal to the difference between the ages of marriage given in Table 4.1.

[5] J. Bongaarts, 'The Projection of Family Composition over the Life Course with Family Status Life Tables', in Bongaarts *et al.*, op. cit. (n. 3).

[6] R. Schoen, *United States Marital Status Life Tables for Periods 1910–75 and Cohorts 1880–1945*

[7] A. J. Coale and P. Demeny, *Regional Model Life Tables and Stable Populations* (Princeton, NJ, 1966).

[8] Op. cit. (n. 6).

5 Remarriage: A Life-Cycle Perspective

PETER UHLENBERG
University of North Carolina

Introduction

Early discussions of the life cycle of the family focused on the mean ages at which selected events occurred (marriage, birth of children, departure of children from the home, and dissolution of the marriage).[1] These discussions are useful in directing attention to changes in the timing of life transitions, but they are too simplistic to capture the full complexity of historical change.[2] The life course is not, nor has it ever been, a neat and orderly process. Each member of a cohort does not experience each family event, and the events which are experienced may occur at different stages of life and in variable sequences for different individuals. A challenge which now confronts demographers interested in families and households is to develop better ways of dealing with the complexity of the life course without being overwhelmed by the diversity of individual experiences.

The focus of this chapter, remarriage, has received scant attention from demographers. Two developments, however, are stimulating increased interest in this topic. First is the expanding availability of historical demographic data and the recognition that 'remarriage is more important in populations of the past than is apparent at first sight'.[3] Second is the increasing frequency of remarriage in recent years.[4] As research on remarriage becomes more common, it is useful to examine what is known and what questions most need answering. A life course perspective provides a good framework for such a task. It suggests a way of organizing the existing literature, reveals gaps in existing knowledge, and directs attention to relevant questions.

[1] P. C. Glick, 'The Family Cycle'. *American Sociological Review*, 12 (1947); *American Families* (New York, 1957).

[2] P. Uhlenberg, 'A Study of Cohort Life Cycles: Cohorts of Native-born Massachusetts Women, 1830–1920', *Population Studies*, 23 (1969); 'Cohort Variations in Family Life Cycle Experiences of US Females', *Journal of Marriage and the Family*, 36 (1974).

[3] J. Dupâquier E. Hélin, P. Laslett, M. Livi-Bacci, and S. Sogner (eds.) *Marriage and Remarriage in Populations of the Past* (New York, 1981).

[4] F. F. Furstenberg and G. B. Spanier, *Recycling the Family: Remarriage after Divorce* (Beverly Hills, CA, 1984).

Perspective on Remarriage

Remarriage is an event experienced by a select portion of each cohort as it moves through time. As with other life-course events (e.g. marriage child-bearing, divorce), there are a number of questions that relate to its determinants and consequences. These questions can be grouped around three aspects of the process: exposure to the risk of remarriage, the propensity to remarry among those at risk, and the aftermath of remarriage compared with no remarriage.

In addition to identifying several aspects of remarriage, a life course perspective also sensitizes the researcher to important contextual variables. These may be pictured as different facets of one's location. First, each individual is located at a particular place in her or his unique life course. Secondly, each person occupies a place within the larger social structure. And thirdly, each individual occupies a position in historical time. These locational factors structure the way in which individuals (or cohorts) encounter and respond to the various aspects of the remarriage process.

Regarding life-course location, remarriage is a transitional event that is preceded and followed by a variety of other events. Recognition that earlier childbearing, employment, education, kin involvement, etc. influence remarriage suggests a series of questions for research. Similarly, the potential impact of remarriage on subsequent life (childbearing, kin involvement, etc.) raises a variety of interesting problems. The second aspect of location, position in the social structure, is multi-faceted. It involves such familiar variables as sex, social class, racial–ethnic identity, religion, and place of residence. As with the other locational parameters, position in the social structure cuts across all three aspects of the remarriage process. Individuals in different social locations are exposed to different risks of remarriage, respond differently to the option of remarriage, and experience different consequences of their decisions. Finally, location in historical time reminds us that each individual (or cohort) lives during a particular period of history. In European and American societies, a larger proportion of members of recent cohorts than of earlier ones will be exposed to the risk of remarriage because of divorce, rather than through the death of a spouse. Other relevant changes have occurred in sex roles, living arrangements, norms and social policies affecting the family, and length of life.

The discussion that follows is structured around the life-course perspective on remarriage outlined above. The effects of one's location (position in the life course, social structure, and historical setting) on each step of the remarriage process are explored.

Exposure to Remarriage

Remarriage in Europe and North America appears to have been relatively common in earlier eras, but declined in frequency during the eighteenth and nineteenth centuries.[5] Since 1900, on the other hand, the incidence of remarriage has been increasing. According to estimates by Jacobson,[6] almost 90 per cent of all marriages in the USA at the turn of the century were first marriages. By 1981 this proportion had declined to 55 per cent, and in almost one-quarter of the marriages both the bride and groom had been previously married. What accounts for the rising incidence of remarriage? Theoretically, the increase could be the result of an increasing number of individuals exposed to the risk of remarriage, or an increasing propensity to remarry among those exposed to the risk, or both. In this section we examine changes in exposure to the risk of remarriage.

First Marriages

Some individuals in every population are never exposed to the risk of remarriage, because they never marry for a first time. A simple way to assess the direct effect of non-marriage upon the level of remarriage is to ask what difference it would make if all bachelors and spinsters had married at the same rate as the rest of the population. Under this hypothetical condition, the pool of eligibles for remarriage in a cohort would increase by a factor equal to the proportion never married.

Using this approach, it appears that non-marriage has not played a significant role in changing the frequency of remarriage in the USA during the past 100 years. Over 90 per cent of all men and women in cohorts reaching middle age during the past 100 years have married at least once, and hence have been at risk of having their marriages end. The proportion never married among those aged 65 and over ranges only from 5.6 to 9.8 per cent, and the changes in propensity to remain unmarried have not been monotonic. Further, age at first marriage may influence exposure to remarriage since, *ceteris paribus*, those who marry earlier may expect a larger number of years remaining after their first marriage has ended. But again, shifts in age at first marriage are not large enough to have much effect. Median age at first marriage for women declined from 22.0 in 1890 to a low of 20.3 around 1960, and then climbed back up to 21.8 by 1980. Basically, variations in first-marriage patterns have been too small to have had significant consequences for historical changes in remarriage levels in the USA.

In Europe, more variability in non-marriage exists. At one extreme is Ireland, where throughout most of the twentieth century over one-quarter of the population aged 45 and over had never married. As Hajnal has shown,[7]

[5] Dupâquier, *et al.*, op. cit. (n. 3); J. Demos, *A Little Commonwealth: Family Life in Plymouth Colony* (New York, 1970); J. D. Griffith, 'Economy, Family and Remarriage: Theory of Remarriage and Application to Preindustrial England', *Journal of Family Issues*, 1 (1980).

[6] P. H. Jacobson, *American Marriage and Divorce* (New York, 1959).

[7] J. Hajnal, 'European Marriage Patterns in Perspective', in D. V. Glass and D. E. C. Eversley (eds.), *Population in History* (London, 1965).

relatively high proportions of non-marriage (15 or more) and late age at marriage have been common in many European countries in recent history. When comparing the incidence of remarriage in different countries, it may be relevant first to account for variations in exposure due to variations in first-marriage patterns. Further, recent increases in the proportion entering first marriage in most European countries[8] have contributed to the increasing occurrence of remarriage. The effect of this change is however relatively minor.

Death and Divorce as Factors in Remarriage

Two events result in individuals moving from the category of 'married' to 'formerly married': death of spouse and divorce. During the past 100 years, the first cause of marital disruption has decreased in importance while the second has increased. Several authors[9] have noted that from 1860 to 1970 the decrease in mortality roughly balanced the increase in divorce, so that the annual rate of marriage dissolution in the USA remained almost unchanged (at about 30 dissolutions per 1,000 existing marriages). While this observation regarding the relative stability of marital disruption is useful for some purposes, it is misleading to view the two different kinds of marriage termination as interchangeable. (Also, the dissolution rate *has* increased substantially since 1970, to more than 40 per 1,000 existing marriages by 1980.)

The major contrasts between divorce and death of spouse as events leading to the potential for remarriage include the following:

(i) Historical trends move in opposite directions. With a few brief exceptions, in the USA the annual rate of marriage dissolution due to death has declined since 1860, while the rate due to divorce has increased. Divorce was uncommon around 1860, causing only between 3 and 4 per cent of the dissolutions of marriage in that year. The proportion of marriage dissolutions caused by divorce increased thereafter, exceeding 25 per cent by 1920, 50 per cent by 1974, and 55 per cent by 1980. These period rates are not, however, the preferred measure to use when approaching the topic from a life-course perspective. Annual rates reflect the age composition of the married population and short-term fluctuations.

Using a cohort approach to describe causes of marriage dissolution, the same historical pattern is observed. Table 5.1 shows the relative contributions of death and divorce in terminating marriage for several different marriage

[8] D. A. Coleman, 'Recent Trends in Marriage and Divorce in Britain and Europe', in R. W. Hiorns (ed.), *Demographic Patterns in Developed Societies* (London, 1980).

[9] K. Davis, 'The American Family in Relation to Demographic Change', in Commission on Population Growth and the American Future, Research Reports, vol. i, *Demographic and Social Aspects of Population Growth* (Washington, DC, 1972); A. Cherlin, *Marriage, Divorce, Remarriage: Changing Patterns in the Postwar United States* (Cambridge, Mass., 1981); M. J. Bane, *Here to Stay: American Families in the Twentieth Century* (New York, 1976).

cohorts. The proportion of marriages ended by divorce increases steadily from 5.3 per cent for the marriage cohort of 1867 to a projected 49.6 per cent for the cohort of 1976. Since in the USA propensity to remarry after divorce is higher than after widowhood, this trend has contributed to the overall rise in the frequency of remarriage.

Table 5.1 Proportion of marriages dissolved by death and divorce for US marriage cohorts, 1867–1976 (per cent)[a]

Year	Marriages ended by	
	Death	Divorce
1867	94.7	5.3
1870	93.3	6.7
1880	91.8	8.2
1890	90.2	9.8
1900	88.0	12.0
1910	86.1	13.9
1920	82.0	18.0
1930	76.3	23.7
1940	74.6	25.4
1950	72.9	27.1
1960	66.2	33.8
1977	50.4	49.6

[a] For more recent cohorts, the proportions ending in divorce are projected using current duration of marriage specific divorce rates.

Sources: Preston and McDonald, op. cit. (n. 18); J. A. Weed. 'National Estimates of Marriage Dissolution and Survivorship': United States' *Vital and Health Statistics*, series 3, Analytic Studies 19 (1980).

Throughout West European and Scandinavian countries divorce rates have increased rapidly since the 1960s.[10] Large variations exist between European countries, partially reflecting differences in the restrictiveness of divorce law in different countries. In none of these countries do divorce levels match those in the USA, but divorce rates are very high in England and Wales, Sweden, and Denmark. Thus, recent trends are in the same direction for all Western societies, where exposure to remarriage is increasingly a result of divorce rather than death of spouse.

(ii) The duration-specific probabilities of death or divorce occurring after marriage move in opposite directions. In the USA, the probability of divorce peaks around the third year after the wedding and then declines continuously

[10] P. Festy and E. Prioux, 'Le Divorce en Europe depuis 1950' *Population*, 30 (1975).

with duration. In Germany and Austria, the peak for divorce also occurs during the third year after marriage, while in other European countries it happens between the fourth and sixth years.[11]

In contrast, the probability of death dissolving a marriage is very low during the first few years after the wedding and then increases continuously. Thus marriages dissolved by divorce, in contrast to those dissolved by death, are more likely to end early in the life course, leaving individuals exposed to the risk of remarriage for longer, and at ages when the propensity to remarry is higher.

(iii) Death leaves one marriage partner 'formerly married'; divorce leaves two. Marriages dissolved by divorce produce twice as many individuals at risk of remarriage as to marriages dissolved by death. Thus, as divorce becomes an increasingly important cause of marriage disruption, the pool of eligibles for remarriage grows disproportionately larger. Equally important, divorce is not sex-selective, while mortality is. Because men's mortality exceeds that of women and because of the age differences between spouses, marriages dissolved by death produce many more widows than widowers. Divorces, on the other hand, produce an equal number of divorced men and women.

(iv) Widowhood occurs in one step, divorce in two. From a demographic perspective, death is a clear-cut event that transfers the survivor of the marriage into the category of 'widowed', thereby placing her or him at risk of remarriage. Divorce is more ambiguous because legal divorce is preceded by a period of separation of varying length. As phrased by Thornton: 'Is a separated woman married or unmarried? Is the re-marriage process best seen as beginning with separation or divorce?'[12] A proportion of marriages ended by separation (and this proportion varies over time and between groups) is never legally terminated by divorce. Thus, a comparison of remarriages following widowhood with those following divorce may be misleading if the 'separated but not divorced' are excluded from the analysis.[13]

(v) Social complications following divorce tend to be greater than those following death. Until quite recently in American society, there was general agreement that marriages should only be ended by the death of one partner,[14] and death was indeed the cause of most dissolutions. Consequently, legal and social norms governing widowhood were institutionalized and the status of the widowed was clearly defined. Social and economic support was expected to be forthcoming from kin and community, and the rights of the widowed to social security benefits and to the property of the deceased spouse were fairly explicit. In contrast, the aftermath of divorce has not been fully institutionalized, and considerable ambiguity exists regarding the status and rights of the

[11] Coleman, op. cit. (n. 8).

[12] A. Thornton, 'Decomposing the Re-marriage Process' *Population Studies*, 31 (1977).

[13] Ibid. Cf. also J. A. Sweet, 'Differentials in Remarriage Probabilities', working paper, Center for Demography and Ecology, University of Wisconsin, Madison (1973).

[14] L. S. Weitzman, *The Marriage Contract* (New York, 1981).

divorced. Aspects of the ambiguity in the social position of divorced men and women discussed by Goode, Bernard, and Cherlin[15] include: ties with former spouse and his or her kin, ties with children for the parent not given custody, relationships with friends, rights to social security and pension benefits, and roles in such social organizations as Church, community, and clubs. Differences between the social position of divorced and widowed individuals have important implications for remarriage. While social disapproval of divorce has recently declined, the various ambiguities in the social position of the divorced have not disappeared.

Dissolution of Marriage by Death

As noted above, death was almost always the cause of dissolution of marriage 100 years ago, and consequently remarriage generally involved the widowed. Mortality declines during the past century have several implications for remarriage patterns. If death were the only cause of marriage termination, and if propensity to marry following widowhood had remained unchanged, the frequency of remarriage would have declined substantially over time. Three aspects of the mortality decline contribute to this outcome.

Data from the USA illustrate the effects of recent mortality changes (see Table 5.2). First, declining death rates lead to a later mean age at widowhood. An increase in the age at which a significant number of individuals are exposed to the risk of remarriage is important because remarriage rates decline sharply with age. In 1980, for example, the remarriage rate fell from 119.7 for women aged 25–44 to 19.9 for those aged 45–64 and 2.3 for those aged 65 and over.[16] Secondly, the average number of years between the deaths of the spouses has diminished. A shorter period of survival following widowhood means fewer years of exposure to the risk of remarriage. And thirdly, the much greater decline in women's mortality than in that of men has increased the imbalance between widows and widowers. As the ratio of widows to widowers increases, the marriage market becomes less favourable for overall levels of remarriage.

While the direct effect of mortality change upon remarriage has been negative, there has been one positive indirect effect. The continuous rise in the average number of years lived after marriage has increased the years of exposure to the risk of divorce. In 1890, the average length of a marriage that was ended by the death of one of the spouses was 28.2 years; in 1977 it was 43.4 years.[17] Preston and McDonald[18] have estimated that if members of the 1867

[15] W. J. Goode, *After Divorce* (New York, 1956); J. S. Bernard, *Remarriage: A Study of Marriage* (New York, 1956); A. Cherlin, 'Remarriage as an Incomplete Institution', *American Journal of Sociology*, 84 (1978).

[16] National Center for Health Statistics, 'Advance Report of Final Marriage Statistics, 1981', *Monthly Vital Statistics Report* 32(11), supplement (1984).

[17] N. Goldman and G. Lord, 'Sex Differences in Life-cycle Measures of Widowhood', *Demography*, 20 (1983).

[18] S. H. Preston and J. McDonald, 'The Incidence of Divorce within Cohorts of American Marriages Contracted since the Civil War', *Demography*, 16 (1979).

Table 5.2 Aspects of widowhood and widowerhood, 1890, 1940, 1977

Aspect	Year		
	1890	1940	1977
Median age at			
widowhood	49	59	65
widowerhood	55	62	68
Mean years remaining after			
widowhood	22	19	19
widowerhood	20	15	13
Ratio of survivors			
widows/widowers	1.3	1.6	2.2

Source: Goldman and Lord, loc. cit. (n. 17).

marriage cohort had experienced contemporary levels of mortality, the number of divorces would have been 29.5 per cent higher than its actual level. However, since divorces were uncommon in the cohorts in which mortality was high, the absolute increase in the proportion of marriages ending in divorce would have been rather trivial (from 5.3 to 6.9 per cent for the cohort of 1867). Thus, factors other than extension of life must be found to account for the increasing incidence of remarriage over the past century.

Dissolution of Marriage by Divorce

In contrast to the mortality decline, the increasing incidence of divorce has greatly increased overall exposure to the risk of remarriage in the population. Some significant effects for remarriage of the increasing proportion of marriages dissolved by divorce have already been indicated. First, divorce places twice as many individuals, and an equal number of men and women, into the remarriage market. Secondly, divorce tends to occur early in married life and hence exposes individuals to the risk of remarriage while they are still young and most likely to remarry. Thirdly, controlling for age, the propensity to remarry has always been higher following divorce than following widowhood.[19] (In 1981, for example, the marriage rate was 30.2 per 1,000 for previously divorced women aged 45–64, compared to 7.9 for comparable never-married women and 12.0 for the previously widowed.[20] As noted by Furstenberg and Spanier,[21] 'divorce is generally a transitional rather than a terminal event'.

[19] P. C. Glick and A. I. Norton, 'Marrying, Divorcing and Living Together in the US Today', *Population Bulletin*, 32(5) (1977).

[20] Op. cit. (n. 16).

[21] Op. cit. (n. 4).

Propensity to Remarry

All who survive the dissolution of first marriage face, in some sense, a decision regarding remarriage. In some cases the odds against it are so extreme that no serious notion of remarriage may be entertained. For example, a very old, sick widow will not, except in most unusual circumstances, remarry. On the other hand, an attractive, young, divorced man will almost certainly remarry, and the only question is how soon the remarriage will occur. Between these extremes lies a long continuum of positions. Some will ardently seek a new mate, some will passively wait to see what 'might come by', some will hardly give it a thought, and some will irrevocably reject the idea of remarriage. As with first marriages, some who desire to remarry will fail in their search for an acceptable partner. The basic question underlying the discussion in this section is: what determines the differential propensity to remarry among those at risk?

One's life course, social, and historical locations at the time of dissolution of the first marriage influence the likelihood of remarriage. Factors that have been found significantly related to the probability of remarriage include: age, sex, race, educational attainment, presence of dependent children, cause of disruption of the first marriage, availability of welfare support, and time period.[22] (In addition to these easily quantifiable characteristics, personality —which will not be discussed here—certainly influences the remarriage decision.) To understand better the observed trends and differentials mentioned above, a simple theory of remarriage propensity can be structured around three considerations: the meaning and function of marriage (i.e. what are the attractions of marriage?); the alternatives to marriage (i.e. what are the attractions of remaining single?); and the marriage market for the formerly married (supply of eligible partners and one's own attractiveness to the eligibles).

Function and Meaning of Marriage

Remarriage is marriage, and the cultural meaning of marriage is relevant in determining the motivation to remarry. The functions and meaning of marriage have changed during the past 100 years in all Western countries. While significant differences between countries persist, changes in the USA may serve as a general indicator of more recent historical trends.

Burgess and Locke, writing in the 1940s, referred to the basic transformation of the family as a movement from 'institution' to 'companionship'.[23] In

[22] Cf. J. Chamie and S. Nsuly, 'Sex Differences in Remarriage and Spouse Selection', *Demography*, 18 (1981); Cherlin, op. cit. (n. 9); R. M. Hutchens, 'Welfare Remarriage and Marital Search', *American Economic Review*, 69 (1975); G. B. Spanier and P. C. Glick, 'Paths to Remarriage', *Journal of Divorce*, 3 (1980).

[23] E. W. Burgess and H. J. Locke, *The Family: From Institution to Companionship* (New York, 1945).

the pre-industrial era the functions of marriage were diverse and instrumental. Marriage created a family that was an important unit for economic production, education, and political control. With urbanization and industrialization, economic production moved out of the household and men hired themselves out for wage labour. Schools developed and the education of children moved out of the home. The modern state grew in political power, reducing the political function of the household. In response to these developments, by the late nineteenth century the ideal of the bourgeois family had evolved, with its emphasis on the home as a refuge designed to meet the emotional needs of its members. During the early twentieth century, boarders, lodgers, and servants disappeared from the household, and the family became increasingly private and nuclear. With these changes, marriage has increasingly come to be viewed in such terms as companionship, intimacy, and self-fulfilment. The exclusive justification for marriage has become romantic love, and the standard used to measure marital 'success' is personal happiness.

As the functions of marriage move from more instrumental to more expressive ones, there is no reason to assume that motivation of individuals to re-enter marriage should decline. As long as marriage is the exclusive means for the achievement of desired ends, whatever these may be, one may expect the unmarried (whether single, divorced, or widowed) to desire to marry. However, there may be interesting changes over time in which segments of the formerly married population are most eager to remarry. When economic factors are a more central aspect of marriage, those in economically precarious positions should be highly motivated to remarry. When the emphasis is placed on intimacy and companionship, those who are economically secure but lacking in social support networks might be expected to desire marriage most strongly.

Over time and across social groups, two aspects of life cycle location—presence of dependent children and age—stand out as significant influences on the decision to remarry. Having responsibility for the care and support of young children will tend to increase the salience of concerns that a new spouse be a 'good provider', 'good homemaker', or 'good step-parent'. As a result, single parents have additional concerns that compete with their personal desires for companionship and intimacy. Thus, child-free and single parents may differ in what they desire from remarriage, but there is no a priori reason to assume that they will differ in overall strength of motivation for remarriage.

Whenever and wherever remarriage rates are compared for different ages, a consistent pattern of decline with age is found. Reduced propensity to remarry among older persons may be the result of involuntary factors (discussed later), but it may also be related to reduced motivation. The old may be discouraged from remarrying by their adult children (who are concerned about their inheritance) and by prevalent negative stereotypes about the elderly (e.g. that the old are asexual or unattractive) held by the elderly themselves. There are also life-cycle variations in the salience of various needs experienced by individuals, and in the availability of alternative sources for satisfying these needs.

Alternatives to Remarriage

Normatively, within marriage there is economic interdependence, division of labour, sexual intimacy, and procreation. An important determinant of motivation for marriage or remarriage is the extent to which these 'benefits' are available exclusively through marriage. In other words, if socially acceptable alternatives to marriage develop which allow individuals to have their basic needs and desires met, then the attractiveness of marriage will decline.

Until recently, alternatives to marriage have not provided socially attractive ways of meeting basic needs and desires, and marriage still remains the preferred state for a majority of the population. However, significant changes are occurring which might be expected to reduce the motivation of the divorced and the widowed to remarry. The women's movement has encouraged removal of barriers to sexual equality in the labour force, which in turn has decreased the economic dependence of women upon marriage. The liberalization of sexual attitudes and behaviour is removing the importance of marriage as a pre-condition for sexual relationships. The growth of cohabitation implies that enduring, sexually intimate relationships without remarriage are tolerated. Improved contraceptive methods and greater acceptance of abortion increasingly allow individuals to separate sexual activity from reproduction. Rising illegitimacy and single parenthood indicate that, for many, marriage is not even viewed as necessary for childbearing. The expansion of state-supported social welfare has increased the economic security of single parents and older, retired, single persons. The growth of the service sector means that labour for household tasks formerly performed by wives (cooking, cleaning, laundry, etc.) can easily be purchased. Overall, these various trends are increasing the viability of a single life-style for a growing number of unmarried persons.

The growth during the past two decades of alternative sources for meeting the traditional functions of marriage fits well with the observed trends in remarriage (and marriage). US remarriage rates peaked in 1969 at 135 per 1,000 divorced women aged 14 and over and then steadily declined to 91 by 1982.[24] Concomitant with the fall in remarriage rates is the rise in frequency of cohabitation. Perhaps the best indicator of future trends is Sweden, where cohabitation has become the norm among young people, and where marriage rates have plummeted.[25] At present, there is little basis for predicting how far remarriage rates might fall; no adequate theory of remarriage exists, and

[24] Population Reference Bureau, 'US Population: Where We Are, Where We're Going', *Population Bulletin*, 37(2) (1982); National Center for Health Statistics, op. cit. (n. 16).

[25] M. Gendell, 'Sweden Faces Zero Population Growth', *Population Bulletin*, 35(2) (1980).

future trends in the many social variables influencing remarriage are unknown.

Remarriage Markets

The remarriage market and an individual's position in it, in addition to strength of motivation, determine the probability of remarriage. The pool of potentially eligible marriage partners is determined by demographic, geographical, and social factors. Population structure is an appropriate starting-place, since it sets an upper boundary on the pool of eligibles.

The maximum pool of eligibles consists of all unmarried adults of the opposite sex in the population. Because of differential mortality, the market favours men over women, and men's advantage increases with age. Widening sex differences in death rates have increased the advantage of men throughout this century. Sex ratios at a national level are not, however, entirely relevant. Marriage markets are primarily local, and substantial variations exist between the sex ratios in different areas. Sex ratio variability may be an important determinant of regional or urban–rural differences in remarriage rates, but empirical studies of this factor are lacking.

Social norms greatly reduce the actual supply of eligibles in the remarriage market from the larger supply implied by narrow demographic and geographical considerations. In every society a cluster of norms regulates who is considered eligible as a marriage partner. Most of the homogamy norms governing first marriages apply to remarriages as well (although there may be some reduction in sanctions against violations, since remarriage is less institutionalized). For example, age, religion, race, and social class operate to define who, among all unmarried of the opposite sex, are really available. Special note should be made of social class and age, since these function differently for men and women.

Norms encouraging marriage only to those of equal or higher social status apply to women, but not to men. As a result, there is a decided market disadvantage encountered by widows of high status or highly educated divorced or widowed women. Age constraints are even more important. Norms regarding acceptable age difference between spouses are asymmetrical and vary with age. The pool of eligible partners for older men, who may choose women much younger than themselves, is much larger than that for older women, who are basically restricted to men older than themselves. In a recent article availability ratios for the US unmarried population have been calculated based on certain age and educational constraints.[26] At ages 40–4, the availability of a marriage partner favours unmarried men over women by an odds ratio of 2.5, and men's advantage increases to an odds ratio of 13.7 for

[26] N. Goldman, C. F. Westoff, and C. Hammerslough, 'Demography of the Remarriage Market in the United States', *Poulation Index*, 50 (1984).

those aged 60–4. Clearly the higher remarriage rates for men (found in every society) are in part a consequence of the different marriage markets for men and women.[27]

Among those who are eligible and motivated to remarry, some are more attractive than others (we use 'attractive' in its broad sense, encapsulating socio-economic status as well as physical appeal). Tangible characteristics giving an advantage include the following: economic resources and social status (especially for men); physical appeal (generally more important for women than for men); absence of dependants (who may be viewed as a burden); and age (*ceteris paribus*, youth is preferred). Additionally, men have an advantage over women not only because of market differences in supply, but also because of the greater economic and political power enjoyed by men in all societies.

Aftermath of Remarriage

Although remarriages are marriages, they differ in important ways from first marriages. People carry with them the experiences, as well as the children and kin, created by their first marriage. And they have a former spouse, either living or dead. Thus, it would be expected that the consequences of a remarriage would differ from those of a first marriage. The consequences of remarriage in three domains are explored in this section: economic, demographic, and kinship. At the outset it can be noted that solid empirical research on the outcomes of remarriage is sparse. This is unfortunate, since the consequences affect a large number of people directly, and all of us indirectly, through their societal effects.

Economic Consequences

Widowhood, divorce, and remarriage have economic implications for individuals, families, and societies. In both historical and contemporary situations, the economic consequences are most serious when adults whose marriage ends have dependent children. In the past, when most marriages were terminated by death, widowhood frequently occurred at a stage of the life cycle when there were dependent children present. Widows with children were left in the precarious economic position of needing to provide for their families in an environment where few employment opportunities and few welfare programmes were available. Widowers with children, like their present-day divorced female counterparts, were faced with the challenging task of combining work and child-rearing. In either case, remarriage provided a solution to the economic problems created by the death of a spouse.

In more recent times, few young children experience the death of a parent.

[27] Chamie and Nsuly, op. cit. (n. 22).

Divorce, however, disrupts a large and growing number of families which contain children. If current US levels persist, about 40 per cent of the children born to members of recent cohorts will experience disruption before they reach the age of eighteen.[28] In about 90 per cent of the cases the mother assumes custody of children following divorce. The drastic decline in the economic welfare of these mothers and their children in the aftermath of divorce has been documented in a number of studies.[29]

How do women and children fare upon remarriage and the establishment of a reconstituted family? Unfortunately, longitudinal studies of this question with a sufficient number of cases to provide solid answers are lacking. But there is no reason to assume that remarriage does not provide an escape route from the poverty created by divorce. Indeed, in a study comparing occupational status of second husbands to that of first ones it was found that 'women generally marry second husbands equal to or higher in status than the first husband's status at marriage'.[30] On the other hand, it is unreasonable to assume that everyone benefits economically from remarriage and that no one loses. Men who marry women with dependent children may experience a loss in economic welfare. Children may find their potential inheritance reduced or lost upon the remarriage of their parents, and, not uncommonly, divorced fathers stop child-support payments to their original families upon remarriage.

At a societal level, the propensity to remarry among those with dependent children will affect welfare expenditures. Child support by fathers after divorce is not, in general, adequate to meet expenses, and mothers who have custody of children rely heavily on state welfare.[31] If it were not for remarriage removing many dependent children from public assistance, the state's welfare expenditures would be much larger than they are. Similarly, as welfare systems expand to cushion the negative economic impact of divorce upon women and children, the total societal welfare burden grows.

Demographic Consequences

Remarriage almost always alters household structure, and it may influence fertility and mortality. Demographic consequences vary, of course, depending on historical and cultural settings and the life cycle stage of those who remarry.

Remarriage, except when it is preceded by cohabitation, leads to the

[28] L. L. Bumpass, 'Demographic Aspects of Children's Second-family Experience', working paper, Center for Demography and Ecology, University of Wisconsin, Madison (1983).

[29] T. J. Espenshade, 'The Economic Consequences of Divorce', *Journal of Marriage and the Family*, 41 (1979); S. Hoffman, 'Marital Instability and the Economic Status of Women', *Demography*, 14 (1977); R. Weiss, 'The Impact of Marital Dissolution on Income and Consumption in Single-parent Households', *Journal of Marriage and the Family*, 46 (1984).

[30] C. W. Mueller and H. Pope, 'Divorce and Female Remarriage Mobility: Data on Marriage Matches after Divorce for White Women', *Social Forces*, 58 (1980).

[31] Weiss, op. cit. (n. 29).

formation of a new household. When the formerly married live alone or in single-person households, remarriage combines smaller households into larger ones. Thus, for adults the transition precipitated by remarriage often involves entrance into a larger and more complex domestic unit where possibilities exist for economies of scale, division of labour, and more intense social interaction. For children, remarriage changes the environment within which socialization occurs. At an aggregate level, remarriage increases average household size and the proportion of the population living in families. To assess the total impact of remarriage on households, it would be possible to compare the actual distribution of individuals' living arrangements with that which would exist if no remarriage occurred. In the USA today, where 20 per cent of the married population are living in households in which one or both spouses have been previously married, the effect of no remarriage would be dramatic.[32] Such a comparison is flawed, however, to the extent that remarriages occur at the expense of marriages among the never-married.

The effect of remarriage on fertility is more complex. If one makes the simplifying assumptions that no fertility occurs outside marriage and that remarriage markets operate independently of first-marriage markets, then the overall impact of remarriage might be calculated directly. All that would be required would be a calculation of the proportion of all births which occur to women who are in second or later marriages. This would be an interesting statistic for an initial comparison between populations. But a precise measure of the impact of remarriage on fertility requires a more sophisticated model.

Three factors complicate the assessment of fertility consequences, even when good data on fertility by marital status exist. First, it is incorrect to assume that all remarried women would not have borne children had they not remarried.[33] Some women who remain divorced or widowed have illegitimate children. The frequency of childbearing outside marriage by the formerly married varies, depending on life-cycle social, and historical location. Secondly, divorced and widowed women may compete with never-married women for marriage partners. Hence, remarriage for women of childbearing age may exclude the first marriage of some younger women, and thereby reduce potential childbearing. Thirdly, if older divorced and widowed men choose younger, fecund women to marry, younger men (who might father more children than the older men) may be excluded from marriage. Merely stating these various considerations does not advance our knowledge of empirical reality. Demographers face the challenge of developing models which incorporate these relevant factors, perhaps experimenting with simulation models where assumptions can be altered.

The effect of remarriage on mortality is also an area open for further

[32] A. Cherlin and J. McCarthy, 'Remarried Couple Households', paper presented at the Annual Meeting of the Population Association of America, Pittsburgh, 1983.

[33] R. Rindfuss and L. Bumpass, 'Fertility during Marital Disruption'. *Journal of Marriage and the Family*, 39 (1977).

exploration. It has repeatedly been found that death rates of the married are lower than those of similarly placed divorced and widowed persons.[34] If marriage offers some protection against death (e.g. by reducing stress, improving economic welfare, or altering life-style), then remarriage may be viewed as a life-extending mechanism. Reasonable estimates of its effect, however, have not been made.

Kinship Consequences

Remarriage, like marriage, creates new kinship ties. Remarriage, however, has an added complexity because kin acquired by the first marriage are not automatically dropped when that marriage is dissolved. This is particularly true when children are involved, and the wide ripple effect of remarriage can be seen by looking at the kin network from the perspective of children. Divorce and remarriage lead to an expanding web of potential kin for children, including step-parents, half-siblings, step-siblings, step-grandparents, and a wide assortment of more distant step-relatives (aunts, uncles, cousins, etc.). Considerable ambiguity exists concerning appropriate relationships between child and both the 'quasi-kin' created by remarriage[35] and the former kin associated with the non-custodial parent.[36] Since relationships involve two-way interactions, one child of a parent who remarries may alter the kin network of a very large number of individuals. What patterns of kin interaction in fact develop after remarriage is an issue of current research interest.[37]

The effect of marriage dissolution and remarriage on kin networks among adults varies by sex and by cause of dissolution. Women, who tend to be the kin-keepers and who generally retain custody of children after divorce in Western societies, are less vulnerable than men to kin disruption by marital-status transitions. For men and women, remarriage following the death of a spouse tends to create less kin ambiguity than remarriage after divorce, since the presence of an ex-spouse complicates the latter situation. The deliberate and often acrimonious nature of divorce, in contrast to widowhood, is likely to have a lasting effect on kinship ties with the former spouse's family, both before and after remarriage. The strength and quality of ties with the family of a new spouse, which are to some extent discretionary anyway,[38] may also vary with the marital status (single, divorced, or widowed) of both parties.

[34] L. March, 'Some Researches concerning the Factors of Mortality', *Journal of the Royal Statistical Society*, 75 (1912); M. C. Sheps, 'Marriage and Mortality', *American Journal of Public Health*, 51 (1961); K. J. Helsing, M. J. Szklo, and G. W. Comstock, 'Factors Associated with Mortality after Widowhood', *American Journal of Public Health*, 71 (1981).

[35] P. Bohannon, *Divorce and After* (Garden City, NY, 1970).

[36] Cherlin, op. cit. (n. 15).

[37] Furstenberg and Spanier, op. cit. (n. 4); G. O. Hagestad, 'Continuity and Connectedness', unpublished paper (1984).

[38] D. M. Schneider, *American Kinship: A Cultural Account* (Englewood Cliffs, NJ, 1980).

Conclusion

Since remarriage is an increasingly common event in the life cycle of members of recent cohorts, it may be expected that demographers will show an increasing interest in it. In response to the methodological challenges, advances in measurement of both exposure to and incidence of remarriage are sure to be forthcoming. It is less certain that demographers will contribute toward the development of a theory of remarriage. In this chapter I argue that a life-cycle perspective offers a very useful starting-point for developing such a theory. It makes clear that historical, social, and life-course location all have important implications for the marriage process. Location affects exposure to the risk of remarriage, as well as propensity to remarry and consequences of remarriage. It is to be hoped that advances in theory will accompany the collection and analysis of new data.

6 The Contemporary Pattern of Remarriage in England and Wales

D. A. COLEMAN

Department of Social and Administrative Studies, University of Oxford

Introduction

Present divorce rates in England and Wales imply that more than one-third of marriages will end in divorce within 25 years,[1] and that almost 30 per cent of men and 25 per cent of women who marry for the first time will remarry at some stage of their lives. Yet, remarkably little is known about the emotional, social, and demographic consequences of remarriage. In the past, the risks of dissolution of a first marriage within 25 years and of the foundation of a new family were, in Western populations, surprisingly similar to those of the present day.[2] However, in the past, the premature dissolution of a marriage among younger couples was most frequently caused by the death of one of the spouses, whereas nowadays divorce is the main cause of the dissolution of marriage where the spouses are under 60 years old. In most of these cases, the previous partner will be alive and may even be living in the same locality.

In 1980, there were some 3.3 million previously married persons who had not remarried in a total population of 25.5 million married and divorced persons.[3] More importantly, 160,000 children are each year deprived of a parent by divorce—by far the biggest section of the child population in one-parent families. Such children either remain in a one-parent family and may need support from the state, or else will have to adapt to the presence of a step-parent. About 7 per cent of all children below the age of 16 in England and Wales now live with a step-parent.[4] According to Haskey,[5] current divorce rates imply that one child in five may expect to experience the divorce of its parents before reaching its 16th birthday.

Remarriage and its attendant problems do not fit in well with notions of the

[1] J. Haskey, 'The Proportion of Marriages Ending in Divorce', *Population Trends*, 27 (1982)

[2] M. Anderson, 'The Relevance of Family History', in C. Harris (ed.), *The Sociology of the Family: Contemporary Developments* (Keele, 1979). Cf. also M. Anderson (ed.), *Sociological Review Monographs* (Keele University, 1980), and 'What Is New about the Modern Family? An Historical Perspective', in British Society for Population Studies/Office of Population Census and Surveys, *The Family* (London, 1983).

[3] Office of Population Censuses and Surveys (OPCS), *Marriage and Divorce Statistics*, 1980 (London).

[4] OPCS, *General Household Survey* (London, (OPCS) 1982).

[5] Haskey, op. cit. (n. 1).

family life cycle, or with more recent concepts of the individual life course.[6] Divorce short-circuits the normal cycle, taking at least one partner from commencement straight to dissolution and the 'empty-nest' stage. Because of divorce and remarriage, entry into and exit from the married state can occur at very different ages and periods of earning capacity or fecundity, and new parallel systems of family life cycles are created among different persons of similar ages. When more than one-half of marriages end in divorce, as in the case in the contemporary USA,[7] parallel family streams of first marriages and remarriages become numerically almost equal.

One of the fundamental problems in the study of remarriage is to establish whether it represents a new beginning at an older than usual age or, conversely, whether it is a new, different, and inherently less well defined and less stable type of association than first marriage. This is considered in more detail later. There is an obvious difference, for example, between the normal expectation that a new marriage will result in children and the problems experienced by new couples in their late thirties and even forties in resuming reproduction.

This chapter has two objectives: to review the present state of knowledge about remarriage in contemporary England and Wales, and to identify the major outstanding problems on which further research is needed. I begin by considering some problem areas in the study of remarriage, review its dynamics as shown by vital statistics, and consider what little is known about the causes of the patterns that are observed. The conclusion will suggest where further work could most usefully be concentrated. Throughout, I shall use the term 'remarriage' for any marriage in which either one or both spouses have previously been married. Shortage of space makes it impossible to consider some important aspects of remarriage, such as its effect upon fertility, or upon the marriage chances of bachelors.

Problems in the Study of Remarriage

Because in many cases strong ties and commitments exist which go beyond the new spouses and their own children (e.g. to former spouses and in-laws, or to children of former marriages), remarriages may be less nucleated and clearly bounded than are first marriages.[8] The different connections to full and

[6] J. Bongaarts, 'The Formal Demography of Families and Households: An Overview', *IUSSP Newsletter*, 17 (1983); G. Elder, 'History and the Family: The Discovery of Complexity', *Journal of Marriage and the Family*, 43 (1981); M. Murphy, 'The Life Course of Individuals in the Family: Describing Static and Dynamic Aspects of the Contemporary Family', in *The Family*, op. cit. (n. 2).

[7] J. Weed, *National Estimates of Marriage Dissolution and Survivorships* (Washington, DC, 1980).

[8] International Union of Family Organizations, *Report of the Commission on Marriage and Family Guidance* (Nuremberg, 1983).

partial members of the family may be conflicting and unequal in strength.[9] As Cherlin has put it,[10] 'remarriage is an incomplete institution.' For others, however, remarriage may represent a release from a previous gross mistake and an opportunity to enjoy what they had expected from their first marriage.[11] The variety of circumstances and experiences of those who have previously been married, unlike the naïvety of the single, is one of the many aspects which not only makes remarriage different from first marriage, but is itself heterogeneous—a major problem both in its comprehension as an institution, and in its statistical study.

Heterogeneity

The varied experiences in their previous marriages of persons who have remarried make possible a multiplicity of comparisons with first marriages. The dispersion of ages is much greater, and the differences between the ages of the parties may be greater.[12] This heterogeneity makes it more difficult to generalize about remarriage than about first marriage. At a more practical level, samples in studies of remarriage need to be large enough to cover each of the three most frequent types: those between divorced men and divorced women, divorced men and spinsters, and bachelors and divorced women. These are between five and ten times as frequent as the least common types of remarriage, all of which involve widowed persons (widowers and spinsters, bachelors and widows, and widowers and divorcees). The social origins and personal attributes of partners in remarriages which have a bearing on their stability have been very little studied. In England, for instance, very little is known about the type of relations between spouses in remarriages compared with first marriages, e.g. whether they are more commonly traditional or egalitarian.[13] Moreover, at current remarriage rates, at least 10 per cent of those who are divorced and about 20 per cent of those who are widowed by their 35th birthday will not remarry. We know little about personality differences between members of this group and those who do remarry.

Stability and Substitution

At current English nuptiality rates, one-quarter of those who ever marry will marry twice, and an unknown number among them will marry for a third time.

[9] L. Bumpass, 'Children and Marital Disruption: A Replication and Update', *Demography*, 21 (1984).

[10] A. Cherlin, 'Remarriage as an Incomplete Institution', *American Journal of Sociology*, 84 (1984).

[11] J. Burgoyne and D. Clark, 'Parenting in Step-families', in R. Chester, P. Diggory, and M. B. Sutherland (eds.), *Changing Patterns of Childbearing and Child Rearing* (London, 1981).

[12] R. Leete, *Changing Patterns of Family Formation and Dissolution in England and Wales 1964–1976* (London, 1979).

[13] B. Schlesinger, 'Husband–wife Relationships In Reconstituted Families', *Social Science*, 52(3).

The number of formal partners a person may have during his or her lifetime is limited by age, money, and the demands of children, but current experience in the USA suggests that the limit may not yet have been reached. New cohabiting partnerships will not be noted in many statistical systems, but tend to rival formal remarriage as a way of life after first marriage. Two out of three remarriages are preceded by cohabitation: one-third of women who live with a second or subsequent partner are cohabiting rather than remarried.[14]

The Image and Self-image of Remarriage

There is no adequate vocabulary in the English language to describe the variety of step- and half-relationships and in-laws which multiple parentage and successive marriages may produce. This is an indication that there exists no normative framework for remarriage or for the behaviour of step-relations, and little legal obligation or informed professional guidance.[15] The first national charitable organization for the support of step-families has only just been formed.[16] Much of a step-parent's energy is likely to be spent in countering the prejudice against him or her which has resulted from tradition, literature, and law. The absence of norms governing step-family relationships is reported in one of the few statistical studies of step-parents in England[17] to be the biggest obstacle to successful family reconstitution. About one-fifth of all children in Britain and two-fifths in the USA will have to learn to live with a new parent before they are 16, and neither the effect on them nor the effect on the second marriage itself have yet been adequately explored.[18]

Problems of Theory

The modern increase in the number of remarriages has taken both the academic world and the practitioners of law and marriage guidance unawares.[19] Most of the demographic and sociological literature on remarriage in English comes from the USA,[20] especially that dealing with the development of suitable methods of study,[21] although there is a substantial

[14] A. Brown and K. Kiernan, 'Cohabitation in Great Britain: Evidence from the General Household Survey', *Population Trends*, 25 (1981).

[15] D. Brown, *The Step Family: A Growing Challenge for Social Work* (Norwich, 1982).

[16] E. Hodder, *The Step Parent's Handbook* (London, 1985).

[17] E. Ferri, *Step-children: A National Study* (London, 1984).

[18] Y. and S. Burns, *Divorce: The Child's Point of View* (London, 1984).

[19] A. Goodie, 'The Aftermath of Divorce', *Marriage Guidance* (Spring 1984).

[20] J. Bernard, *Remarriage: A Study of Marriage* (New York, 1956); S. B. Cohen and J. A. Sweet, 'The Impact of Marital Disruption and Remarriage on Fertility', *Journal of Marriage and the Family* 36(1) (1974);P. C. Glick, 'Remarriage: Some Recent Changes and Variations', *Journal of Family Issues*, 1(4) (1980); A. Cherlin, *Marriage, Divorce, Remarriage* (London, 1981); T. J. Espenshade, 'Marriage Trends in America: Estimates, Implications and Causes', *Population and Development Review*, 11(2) (1985).

[21] T. J. Espenshade, 'Marriage, Divorce and Remarriage from Retrospective Data: A Multi-regional Approach', *Environment and Planning*, A15 (2) (1983).

tradition of work on the subject in France.[22] British work dates mainly from the last decade.[23] Elsewhere, otherwise substantial reviews of the sociological and psychological problems of marriage have not found space for the specific problems of remarriage.[24]

Data Problems

The complexity of remarriage puts considerable demands on data sources which transcend those relating to the analysis of first marriages. Although marriage and divorce statistics in England and Wales must rank among the best in the world, the study of remarriage is none the less hampered by deficiencies in data. For instance, the annual population estimates by marital status published by OPCS do not provide information about the distribution of the currently married population by order of marriage. This distribution is known in census years, although it was only in 1981 that it became available for all age groups of men and women.[25] Hardly any routine tabulations specify the remarried as a separate category, except for those in the annual *General Household Survey*[26] relating to women of childbearing age. The gradual nature of the process of divorce and the frequency of cohabitation before, or instead of, remarriage, even when the individual is still legally married to another partner, lead to difficulties in interpreting answers to questions on marital status asked in censuses and surveys. An analysis of remarriage rates, or of fertility rates within remarriage, or of the dissolution of remarriages requires information about the beginning, the duration, and the end of the previous marriage of each partner, as well as information about the time elapsed between the end of the previous and the beginning of the new marriage. Such detailed information is not required to be furnished by the vital registration system. Complex linkage operations would be needed to construct it.[27]

The most important longitudinal survey at present in progress in Britain, the Longitudinal Study of a 1 per cent sample from the Census of 1971, contains no information about subsequent marriages, divorces, or remarriages of the persons included in the sample, because no information about

[22] R. Pressat, 'Le Mariage des veufs et des veuves', *Population* 1956 (11(1)); L. Roussel, 'Le Remariage des divorcés', *Population*, 1981 (36(4–5)).

[23] R. Rapoport and R. N. Rapoport, *Families in Britain* (London, 1981); J. Haskey, 'Remarriage of the Divorced in England and Wales: A Contemporary Phenomenon', *Journal of Biosocial Science*, 15 (1983); *The Family* (op. cit., n. 2).

[24] M. Argyle and A. Furnham, 'Sources of Satisfaction and Conflict in Long-term Relationships', *Journal of Marriage and the Family* (1983); J. Schmid, 'The Family To-day: Sociological Highlights of an Embattled Institution', BSPS Exeter conference (1981).

[25] OPCS, *Census, 1981: Sex, Age and Marital Status Tables* (London, 1982).

[26] OPCS, *General Household Survey, 1982* (London, 1984).

[27] R. Leete and S. Anthony, 'Divorce and Remarriage: A Linkage Study', *Population Trends*, 16 (1979).

birth dates is available in vital records, information which is needed for routine linkage.[28]

An Outline of Remarriage in England and Wales

What little we know about remarriage in earlier times has been gleaned from the parish register studies by Wrigley and Schofield,[29] and from some of the more complete genealogical records which relate to families of the gentry and the aristocracy.[30] The figures suggest that before the nineteenth century, between 25 and 30 per cent of all marriages were remarriages.[31]

Rapidly declining mortality rates during the earlier years of this century, before divorce replaced widowhood as the most common cause for the dissolution of marriages at younger ages, have tended to reduce both the numbers and the incidence of remarriages, especially during the 1930s, to only about 10 per cent of all marriages (Table 6.1). This process was reinforced by rapidly rising rates of first marriage after the Second World War, which was accompanied by a fall in the average ages of brides and grooms, but particularly the former.[32] Before the reversal of this trend during the early 1970s, the proportion of women who married at least once before their 50th birthday had increased from about 85 to about 95 per cent; hence the increasing number of remarriages of the divorced made little impact on the proportion of remarriages among all marriages. But the high post-war level of first marriage has not been sustained. The fall in the numbers of first marriages after 1972, together with the accelerating increase in the numbers at risk of remarriage caused by divorce, has brought the proportion of remarriages back to the level of the eighteenth century and beyond, in just 15 years. By the early 1980s, 36 per cent of all marriages in England and Wales were remarriages, the highest proportion since the collection of reliable marriage statistics began (Table 6.2). Moreover, among men who had passed their 35th birthday, remarriages in 1980 outnumbered first marriages (Table 6.3). The present proportion of remarriages in England and Wales is substantially exceeded only in the USA (where it amounted to 44 per cent in 1980) and, in Europe, marginally in Sweden and Denmark.[33] In other parts of the UK the rise has

[28] J. Fox and P. O. Goldblatt, *Longitudinal Study 1971–75: Socio-demographic Mortality Differentials* (London, 1982).

[29] E. A. Wrigley and R. S. Schofield, *The Population History of England 1541–1871: A Reconstruction* (London 1981).

[30] L. Stone, *The Family, Sex and Marriage in England, 1500–1800* (London, 1977); L. Stone, 'Family History in the 1980s: Past Achievements and Future Trends', *Journal of Interdisciplinary History*, 12(1) (1981).

[31] J. Dupâquier *et al.* (eds.), *Marriage and Remarriage in Populations of the Past* (New York, 1981).

[32] D. A. Coleman, 'Recent Trends in Marriage and Divorce in Britain and Europe', in R. W. Hiorns (ed.), *Recent Demographic Trends in Western Europe* (London, 1980).

[33] J. Chamie and S. Nsuly, 'Sex Differences in Remarriage and Spouse Selection', *Demography*, 18(3) (1981).

been slower: only 18 per cent of Scottish marriages in 1981 were remarriages,[34] and in Northern Ireland in 1980 the proportion was 7 per cent.[35] Limits of data and space preclude further consideration of these figures here.

Trends in Types of Remarriage

Not only have remarriages become much more common within the lifetime of most existing marriages; the proportions of remarriages of different types have changed rapidly too. At marriageable ages, the small and declining numbers of the widowed are numerically overwhelmed by an avalanche of men and women released from their first marriage at an early age by divorce. In this context it must be remembered that each divorce yields two formerly married marriageable persons, compared to one left by widowhood. In 1983, only 5.3 per cent of all remarriages were between widows and widowers, whereas 36 per cent were those of two divorced persons, 28 per cent were marriages between divorced men and spinsters, and almost as many, 25 per cent, were between bachelors and divorced women (Table 6.2). In 1906, by contrast, almost half (46 per cent) of the much smaller number of remarriages were those of widowers and spinsters, whilst roughly equal proportions of widows married bachelors (27 per cent) and widowers (28 per cent). The numerical pre-eminence of these types of remarriage remained unchallenged until the Second World War.

During the last few decades there has thus been something of a transition in nuptiality affecting both first marriages and remarriages. The present distribution of remarriages in the age structure of the population cannot continue; the rapid pace of change must slow down, and the distribution of population by marital status in future decades will reflect the higher rates of recent years.

The Dynamics of Remarriage

The flow of formerly married persons at risk of remarriage changes much more rapidly through divorce than does the number of persons who are at risk of first marriage, which reflects previous changes in the numbers of births. Yet the two groups interact in the same marriage market, at least at younger ages: almost half the remarriages involve one person who was not formerly married. In this section we consider more closely three components of remarriage: the flow into and out of the remarried state, the composition of the remarried population, and its marital stability.

[34] Registrar General for Scotland, *Annual Report, 1981* (Edinburgh).

[35] Registrar General for Northern Ireland, *59th Annual Report of the Registrar General, 1980* (Belfast).

Table 6.1 Proportion of marriages of different types (per 1,000), England and Wales, 1901–1980

Category of marriage	1901–5	1906–10	1911–15	1916–20	1921–5	1926–30	1931–5	1946–40	1941–5	1946–50	1951–5	1956–60	1961–5	1966–70	1971–5	1976–80
Bachelors–spinsters	876	882	884	835	864	882	893	898	865	792	816	843	842	827	730	661
Bachelors–widows	33	32	34	64	41	26	21	19	30	33	20	16	13	11	10	8
Bachelors–divorced women	<1	1	1	1	3	4	5	7	10	37	35	30	32	37	63	81
Widowers–spinsters	56	54	49	57	53	50	47	41	43	36	29	23	19	14	10	8
Widowers–widows	33	30	29	41	32	29	24	22	28	26	26	25	25	24	24	21
Widowers–divorced women	<1	<1	<1	<1	1	1	2	2	3	8	9	9	9	9	13	13
Divorced men–spinsters	1	1	1	2	4	6	7	9	16	46	40	33	35	43	70	88
Divorced men–widows	<1	<1	<1	<1	1	1	1	1	3	9	8	7	7	8	13	14
Divorced men–divorced women	<1	<1	<1	<1	<1	1	1	1	2	14	16	15	18	26	66	106

Source: OPCS, *Marriage and Divorce Statistics* (London, various dates), series FM2, Table 3.2.

Table 6.2 Distribution of types of marriages (per 1,000), England and Wales, 1972–1983

	1972	1973	1974	1975	1976	1977	1978	1979	1980	1981	1982	1983
Bachelors–spinsters	734	719	707	696	680	667	653	653	651	647	644	622
Bachelors–widows	10	10	10	9	9	8	8	7	7	7	6	6
Bachelors–divorced women	61	66	70	73	77	79	83	83	83	83	83	84
Widowers–spinsters	11	11	10	9	9	9	8	8	7	7	7	6
Widowers–widows	23	25	24	24	24	23	21	20	19	19	18	18
Widowers–divorced women	13	13	13	13	14	14	14	13	13	13	13	13
Divorced men–spinsters	27	72	76	78	82	87	89	91	92	94	95	96
Divorced men–widows	14	14	14	14	14	14	14	13	13	13	12	12
Divorced men–divorced women	62	70	77	84	91	100	110	112	114	117	121	123

Sources: As Table 6.1; OPCS *Monitor*, FM2, 84/2, p. 3, Table 2.

Table 6.3 Distribution of types of marriage by marital status and age of groom, England and Wales, 1980

Age of groom	No. of marriages	Proportion per 1,000 of grooms who were		
		Bachelors	Widowers	Divorced men
<20	21,959	1,000	0	0
20–4	145,183	972	0	28
25–9	88,067	826	3	171
30–4	43,854	526	10	464
35–9	22,086	313	26	660
40–9	24,493	181	76	742
50–9	13,554	128	296	577
60–9	7,409	83	604	313
70–9	2,985	43	819	138
80+	432	33	907	60
ALL	370,022	741	39	220

Source: OPCS, *Marriage and Divorce Statistics* (London, 1980).

The flow into the ex-married state

(i) *Divorce.* Now that one-third of English marriages fail before their 25th anniversary,[36] over 250,000 divorced persons join the formerly married population each year. Marriages are most likely to be dissolved during their third year, so that the age group at which divorce is at its peak is 25–9 for both men and women. At those ages about one marriage in 30 fails each year. The new population at risk of remarriage is, therefore, young: almost half of its members are under 35 years old (Table 6.4). In 1980, for instance, about 296,000 men and women left the married state through divorce, and joined 528,000 divorced men, 679,000 widowers, 815,000 divorced women, and 2,904,000 widows who were already in the population. At younger ages, the annual increment of newly divorced men and women amounts to up to one-half of the number of people in the age group who are already divorced. Formerly married men in their early 30s are outnumbered by bachelors by about three to one. When the late 60s are reached, divorced men are outnumbered by widowers, although the recent rise in divorce has led to instability in these distributions.

(ii) *Widowhood.* About two out of three marriages are still ended by death rather than by divorce. Thus, in 1880, 264,000 marriages were ended by the death of one of the spouses, 182,000 (or 69 per cent) by the death of the husband. However, the divorced still dominate the remarriage market, because the high and rising age at widowhood puts many of the bereaved beyond expectation or desire of remarriage. On the supply side of remarriage,

[36] Haskey, op. cit. (n. 1).

Table 6.4 Stock and flow of the male population at risk of remarriage, England and Wales, 1980

Age	Stock: estimated mid-year population			Flow			
				Increments: dissolution of marriage by		Decrements: remarriage of	
	Single	Widowed	Divorced	Widowhood	Divorce	Widowed	Divorced
16–19	1,620,700	—	—	—	54	—	4
20–4	1,364,800	300	8,400	113	8,972	44	2,600
25–9	550,700	1,000	53,400	363	30,498	257	15,083
30–4	271,100	2,800	89,600	646	33,677	443	20,357
35–9	157,100	3,300	83,000	850	24,193	568	14,582
40–4	130,100	6,400	75,000	1,427	18,039	741	10,618
45–9	124,800	12,200	64,700	2,354	13,010	1,114	7,571
50–4	133,600	24,900	53,400	4,124	14,148	1,703	4,824
55–9	126,800	48,400	44,100	7,255		2,302	2,996
60–4	91,700	63,900	29,400	8,730	5,710[a]	2,178	1,503
65–9	85,700	100,900	21,000	12,723		2,301	820
ALL	4,788,500	678,800	538,300	81,190	148,301	14,486	81,396

[a] Figure for age 60 and over.

Source: OPCS, *Marriage and Divorce Statistics*, series FM2 (London, various years), no. 7, Tables 1.1, 3.6(*a*), 4.1(*a*), 5.1.

widowed persons do not predominate over those who are divorced until the age of 60 is reached for men and 50 for women; ages when remarriage rates are low. Thus, although only one marriage in three is ended by divorce, these marriages provide just over one-half of the men and women who enter the previously married state each year (because each divorce releases two remarriageable persons, whilst widowhood provides only one survivor, as mentioned above). The lower remarriage rates of the widowed strengthen this effect still further.

The total number of newly widowed men each year has remained constant at about 85,000 since the 1960s and the rate (seven per 1,000) has hardly changed since the 1950s. The number of women who are widowed each year has increased somewhat, from 176,000 in 1965 to a peak of 196,000 in 1972. The rate at which women are widowed has increased since the 1950s to about 15 per 1,000. Thus patterns are typical of developed societies in general.

As Haskey has pointed out,[37] the proportion of widowers has fallen substantially, but that of widows has increased. This is a consequence of the increasing difference between the expectations of life of men and women; since the 1930s men's expectation of life on their 16th birthday has increased by six years, that of women by nine years. The median age at widowhood was 68 years for men and 64 for women in 1978. The increase in the expectation of life has pushed the widowed ever further to the fringes of the remarriage market. The asymmetry in these death rates shows up in Haskey's figures of the proportion widowed in different birth cohorts by given ages. Improvements in women's survival rates have reduced the risk of being widowed for men by 40 per cent compared with the situation 30 years ago, whereas the analogous risk for women stands at 62 per cent of its then value. Other things being equal, the interaction between widowhood and divorce (to some extent the pre-emption of widowhood by divorce) has tended to reduce the population which is currently widowed.[38]

Remarriage rates

Three important points stand out in a study of remarriage rates. First, the huge growth in remarriage is entirely due to the increased flow of formerly married persons whose marriages have ended in divorce and who are looking for new spouses, a result of the increase in divorce rates during the last 20 years. Age-specific remarriage rates have not increased; in fact those of men (though not those of women) have fallen somewhat during the last ten years (see Figs. 6.1 and 6.2), though the decline has been slower than that of rates of first marriage. Most of the rising trend in the number of remarriages up to 1971 (Fig. 6.1) was caused by the younger age structure of the divorced population.[39]

[37] J. Haskey, 'Widowhood, Widowerhood, and Remarriage', *Population Trends*, 30 (1982).
[38] Bongaarts, op. cit. (n. 6).
[39] Leete, op. cit. (n. 12).

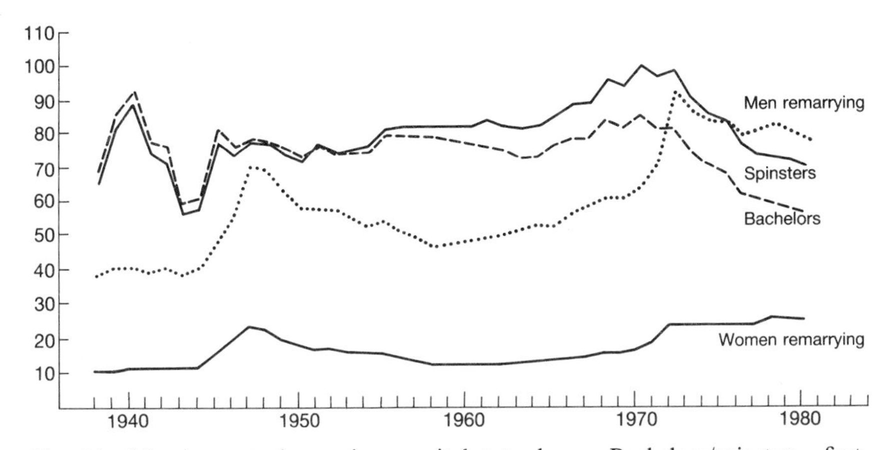

Fig. 6.1 Marriage rates by previous marital status by sex: Bachelors/spinsters—first-marriage rates per 1,000 single, widowed, and divorced, England and Wales, 1938–1980.
Sources: Registrar-General's Statistical Review, vol. ii (London, 1969), Table H1; OPCS, *Marriage and Divorce Statistics*, series FM2 (London, various years), Table 2.1.

Secondly, divorced and widowed men and women are much more likely to marry again—at almost any given age—than are unmarried men and women to marry for the first time. In 1980, remarriage rates for divorced women between the ages of 20 and 24 were about four times as high as the marriage rates of spinsters of the same age; they were twice as high between the ages of 30 and 34, four times as high between the ages of 40 and 44, and the ratios were even greater at later ages. The disparity between the low marriage rates of bachelors and the high remarriage rates of divorced men is even more pronounced, especially at older ages.

Thirdly, at all ages remarriage rates of divorced persons substantially exceed those of the widowed of the same sex. The contrast is greatest among women (Fig. 6.3); at all ages the remarriage rates of divorced women are up to twice those of widows. Marriage rates of widows in their 20s are only about 15 per cent higher than those of spinsters of the same age, but by the time that they have reached their 40th birthday, widows' remarriage rates are nearly four times those of the (very low) marriage rates of spinsters (Table 6.5).

Divorced men are more likely to remarry than divorced women, and widowers more likely than widows. Higher remarriage rates among men are found almost everywhere in Europe, except in Austria, Finland, the Netherlands, and the German Democratic Republic. In the Netherlands and in some other European countries, the remarriage rates of divorced men are lower than those of widowers,[40] but this apparent deficiency may be compensated by cohabitation.

[40] Chamie and Nsuly, op. cit. (n. 33).

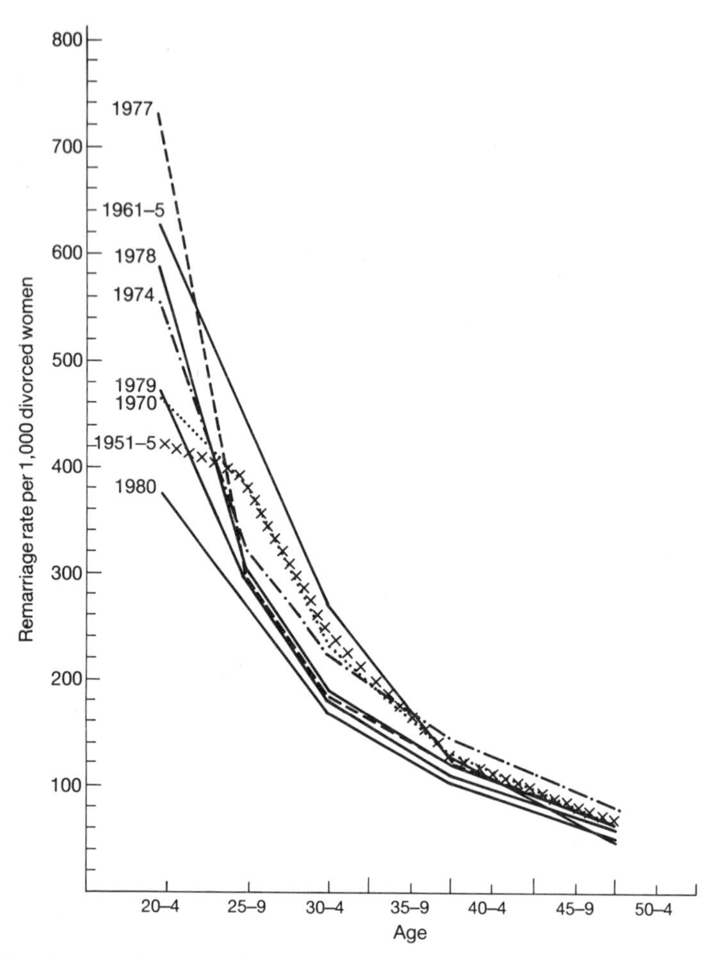

Fig. 6.2 Age-specific remarriage rates for divorced women, England and Wales, 1951–1980.
Source: OPCS, *Marriage and Divorce Statistics*, series FM2 (London, various years), Table 3.30.

Remarriage of the Divorced

To begin with, we need to know how remarriage rates change with the ages of formerly married persons and with the length of time that has elapsed since the end of their first marriage. Statistics about ages are much more easily obtainable. Age-specific remarriage rates combine the experiences of persons of the same age who have been widowed or divorced for the same length of time; duration-specific rates combine the experiences of persons of different ages. By contrast, all those who marry for the first time become eligible for first

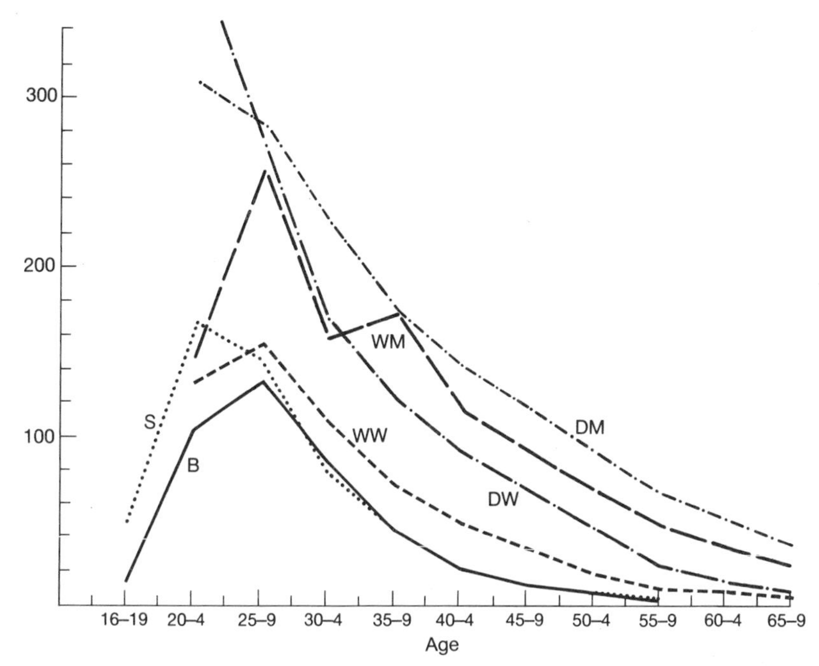

Fig. 6.3 Age-specific marriage rates for single, widowed, and divorced men and women, in five-year age groups, England and Wales, 1980. B = bachelors; S = spinsters; DM = divorced men; DW = divorced women; WM = widowers; WW = widows.
Source: OPCS, *Marriage and Divorce Statistics*, series FM2 (London, various years), Tables 3.3a, 3.3c, 3.6a, 3.6b, 1.1.

marriage merely by passing their 16th birthday, and the length of time that they have spent in the single state exactly matches their age.

Previous marital condition is recorded on marriage certificates, but the dates of the beginning and end of the previous marriage are not. Thus, information about the time elapsing between divorce or widowhood and remarriage must be obtained either from surveys in which questions on this subject are asked (e.g. the General Household Survey or the Family Formation Survey), or from record linkage studies (which can only be undertaken in collaboration with the Office of Population Censuses and Surveys), in which certificates of divorce or of the deaths of spouses are linked to subsequent marriage entries. This is a very large operation for anything other than a short span of years.

In cohort analysis, the same problem of insufficient information from marriage entries is encountered. In the Longitudinal Study, a sample consisting of 1 per cent of persons was taken from the Census of 1971 and all available registration data relating to vital events that occurred to individuals

Table 6.5 Age-specific remarriage rates per 1,000 persons in each sex/age group

Age	Men			Women		
	Widowed	Divorced	Both	Widowed	Divorced	Both
16–19	147	310	304	132	375	385
20–4	147	310	304	132	375	385
25–9	257	282	282	147	271	265
30–4	158	227	225	110	169	166
35–9	172	176	176	72	122	117
40–4	116	142	140	49	91	82
45–9	91	117	113	33	69	55
50–4	68	90	83	19	46	29
55–9	48	68	57	10	24	13
60–4	34	51	40	6	4	9
65–9	23	39	26	4	8	4

Source: OPCS, *Marriage and Divorce Statistics*, series FM2, calculated from Table 1.1 and Tables 3.6(*a*) and (*b*).

included in the sample were linked. But neither divorce nor marriage entries contain information relating to an individual's date of birth which was used for linkage, so that marital histories cannot be obtained from information in this study (except widowhood, about which information is available on death certificates). Of the three other major British cohort studies—the National Survey of Health and Development (1946), the National Child Development Study (1958), and the Child Health and Education Study (1970)—only members of the cohort of 1946 are old enough to have experienced a sufficient number of divorces and remarriages, and this study may in future yield valuable information.

Life-table Approaches

Life-table methods are a useful way of showing the implications of current remarriage rates. As the age distributions of those who divorce and those who remarry have been reasonably constant for more than a decade, age-specific rates provide a useful basis for calculation. Most remarriages occur relatively soon after the end of the first marriage. Life tables can show the current probability of ever remarrying after a given birthday, the chance of remarrying within a specified period after a given birthday, and the average number of years spent in the divorced or widowed state before remarriage.

The results (Table 6.6, Fig. 6.4) have been calculated from unpublished information on remarriages collected by OPCS for divorced men and women in England and Wales in 1981 by single years of age up to the age of fifty, and then by five-year age groups to the age group 65–9. The table is a gross nuptiality table in which no account is taken of mortality. It shows chances of remarrying up to the age of 65, but remarriage rates are very low at older ages. Age-specific remarriage rates were computed from the unpublished statistics on numbers of remarriages of divorced persons and related to estimates of the age structure of the divorced population. The rates were converted into probabilities of remarriage by using the formula:

$$_nq_x = 1 - \exp[-n\,_nm_x - an^3\,_nm_x^{\,2}]$$

where $a = 0.008$ when $n = 5$. The results show the probabilities of remarriage implied by the rates of 1981 within five years of a particular birthday for individuals who had been divorced or widowed before that birthday. The method of computation follows that set out by Saveland and Glick[41] for decrements caused by remarriage only.

Table 6.6 Chances of remarriage for divorced and widowed persons

Age	Divorced men			Widowed men			Divorced women			Widowed women		
	q'_x	$q_0N'_x$	e'_x	q'_x	$q_0N'_x$	e'_x	q'_x	$q_0N'_x$	e'_x	q'_x	$q_0N'_x$	e'_x
20	0.07384	99.8	5.4	0.00995	98.6	9.3	0.19153	99.0	4.8	0.02306	89.9	12.0
25	0.22910	99.5	4.2	0.12646	97.9	6.9	0.20393	96.7	6.3	0.09524	83.4	13.0
30	0.21324	98.3	5.3	0.14815	9.52	7.9	0.15484	90.8	8.9	0.09826	72.0	15.5
35	0.17926	94.8	6.9	0.13084	89.9	9.2	0.12064	80.7	11.1	0.06112	58.2	17.0
40	0.13976	87.6	8.5	0.11232	80.8	10.4	0.08849	66.4	12.8	0.04517	43.7	17.1
45	0.10899	76.1	9.4	0.08901	68.4	10.81	0.06709	49.5	13.1	0.03872	28.5	16.1
50	0.32797	59.6	9.4	0.26554	51.7	10.3	0.17993	31.3	12.0	0.08629	15.9	13.5
55	0.25512	40.0	7.7	0.21504	34.2	8.1	0.10407	16.3	9.1	0.04576	8.0	9.6
60	0.19389	19.4	4.5	0.16164	16.2	4.6	0.06538	6.5	4.8	0.03561	3.6	4.9
65												

Key: q'_x chance of remarriage from birthday x to birthday $x+5$
$q_0N'_x$ percentage of persons remarrying between birthday x and 65th birthday
e'_x average number of years spent unmarried between birthday x and 65th birthday

Source: $\bar{q}_x$ values derived from unpublished OPCS statistics on numbers of remarriages by previous marital status, and census estimates of distribution of the population by sex, age, and marital status.

According to Table 6.6, men who are divorced whilst in their 20s are almost certain to remarry; their marriage rates are higher than those of single men of the same age. Divorced men in their 30s are more likely to remarry (95 per cent at birthday 35) than are bachelors aged 20 (of whom 87 per cent are married by their 50th birthday), according to the gross nuptiality of 1980. This proportion falls to 60 per cent of men aged 50 and to 20 per cent of men aged 60 ever remarrying before their 65th birthday. Once more, these rates

[41] W. Saveland and P. C. Glick, 'First Marriage Tables by Color and Sex for the United States in 1958–60' *Demography*, 6 (1969).

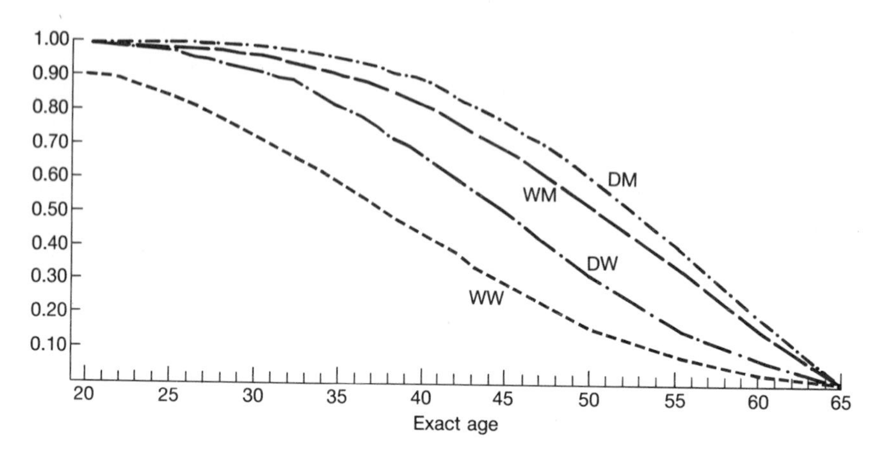

Fig. 6.4 Proportions ever remarrying between birthday x and birthday 65 from divorced or widowed state, England and Wales, 1981. DM = divorced men; DW = divorced women; WM = widowers; WW = widows.
Source: Life-tables calculated from OPCS, *Marriage and Divorce Statistics* (London, various years) and unpublished data.

are much higher than those for single men of the same age. At his 23rd birthday, a divorced man would on average expect to spend no more than four years in the divorced state, but this figure is doubled to nine years for a man who is 40 years old. (The calculations in each case extend to the 70th birthday).

The situation relating to divorced women is different. During their early twenties they remarry even more quickly then divorced men. But their remarriage prospects worsen more rapidly. The probability of remarriage reaches a maximum at age 22, and the expectation of life in the divorced state (the calculations again go up to the 70th birthday) lengthens continuously from then to a peak value of 14 years. None the less, 91 per cent of those divorced by their 30th birthday will eventually remarry (a rather higher proportion than that of spinsters of the same age who marry for the first time). The figure is 66 per cent by their 40th birthday, 31 per cent by their 50th (half the chance for divorced men of the same age), and less than 10 per cent after their 60th.

The radix of the synthetic life-table, of course, represents 100,000 persons who are divorced on their 20th birthday. In reality, few men are divorced at that age; many of them will not even have married for the first time. New divorce cohorts of increasing size are added to the pool of formerly married at each age, so that the figures quoted above relate to divorced persons who remain unattached on each birthday, and not to the rather unimportant radix of 100,000 divorced men on their 20th birthday.

Longitudinal Studies

Duration-specific statistics are clearly needed. Leete and Anthony[42] have linked remarriage and divorce records of a pseudo-random sample of 1,000 divorces in 1973. Remarriages occurring up to December 1977 were identified—that is, an average period of four and a half years. During that period just over half the men (56 per cent) and fewer than half the women (48 per cent) had remarried (Table 6.7). In the life-table described above, the proportion of divorced men expected to remarry between the ages of 34.5 years (the median age at divorce for men) and 39 years is 56 per cent, exactly the same as in the linkage study. The agreement is less good for divorced women. In the life-table, 45 per cent would have remarried between the ages of 32 years (the median age at divorce for women) and 36.5 years, rather than the 48 per cent found in the linkage study. In 27 per cent of the cases both spouses had remarried, in 23 per cent neither had done so; in 29 per cent the husband only, in 21 per cent the wife only had remarried. Age at divorce affected remarriage rates strongly and differentiated between the sexes very clearly. Sixty per cent of the men and women who had divorced by their 30th birthday had remarried, but only one-third of the women divorced after their 40th birthday had done so, compared with about half the men.

Table 6.7 Percentage of divorced persons who remarried within specific periods after divorce, England and Wales, 1973–1977

Age	No. in sample	Time between divorce and remarriage								Proportion remarrying within $4\frac{1}{2}$ years
		3 mths.	3–5 mths.	6–11 mths.	All <1 yr.	1–2 yrs.	2–3 yrs.	3–4 yrs.	4–$4\frac{1}{2}$ yrs.	
Wives										
Under 30	400	20	7	10	37	13	5	3	1	59
30–9	295	15	9	7	31	7	6	4	2	50
40–9	176	12	4	5	21	7	4	2	1	35
50 and over	129	14	2	6	22	2	2	3	0	29
Total	1,000	16	6	8	30	9	5	3	1	48
Husbands										
Under 30	270	18	7	6	31	11	9	7	2	60
30–9	341	18	7	10	35	13	6	4	2	59
40–9	216	19	6	3	28	10	7	3	2	50
50 and over	173	28	6	3	38	4	2	2	1	47
Total	1,000	20	6	6	33	10	6	4	2	55

Source: Leete and Anthony, op. cit. (n. 27), p. 6, Table 2.

[42] Leete and Anthony, op. cit. (n. 27).

The chances of remarriage are highest very soon after divorce. About one-third of those who remarried did so within three months of their divorce, and it is shown in Table 6.7 that the gap between the proportions of the two sexes who remarried is already apparent then. The enquiry could not, of course, show the number of cases in which the new couple had already known one another during their previous marriage. In this context it may be relevant to note that petitioners for divorce are more likely to remarry within four and a half years than respondents; this is more true of men (59 per cent) than of women (55 per cent).

Remarriage Rates after Separation

Some of the very few statistics available that relate to remarriage and cohabitation after separation can be found in the General Household Survey, although the 'separated' are not adequately distinguished from the 'divorced' by respondents to the survey. Unlike marriage, divorce is a progressive process; legal formalities matter less to many respondents than physical separation from their spouse. Likewise, couples who describe themselves as 'remarried' are often cohabitating and have not gone through a formal marriage; one-quarter of the 'remarried' respondents in the Family Formation Survey were found to be cohabiting.[43] The time elapsed since separation gives a better indication of the interval between the failure of the first marriage and remarriage, even though the timing is in part dictated by the law.[44] Accordingly in the data from the General Household Survey the interval between the end of the first marriage and the peak period for remarriage is much longer—about three years—than when the legal definitions for the end and the beginning of marriages are used (Table 6.8). Remarriage progressively replaces cohabitation within four years of separation, although the proportion of couples who remain cohabiting without ever remarrying is unknown. Former spouses may remarry immediately after their divorce. But until the Matrimonial and Family Proceedings Act 1984, a marriage could not be dissolved by divorce, save in cases of exceptional hardship or depravity, until two years had elapsed. Nor was divorce by mutual consent available until after two years of legal separation, nor divorce without consent until five years of legal separation. In 1981, 32 per cent of men and 22 per cent of women divorced on the grounds of two years' separation, and 12 per cent of men and 6 per cent of women on the grounds of five years' separation.

Separation without divorce is extremely common and does not inevitably lead to a divorce; but, of course, unless there is a divorce it cannot be followed by remarriage. Separation results in divorce more rapidly than used to be the case: 65 per cent of separations in 1972–3 were followed by divorce within

[43] K. Dunnell, *Family Formation* (London, 1979).
[44] R. Chester, 'The Duration of Marriage to Divorce', *British Journal of Sociology*, (1971).

Table 6.8 Cumulative percentages of women remarried within given periods of divorce or separation, by date of divorce or separation, Great Britain, 1980

Year of separation	Remarried within						
	1 yr.	2 yrs.	3 yrs.	4 yrs.	6 yrs.	8 yrs.	No.
1965–9	1	7	16	24	45	55	119
1970–2	2	7	17	31	51	—	127
1973–4	3	13	24	39	—	—	108
1975–6	3	7	23	—	—	—	122

Source: General Household Survey (London, 1982), p. 37, table 2.47.

three years, compared with 55 per cent of the separations which occurred between 1961 and 1965.[45] In the General Household Survey of 1982 it was shown that for durations of marriage shorter than six years, the cumulative proportion of partners who were separated was about double the proportion who were divorced. Four per cent of the women who married between 1975 and 1979 had already separated within two years of their marriage, a period during which divorce is normally impossible.

Remarriage rates may be falling, but the tempo of remarriage and cohabitation after divorce or separation is increasing a little. In her survey in 1976 Dunnell showed that over one-quarter of the women who were separated between 1961 and 1965 had found a new partner within three years. This figure compares with one-third for the women separated between 1970 and 1973. Among women who described themselves as 'separated' during the 1970s (some of whom may already have been widowed or divorced) between 2 and 3 per cent had remarried within the first year of separation, 7 per cent within two years, up to 24 per cent within three years, and up to 39 per cent within four years. Fifty-one per cent of members of cohorts who were separated between 1970 and 1972 had remarried within six years. The statistics for the cohort 1970–2 were exceptional, however, because its members were the first to benefit from the provisions of the Divorce Reform Act 1971, which made it possible for a divorce to be obtained after five years' separation, without the consent of the other spouse. The Act resulted in the legal termination of many marriages which had existed in name only, and where the couple had separated years earlier, but where one spouse had refused a divorce. There was, therefore, a rush of divorces and remarriages during the early 1970s.

Remarriage Rates of the Widowed

Problems similar to those discussed in the previous section arise in the analysis of remarriage after widowhood. Age-specific remarriage rates can be

[45] Dunnell, op. cit. (n. 43).

calculated quite easily, but there are no regular statistics on the interval that elapsed between the death of a spouse and the remarriage of the survivor, nor indeed is it known what proportion of widowed persons remarry at all.

A life-table analysis shows that the chance of remarriage after widowhood is lower than that after divorces at all ages, and particularly so among older women. Ninety-eight per cent of men and 83 per cent of women widowed by their 25th birthday will remarry before they reach the age of 70. The proportion of women is no greater than that of spinsters of the same age who marry for the first time. Ninety-five per cent of widowers aged 30 can expect to remarry, but only 72 per cent of widows of the same age. At the 40th birthday, the difference between the proportions of widowers and widows who remarry has become much greater: 80 per cent of widowers, compared with 44 per cent of widows, two-thirds of the corresponding proportion of divorced women of the same age. But the low levels of remarriage of widows among those who were recently married seem particularly strange. Possibly there is some socially selective effect here.

Other things being equal, individuals who lose their spouses at earlier ages than average may be expected, as a result of sharing the same household, or through assortative mating, to be less healthy and possibly less marriageable themselves. The lower social groups will be disproportionately represented among them, because of their higher mortality rates. On the other hand, Haskey has shown[46] that women in the lower social classes are more likely to marry than others. However, we shall present reasons why this may not hold true of remarriages.

There has been no study in which remarriage rates of the widowed are linked with information on their spouses' death certificates, analogous to that carried out by Leete and Anthony for remarriages of the divorced. But Haskey has used another source of data on remarriages of 1980–1[47] to show the attrition of the population of widowed caused by remarriage. The Department of Health and Social Security pays widows' benefit which ends on remarriage, so that some figures are available, though they give the date of remarriage rather than that of widowhood.

In Table 6.9 we show that younger widows remarry much sooner than older ones. Ninety-three per cent of widows who had remarried by their 40th birthday and who had, therefore, been mainly widowed when they were in their 30s had remarried within ten years of being widowed, and 77 per cent did so within six years. These proportions become progressively smaller for older women: the proportion of widows who remarried between the ages of 55 and 59 and who had been widowed for ten and six years respectively were 77 and 59 per cent. In the same age range, the median period between widowhood and remarriage increased from 4.0 to 5.0 years (Table 6.9). The interquartile range

[46] J. Haskey, 'Social Class Patterns of Marriage', *Population Trends*, 34 (1983).
[47] Haskey, op. cit. (n. 37).

was much greater for later remarriages. This is caused by greater variations in the age at widowhood for women who remarried late; some who were widowed early, but who put off remarriage, will have been included in this group. Unfortunately, it is not possible to tabulate these data by age at widowhood. Furthermore, they refer only to widows who remarried, and cannot therefore yield proportions of widows ever remarrying or never remarrying. Presumably, remarriages of older women will form a smaller proportion of the cohort of widows. But an analysis by widowhood cohort or by duration of widowhood is not easily possible.

Table 6.9 Cumulative percentages of widows who remarried before selected anniversaries of their widowhood

Age at remarriage	No.	Cumulative % remarried before given widowhood anniversary					Expectation of widowhood			
		2	4	6	8	10	Q_1	M	Q_3	Range
<40	148	16	49	77	88	93	2.4	4.0	5.8	3.4
40–4	96	15	55	75	83	90	2.4	3.7	6.0	3.6
45–9	146	6	40	64	79	86	3.1	4.7	7.3	4.2
50–4	176	7	35	59	68	81	3.1	5.3	8.8	5.7
55–9	162	9	33	59	69	77	3.0	5.0	9.6	6.6

Notes: Q_1 = first quartile; Q_3 = third quartile; M = median; Range = interquartile range.

Source: Haskey, op. cit. (n. 37), Table 3.

Some Factors which Influence Remarriage Rates

There is little information on the major factors that affect remarriage chances, other than age, sex, and reason for the dissolution of the previous marriage, all of which have been discussed above. We do however have some information about the effect of children of previous marriages and of social class.

Asymmetries in chances of remarriage

It is not surprising that the divorced find a new partner more easily than the widowed. According to Holmes and Rahe's scale of life events,[48] divorce is less stressful than bereavement, and the mortality of divorced persons is lower than that of widows or widowers.[49] Most bereavement is unexpected, but

[48] T. H. Holmes and R. H. Rahe, 'The Social Readjustment Rating Scale', *Journal of Psychosomatic Research*, 11 (1967).

[49] *The Registrar General's Statistical Review of England and Wales, 1967*, pt. iii, *Commentary* (London, 1971); Fox and Goldblatt, op. cit. (n. 28).

many men and women get divorced in order to remarry or live with a new partner. This phenomenon is difficult to quantify: in England and Wales adultery was cited as one of the facts proven against the husband in 43 per cent of all divorces in 1981 (and in 53 per cent of those in which the husband was between 35 and 39 years old), but less frequently against the wife (25 per cent overall and 30 per cent between the ages of 30 and 34). But with the availability of 'no-fault' divorce, the need to prove adultery is less pressing that it used to be; furthermore, it is not certain that the new spouse will be the former sexual partner. Recent research in Australia suggests that about one married man in three is currently engaged in an extramarital affair.[50] The high proportion of remarried couples who lived together before their remarriage (67 per cent compared with 20 per cent in first marriages, and more when both spouses had previously been married) suggests that a new partner is already lined up in many cases.

Few divorced men have to bear the burden of child care; the wife is given custody of children in about 90 per cent of all cases,[51] though men will of course always be responsible for the care of children if the marriage has ended by the death of their wife.

Average remarriage rates of divorced persons conceal big differences in the chances of remarriage of former spouses, not just according to their sex but also according to which partner initiated the break. Those who abandon their current marriages in many cases eagerly take on new partners for the next marriage—for which they have high hopes despite their previous experience, as is shown by the couples quoted by Burgoyne and Clark.[52] But the abandoned partner may have poor prospects and less motivation for meeting and marrying new partners, as witness the comments of Hart's respondents.[53] For them, divorce may be more like widowhood. Clearly, the best time to find a new partner is when one is still safely married to one's first spouse and functioning properly in a normal and accepted state.

Effect of children on the chance of remarriage

It is generally supposed that the presence of children of a previous marriage affects the chances of divorced women or widows remarrying adversely. Thus, in a multivariate analysis of the effect of children on the remarriage of American women between 1968 and 1978, remarriage rates of women with children were up to 10 per cent lower during the first four and a half years after divorce.[54] However, English data suggest that divorced and widowed women

[50] A. P. Thompson, 'Emotional and Sexual Components of Extramarital Relations', *Journal of Marriage and the Family*, 46 (1984).

[51] J. Eekelaar and E. Clive, *Custody after Divorce* (Oxford, 1977).

[52] J. Burgoyne and D. Clark, 'Why Get Married Again?' *New Society*, 3 Apr. 1980.

[53] N. Hart, *When Marriage Ends: A Study in Status Passage* (London, 1976).

[54] F. L. Mott and S. Moore, 'The Tempo of Remarriage among Young American Women' *Journal of Marriage and the Family*, 45(2) (1983).

with children are slightly more likely to remarry than childless women.[55] This pattern is only reversed for women who were divorced after their 40th birthday. The ages of children seem important; the probability of remarriage is higher for women with children who are less than ten years old. Furthermore, the presence of up to two dependent children under the age of 16 does not affect the interval between the end of the first marriage and remarriage. According to the Fertility Report on the Census of 1971,[56] remarriage rates of childless women in recent marriage cohorts (up to 1971) were not much higher than those of women with one child. This is a marked change from the situation for marriages that occurred between 1936 and 1940. In this group, 58 per cent of women without children had remarried by census date, compared with 46 per cent of women with at least one child. Furthermore, women who had married between 1951 and 1955, or between 1956 and 1960, whose first marriages had lasted for at least five years, and who had had at least one child were actually more likely to have remarried by census date than childless women. More surprisingly, the chances of remarriage did not decline sharply even for women with two or more children (although they were somewhat lower), except at very short marriage duration (less than five years). In older cohorts, these women's chances of remarriage were about one-third or less, and in recent cohorts about two-thirds, of those of childless women or those with only one child. The presence of children, therefore, makes less of an impact on remarriage chances than might be expected, especially in more recent marriage cohorts, except for women of high parities, or for those whose first marriage lasted for a short time only.

The effects of social class

Haskey has used the information on social class which is given on marriage entries[57] and has related them to populations at the risk of marriage in these social classes, as given in the Labour Force Survey. He had demonstrated some interesting social-class patterns in the propensity to marry. Rates of first marriage are higher than average for men in the upper and for women in the lower social groups (although they do not usually intermarry), whilst the reverse is true for women in the upper and men in the lower social groups. After divorce, remarriage rates of both men and women in the upper social groups exceed those of men and women in the lower groups. The division used was a simple dichotomy between non-manual and manual occupations. Indeed, remarriage rates of divorced women in the higher social groups exceed those of men in the manual group at ages below 35 years. Remarriage rates are particularly low for divorced women whose husbands were manual workers, particularly those in their early 30s, and according to the General Household

[55] J. Haskey, 'Remarriage of the Divorced in England and Wales: A Contemporary Phenomenon', *Journal of Biosocial Science*, 15 (1983).

[56] OPCS, *Fertility Report from the 1971 Census*, series DS (London, 1983).

[57] J. Haskey, 'Social Class Patterns of Marriage', *Population Trends*, 34 (1983).

Survey such women are particularly prone to cohabit after divorce and also before remarriage.

In a sample analysed by Coleman and Haskey,[58] it was found that 58 per cent of manual workers cohabited before remarriage, compared with 45 per cent of non-manual workers. There is no evidence about the separate effects of education on the chances of remarriage in Britain. However, the experience of American women studied by Mott and Moore[59] showed that the chances of remarriage during the first four and a half years after divorce were 20 percentage points lower for women with the highest education than for the least educated. The authors thought that remarriage offered fewer advantages to highly educated women, because of their higher earning power. They did not record cohabitation and this may have compensated for lower remarriage rates.

The Stock of Remarried People in the Population

The trends described above have resulted in the proportion of remarried couples in the general married population almost doubling within 30 years. In 1951, when the figures were inflated by war widowhood and subsequent remarriages, 5.3 per cent of women between the ages of 16 and 49 were in second or subsequent marriages. By 1961, this proportion had fallen to 3.1 per cent (5.5 per cent for women of all ages), and the figure had increased to only 3.5 per cent in the Census of 1971 (5.2 per cent of all married women below the age of 60). By 1981, 8.2 per cent of women below the age of 50 were in second or subsequent marriages (8.9 per cent at all ages). The figure for men of all ages was 9.2 per cent.

These erratic changes are the result of three forces. The first is the excess rate of widowhood and remarriage caused by the Second World War. The bulge in remarriages caused by the war can be seen clearly in Fig. 6.5 and moves through successive age groups: 30–40 in 1951, 40–4 in 1961, 50–4 in 1971, and 60–4 in 1981. The second factor is the increase in general marriage rates and especially in first marriages between the end of the war and the 1970s. This increase in the proportions ever marrying, which raised the proportion of ever-married women from 85 per cent in 1951 to 95 per cent in 1972, prevented the remarriages of the slowly increasing numbers of divorced persons making much of an impact on the composition by marital status of the population as a whole. Lastly, the very rapid increase in the numbers of divorces and subsequent remarriages which began during the late 1960s, combined with the decline in rates of first marriage after 1972, has concentrated almost the whole of the post-war change in composition by marital status into the last decade.

[58] D. A. Coleman and J. C. Haskey, 'Marital Distance and its Geographical Orientation in England and Wales, 1979', *Transactions of the Institute of British Geographers*, n.s. 11 (1986).

[59] Mott and Moore, op. cit. (n. 54).

Fig. 6.5 Proportion of remarried women among all currently married women, 1951, 1961, 1971, 1981, and men 1981, by five-year age group, England and Wales
Source: Census Fertility Reports and Tables 1951, 1961, 1971 (London, 1959, 1966, 1979).

Fig. 6.5 also illustrates the precocious nature of the surge in remarriage, which leads to a concentration of remarried persons in the group aged 35–9 years (11 per cent of married women and 10 per cent of men). These proportions decline a little for older age groups which contain members who have survived from a more sedate earlier period. These three processes have disrupted what would have been a more gradual increase in the proportions remarried by age, which stable rates would otherwise have generated. Even by 1961, 9.4 per cent of women between the ages of 70 and 74 were currently remarried, as were 8.4 per cent of women over the age of 75. The figures in the Census of 1981 are not much larger (9.8 per cent of women between the ages of 70 and 74, rising to 11.6 per cent of women over 90 years old). In the Census of 1981, figures relating to the remarriages of men became available for the first time. The proportion of remarried men is roughly the same as that of remarried women up to the age of 70; thereafter, the proportion remarried progressively increases until it reaches a level of 26 per cent for men aged 95 and over.

These proportions reflect the legal marital status claimed by respondents who answer questions in the census, and they take no account of cohabitation. When *de facto* marital status is considered the proportions remarried decline somewhat, as is shown by the figures in Table 6.10. The proportions cohabiting before and after first marriage are considered in Table 6.11.

Table 6.10 *De facto* marital condition by age of woman, Great Britain, 1980 (per cent)

Age	Single	Cohabiting	First marriage	Second marriage	Widowed	Divorced	Separated	Total	No. in sample
18–19	84	2	13	—	—	—	1	100	410
20–4	43	6	47	1	—	1	2	100	994
25–9	13	5	72	4	0	3	2	100	989
30–4	5	2	78	8	0	4	2	100	1,131
35–9	4	3	77	8	1	5	2	100	959
40–4	4	2	76	8	2	5	2	100	898
45–9	5	0	77	7	4	5	2	100	813
ALL AGES	17	3	67	6	1	4	2	100	6,194

Source: General Household Survey, 1980 (London, 1982), p. 27, Table 2.25.

Cohabitation

Today cohabitation is a normal precedent to remarriage and, for some couples, acts as a substitute for it.[60] As it has become a parallel system of informal remarriage, it should ideally be considered in tandem with legal remarriage, but at present too much information is missing.

The term 'common-law marriage', which is often used to describe a cohabiting couple, has no legal meaning in England and Wales. The only non-statutory forms of marriage legally recognized in England and Wales are the customary forms contracted abroad by couples who have become resident in England and Wales. But the courts have increasingly come to recognize the interests of cohabiting partners and their children and, implicitly, these have also been recognized in recent statutes.[61] It is an indication of the ill-defined status of cohabitation that no agreed terms are in common use to describe the partners in such unions.

Brown and Kiernan's analysis of the statistics given in the General Household Survey of 1979[62] showed that the majority of couples who had remarried had lived together before their remarriage, particularly those who had previously been divorced (72 per cent). Cohabitation before remarriage seems to have been fairly common for some time, well before its popularity as a preliminary to first marriage, where it has become prevalent only since the 1970s. In recent marriage cohorts, 20 per cent of bachelors and spinsters had lived together before their marriage, compared with only 1 per cent before 1961. Forty-four per cent of couples who remarried between 1970 and 1974 had lived together before their marriage; 67 per cent of those who remarried between 1979 and 1981 had done so. (These figures relate to women less than 35 years old at the time of marriage.) Cohabitation accounts for some of the decline in rates of first marriage,[63] as well as for some of the less marked drop in remarriage rates.

The proportion of cohabiting women is particularly large among those who are currently divorced, irrespective of whether or not they remarry. In the Family Formation Survey it was estimated that one-third of women in second or subsequent unions of all kinds were cohabiting and two-thirds were remarried. Similar proportions were found in the General Household Survey of 1982[64] (Table 6.11). At any age, divorced and separated women are much more likely to cohabit than widows. In 1981–2, 20 per cent of currently divorced or separated women between the ages of 18 and 24 were cohabiting, as were 23 per cent of those between the ages of 25 and 34, and 18 per cent of

[60] M. D. A. Freeman and C. M. Lyon, *Cohabitation without Marriage* (Aldershot, 1983).

[61] Ibid.

[62] A. Brown and K. Kiernan, 'Cohabitation in Great Britain: Evidence from the General Household Survey', *Population Trends*, 25 (1981).

[63] K. E. Kiernan, 'The Structure of Families To-day: Continuity or Change?' in *The Family*, op. cit. (n. 2).

[64] OPCS, op. cit. (n. 4).

those between the ages of 35 and 49. These figures compare with 8, 17, and 5 per cent respectively of widows in the same age groups. These differences may have had some effect on the propensity of women in these groups to remarry.

The proportions of cohabiting women of different marital status between the ages of 18 and 49 found in the General Household Survey may be weighted by the overall proportions in each marital status of the population enumerated in the Census of 1981 to yield population estimates. These calculations suggest that about one-third of second and subsequent unions are cohabitations: 2.7 per cent of women between the ages of 18 and 49 are in second or subsequent cohabiting unions, compared with 6.0 per cent who are legally remarried. Thus, 1.2 per cent of the female population who have never married are cohabiting. Three-quarters of the second cohabiting unions are those of women who are still in their first marriage, but are living with a partner other than their husband. In all, 3 per cent of currently married women were cohabiting, as were 6 per cent of separated women. We do not know what proportions of these will eventually formalize their union by remarriage.

Cohabitation before remarriage lasts longer than before first marriage. The median length, according to the General Household Survey of 1982, was 21 months, compared with 14 months for cohabiting unions before first marriage. There is a strong concentration of cohabitations lasting between one and five years; 41 per cent of couples who cohabited before remarriage had lived together for between two and five years, compared with 24 per cent of couples who had cohabited before their first marriage. Many of the former will have waited for between two and five years for the divorce from their previous spouse to come through. Only 9 per cent of cohabitations before remarriage lasted for longer than five years.

Cohabitation is common in all social groups. However, rather fewer people in social class I lived together before remarriage, and, generally speaking, cohabitation before remarriage is more common among people in manual rather than among those in non-manual occupations (58 compared with 43 per cent). The proportions who cohabit before remarriage do not vary greatly with age, except for those over the age of 65, where cohabitation is less common, presumably because at this age marriages between widowed persons predominate.

Ermisch's analysis[65] of the economic determinants of marriage rates has led him to suggest that cohabitation before (first) marriage could be regarded as a symptom of indecision about life courses, because women's opportunities for outside work made marriage less unequivocally advantageous to them. Cohabitation, which delays marriage without necessarily delaying some of its comforts, seemed a rational response.[66] No general analysis of the rationality

[65] J. Ermisch, 'Economic Opportunities, Marriage Squeezes and the Propensity to Marry: An Economic Analysis of Period Marriage Rates in England and Wales', *Population Studies*, 35(3) (1981).

[66] Freeman and Lyon, op. cit. (n. 60).

Table 6.11 Percentage of women aged 18–49 currently cohabiting, by current marital status, Great Britain, 1981, 1982

Marital status	Women in given status	Cohabiting in each status	Distribution of cohabitees by marital status
Single	19.7	6	1.2
First married	66.8	3	2.0
Remarried	6.0	3	0.2
Widowed	1.1	2	<0.1
Divorced	4.3	7	0.3
Separated	2.2	6	0.1
ALL	100.0	4	3.9

Sources: General Household Survey 1982 (London, 1984), Table 4.1(*a*); Census 1981.

of different kinds of living arrangements after the end of the first marriage has as yet been attempted in England and Wales.

The Dissolution of Remarriage

Remarriages are more fragile than first marriages. In 1981, remarriages accounted for just 9 per cent of all marriages, but 12.5 per cent of all divorcing men had previously been divorced or widowed, and 18.5 per cent of all divorcing men (including those who had married as bachelors) were not in a marriage which was the first for both parties. The high risk of divorce among unmarried couples has long been documented in the USA,[67] but Haskey's recent analysis was the first to show that this also held true for England and Wales.[68]

Haskey related divorces classified by age and duration of marriage to the appropriate marriages at risk, deriving his figures from the registration statistics for previous years. At most ages and durations of marriage, the cumulative proportion of husbands and wives who divorced after remarriage was about double that of spouses divorcing after a first marriage. Life-table analysis also shows that the risk of dissolution by divorce at any duration is much higher for those who remarry after a divorce. These results are similar to those obtained by McCarthy for the USA.[69]

The difference becomes larger for those who marry at older ages, particularly for women. The chance of the marriage of a divorced man ending in a second divorce is about 10 per cent higher than for a divorced woman of

[67] J. McCarthy, 'A Comparison of the Probability of the Dissolution of First and Second Marriages', *Demography*, 15(3) (1978).

[68] J. Haskey, 'Marital Status before Marriage and Age at Marriage: Their Influence on the Chance of Divorce', *Population Trends*, 32 (1983).

[69] McCarthy, op. cit. (n. 67).

the same age. The chance of remarriage ending in a divorce is also greater when the parties are young. The chance that the remarriage of a divorced woman or man who remarries in their 20s will fail within 20 years exceeds, 0.5, about the same as the chance for a first marriage of teenagers (Fig. 6.6).

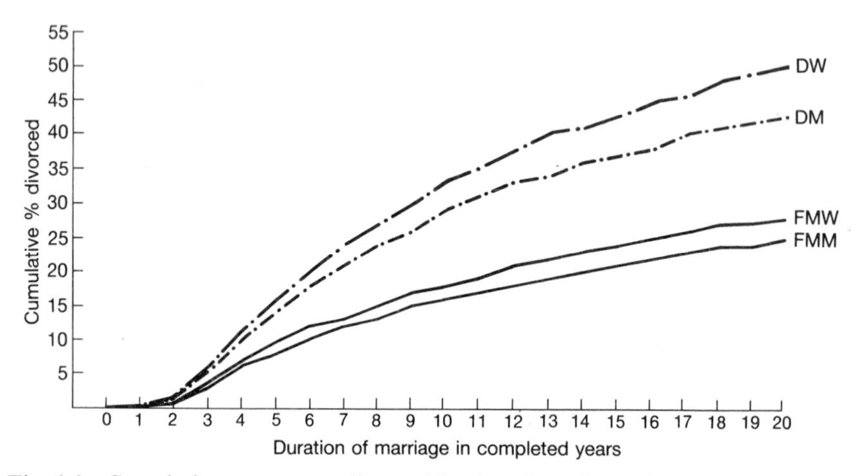

Fig. 6.6 Cumulative percentage divorced by duration of marriage and remarriage implicit in rates current in 1980–1981, England and Wales. Spinster brides and previously divorced brides aged 20–4 at marriage; bachelor grooms and previously divorced grooms aged 25–9 at marriage. FMW = first-married women; DW = divorced women; FMM = first-married men; DM = divorced men.
Source: Haskey, op. cit. (n. 10), Tables 10, 11.

Complementary results may be obtained from a consideration of age-specific divorce rates by previous marital status. The Census of 1981[70] contains a detailed tabulation of persons in second and subsequent marriages, distinguished by sex and age, and age-specific divorce rates for the remarried may be obtained from these statistics. More recent population estimates[71] contain revised numbers of the married population, but do not distinguish them by order of marriage. The ratios of the remarried to the married population given in the Census were applied to the married population in the estimates to yield denominators for the construction of divorce rates in 1981. The rates by order of marriage are shown in Fig. 6.7. They are divorce rates of bachelors and remarried men, and of spinsters and remarried women, not those of bachelor–spinster marriages and others. Some remarriages will therefore be included in the divorce rates of the single, as in Haskey's analysis.

[70] OPCS, op. cit. (n. 25).
[71] OPCS, *Population Estimates* (various dates).

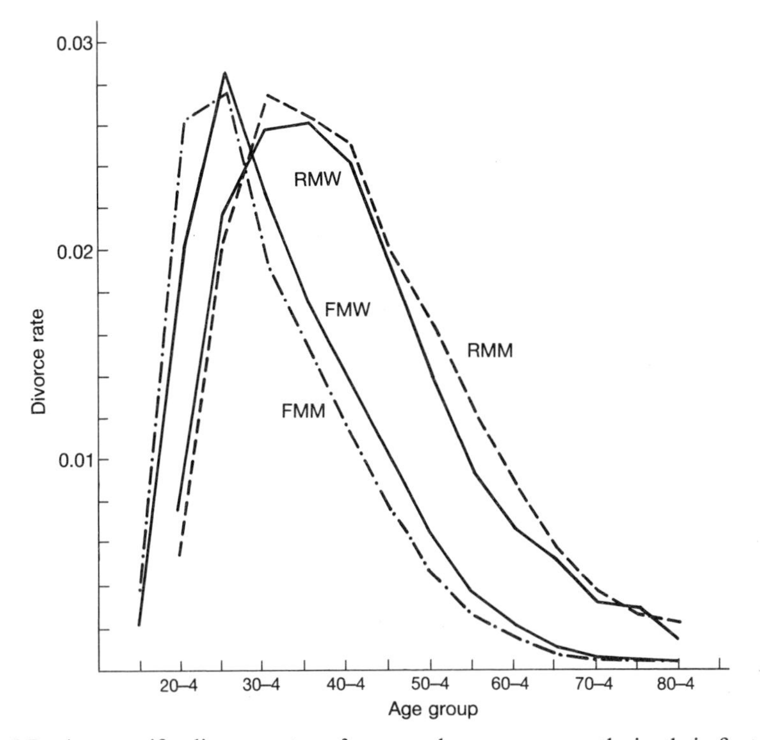

Fig. 6.7 Age-specific divorce rates of men and women currently in their first and subsequent marriages, England and Wales, 1981. FMW = first-married women; FMM = first-married men; RMW = remarried women; RMM = remarried men.
Sources: OPCS, *Marriage and Divorce Statistics*, series FM2 (London, various years); 1981 Census: sex, age, and marital-status tables.

If remarriages at all durations are combined, the divorce rates of remarried persons exceed those of first marriages at ages beyond 30. During the later 30s, they are 50 per cent higher; during the 40s and 50s they are double the rates for first marriages; and at higher ages the ratios are even larger. The lower rates at younger ages are due to the high proportions of marriages of short durations. Men's rates exceed those of women to an increasing extent after the age of 30.

Summarizing the Dynamics of Remarriage

It would be instructive to bring together the results of these studies of the formation and dissolution of remarriages in order to obtain an estimate of their impact on the population and of the extent of remarriage. Leete[72] has

[72] Leete, op. cit. (n. 12).

projected the cohort distribution of remarriages to show that 18 per cent of men born around 1950, and 19 per cent of women in the same cohort can expect to remarry before their 50th birthday, compared with 12 per cent of those of either sex born around 1936. A consideration of the current proportions divorcing, median ages at divorce, and proportions remarrying suggests that current rates imply even higher proportions: 29 per cent for men and 25 per cent for women. An analysis of current remarriage rates in which the model suggested by Willekens[73] was used to construct multi-state life-tables is at present in progress.

Problems of Remarriage

There have been few sociological studies of the reasons for the vulnerability of remarriages. Some demographic risks are obvious: divorced persons who remarry tend to have married for the first time at ages below average and were, therefore, at substantially higher risk of divorce.[74] Other things being equal, those who marry young will also remarry young at an age when the divorce rates of the remarried population are high. As we saw earlier, marriage rates of the divorced are higher than those of the married. Among men divorced in 1981, 13 per cent of those who had married in 1978 were less than 20 years old when they first married, compared with 7 per cent of all men married in that year. The corresponding figures for women are 38 and 22 per cent respectively. The statistics in Table 6.12 taken from the Fertility Report of the Census of 1971 indicate a similar age distribution at first marriage for women who had remarried.

Table 6.12 Distribution of age at first marriage of remarried women, and of women married once only, Great Britain, 1971

Year of first marriage	Age at first marriage					Total
	<20 (%)	20–22.5 (%)	22.5–24 (%)	25–9 (%)	30–4 (%)	
1936–40						
RM	30	34	25	11	—	102,415
FM	16	30	33	21	—	881,195
1956–60						
RM	46	33	12	6	3	53,210
FM	24	35	20	14	8	1,290,135

Note: RM = remarried women; FM = women married once only.

Source: Census 1971, Fertility Report (London, 1983), Table 8.17.

[73] F. Willekens, *Computer Program for Increment–Decrement Life Table Analysis: A User's Manual to LIFEINDEC* (Laxenburg, Belgium, 1979).

[74] M. Murphy, 'Marital Breakdown and Socio-economic Status: A Reappraisal of the Evidence from Recent British Sources', *British Journal of Sociology*, 36(1) (1985).

Other potential risk factors which cannot be quantified with British data include the presence of a child from a previous marriage, complications with the former spouse, financial and material problems discussed below, and age disparities between the new spouses. So far, no information has been available in Britain to show whether the presence of children from a former marriage brings an added risk of instability to a remarriage. Sociological evidence suggests that it does, and it is certainly true in the USA, where 24 per cent of remarriages in which there were children from a former marriage ended within ten years, compared with 20 per cent of remarriages in which there were no such children.[75]

The Law and the Previous Marriage

In England it is claimed that the law has made remarriage more vulnerable by obliging the former husband to support his first wife, often without limit of time or definition of liability, so that the obligations of the second marriage are subordinated to those of the first. Support may continue until the death of the former spouse, who may apply from time to time to have the payments increased (a right which has been restricted by legislation in 1984), and there may be a claim on the husband's estate after his death. Thus, divorce is merely the continuation of marriage by other means, and venturing into a second marriage may be as risky as opening a war on two fronts. Cohabitation is much safer. The Matrimonial and Family Proceedings Act of 1984 makes early divorce easier (after one year), but will only help remarried couples who have not inherited children from previous marriages. Couples who remarry or who are known to be cohabiting risk losing social-security payments in respect of their children. These problems may lead to tensions by impoverishing the new household; they can also cause fierce resentment between former and current spouses, and may absorb a great deal of time and energy in the new marriage. Another source, however, suggests on the basis of a small sample that the poverty of reconstituted families is mainly due, not to payment of maintenance, but to their larger sizes and their over-representation in the lower social classes.[76]

Conclusion and Summary

The increasing frequency of remarriage obliges us to think again about our conception of the family and the sequence of personal relations which many people can now expect to experience during the course of their lives. While the family remains the focus of most people's emotional and domestic life, replacement of spouses in remarriage is further evidence of the primacy of the

[75] McCarthy, op. cit. (n. 67).
[76] M. Maclean and J. Ekelaar, *Children and Divorce: Economic Factors* (Oxford, 1983).

demand for private personal satisfaction over externally imposed traditional expectations, and even of material self-interest.

Almost 40 per cent of marriages in England and Wales now contain at least one partner who has been married before, and remarriage rates are higher than rates of first marriage at all ages. The diversity of ages and previous experience of partners in remarriages makes remarriage a heterogeneous social institution, difficult to study and one which places heavy demands on statistics. Divorced men and women are more likely to remarry than those who were widowed. None the less, cohabitation is a very general preliminary to remarriage and has, to some extent, replaced it. Current rates imply that one-quarter of those who marry once will marry again, and that at least one in ten children will be brought up in reconstituted families. The rapid increase in the number of remarriages has been made possible by the increase in the number of divorces; remarriage rates have remained constant for women, but have declined for men. Although it is conventional to regard high remarriage rates as following on high divorce rates, in terms of real behaviour it is often the desire for a new partner—and the ability to act on this desire—which fuels the divorce rate. Those who find a new partner whilst they are still married to someone else (an unknown proportion of those who divorce) can now remarry promptly after divorcing. The abandoned spouse may be much less able to do so, and this introduces an asymmetry into remarriage rates which cannot be studied with the statistics available (although it may help to explain the lower remarriage rates of the widowed).

All these problems suggest further topics on which research is needed. The first is the natural history of remarriages of different types, their material setting and the psychological satisfactions, expectations, and problems involved. Remarriage commonly occurs during a 30-year period of an individual's life-span (unlike first marriage), yet little can be said about the effect of age—and of disparities in age—on the lives of the partners. A typology of remarriages is needed, based on age and age differences, presence of existing children and desire for new children, previous marital and cohabiting status, and partners' attitudes. This should show the factors which contribute to the high risk of dissolution of remarriages and indicate the types that are most at risk.

Secondly, we know too little about the needs and social characteristics which determine the situation of spouses after the end of their first marriage, whether they are unmarried, cohabiting, or remarried. In particular, nothing is known about the importance of women's employment in affecting remarriage in Britain, despite the prominence which is given to this factor in general studies of marriage. There are no longitudinal studies which are statistically satisfactory of the experiences of individuals in moving between different marital-status groups. A typology of formerly married persons would help, separating the divorced, widowed, abandoned, and abandoning, and showing their financial position and employment status and whether or not they had children.

Fertility in remarriage will become a more important component of total fertility, so that fertility decisions in remarriages will become increasingly important. We know the period fertility rates of remarried persons, but these are not related to their fertility in previous marriages. The rather complex data needed on order of marriage, type of remarriage, and interval between marriages are difficult to come by.

Remarriage has become a major component of the life cycle, with important effects on the chances of first marriage and the proportion of life spent in the married state. Existing knowledge needs to be integrated, for example through the construction of multi-state life-tables (preferably including cohabitation) and of more sophisticated models of the marriage market, perhaps similar to those proposed by Goldman, Westoff, and Hammerslough.[77] Stochastic modelling of individual life courses would also apply a more realistic picture of variability and make better use of longitudinal information.[78]

[77] N. Goldman, C. F. Westoff, and C. Hammerslough, 'Demography of the Marriage Market in the United States', *Population Index*, 50 (1984).

[78] Cf. Bongaarts's chapter in this volume.

7 The Departure of Children

KATHLEEN KIERNAN
Social Statistics Research Unit, City University, London

Introduction

At some stage in the life cycle of a nuclear family the younger generation make the transition from living with their parents to living independently. This transition is almost universal in contemporary industrial societies. As children move through adolescence and become adults their parents move into what has been described as the 'launching stage',[1] and when the last child has left home the parental generation is categorized as being in the post-parental or 'empty-nest' phase of their life cycle.

Conceptually, the nuclear family can be deemed to have a predictable demographic history. It begins with the single husband–wife pair, and expands as children are born. The birth of the last child marks the end of the expanding phase, whilst the departure of the first child marks the end of stable family size. The departure of the first child also heralds the onset of the contraction phase, which is completed when the last child leaves home and the family group shrinks back to the husband–wife pair. Such a profile assumes that all the family members co-reside throughout the depicted phases—i.e. that the disruptive influences of mortality and divorce are minimal.

The severance of co-residence when adult children leave the parental home typically splits the generations in demographic accounting. The timing and intensity with which young people leave their parents' homes are critical elements in household formation rates, and can directly and indirectly influence the stock, size, and composition of families and households in a population.[2]

As well as being of demographic significance, this multi-generation transition, when the young move to living independently and their parents enter the child-free phase of their lives, has social, economic, and psychological significance. Leaving home is one of the set of events involved in the transition to adulthood. During this transition, children move from economic dependence on their parents to economic independence. The relationship and

[1] R. Hill, *Family Development in Three Generations* (Cambridge, Mass. 1970).

[2] W. Brass, 'The Formal Demography of the Family: An Overview of the Proximate Determinants', in *The Family* (Proceedings of the British Society for Population Studies 1983 Conference), (London, 1983); P. Glick, 'Dimensions of the Fields of Family Demography', in *Proceedings of the International Population Conference, Mexico 1977* (Liège, 1977).

interactions between parents and children alter. Young people establish identities and roles outside the family unit, and the child-rearing role of the parents is largely over. After the children have left home, the post-nuclear family is orientated more to the needs of the couple and to establishing different relationships with their children, their children's spouses, and eventually their grandchildren.

The main focus of this chapter is on the demographic aspects of this transition, and particularly on the timing of these transitions during the life courses of parents and children.

Leaving Home

Relatively little is known about the factors which influence young people's separation from their parents' household, and about how parents and children negotiate this transition. The timing of this residential split is probably normatively prescribed, at least within some range, so that beyond a certain age a child is expected to have left home. This range is likely to vary between families, societies, and over time.[3]

It has often been assumed that the majority of children leave home on marriage. In many contemporary Western societies, but especially among the less educated groups and lower social classes, this may still be the case. Age at marriage in many instances is the only available approximation for studying changes in leaving home over time. It has rarely been a precise measure. In the more distant past, many young single people left home to live as servants or lodgers in other households.[4] And during the 1950s, for example, a substantial minority of married couples did not establish a home of their own until after marriage, but lived for a time with their parents or parents-in-law.[5] The closest coincidence between marriage and leaving home probably occurred during the 1960s. During this decade young people in many Western countries were marrying at increasingly younger ages and over a narrower range of ages than previously, and the supply of housing increased. During the 1970s there were factors at work that reduced the link between leaving home and marriage. Rates of first marriage have fallen in most Western countries, and the age at first marriage has increased.[6] Young people in many European

[3] Such generalizations refer to societies with nuclear family systems. For a review of age at leaving home in past societies see R. Wall, 'The Age at Leaving Home', *Journal of Family History*, 3 (1978).

[4] J. Hajnal, 'Household Formation Patterns in Historical Perspective', *Population and Development Review*, 8 (3) (1982); J. Modell and T. K. Hareven, 'Urbanization and the Malleable Household: An Examination of Boarding and Lodging in American Families', *Journal of Marriage and the Family* 35 (1973).

[5] P. Glick, *American Families* (New York, 1957); K. Dunnell, *Family Formation 1976* (London, 1979).

[6] L. Roussel and P. Festy, *Recent Trends in Attitudes and Behaviour Affecting the Family in Council of Europe Member States* (Strasburg, 1979).

countries and the USA are increasingly likely to cohabit before marriage,[7] and there is evidence that in some countries the incidence of young single-person households has increased.[8] Also, throughout the 1970s, in many countries there have been substantial increases in the proportions of young people, and especially of young women, who go on to higher education.[9] Students who leave home to study are likely to leave home at an earlier age than if they only left at marriage. Young people who do not go on to college and they are still a substantial majority in many countries—may also increasingly prefer a period of living on their own between leaving home and marrying. This is certainly the case in Australia, the only country for which we have detailed information on the leaving-home process.[10] All these factors point to a weakening of the link between marriage and leaving home. But in some countries this process may have gone further than in others.

Living Arrangements for Young People

Cross-sectional studies in which the current living arrangements of young people are investigated provide some clues on the timing of leaving home. A document entitled *The Young Europeans*,[11] which was primarily concerned with the perceptions, values, and political views of young people, contained two tables that are relevant to our purpose (reproduced as Tables 7.1 and 7.2 in this text). The data refer to the aggregate experience of just under 4,000 young people, aged between 15 and 24 years in 1982, in ten countries,[12] and the heterogeneity between countries is thus disguised. Yet relatively simple tables of this type for individual nations would have enhanced our knowledge about the leaving-home patterns of young people, within and the between countries, and a time series would have made it possible to look for changes. National multi-purpose sample surveys could easily meet this challenge.

Table 7.1 shows that about 90 per cent of young Europeans aged 18 or younger were living with their parents in 1982. After the 19th birthday the proportions living with their parents decrease fairly rapidly. At ages 23–4 only a minority (21 per cent) of young women, and a more substantial minority of

[7] A. Brown and K. E. Kiernan, 'Cohabitation in Great Britain: Evidence from the General Household Survey', *Population Trends*, 25 (1981); P. Glick and G. B. Spanier, 'Married and Unmarried Cohabitation in the United States', *Journal of Marriage and the Family*, 42 (1980).

[8] F. E. Kobrin, 'The Fall in Household Size and the Rise of the Primary Individual in the United States', *Demography* 13(1) (1976); K. Schwarz, 'Les Ménages en République Fédérale d'Allemagne: 1961–1972–1981', *Population* 1983 (38(3)).

[9] UNESCO, *Statistical Year Book* (Paris, 1982).

[10] C. Young, 'Leaving Home and Returning Home: A Demographic Study of Young Adults in Australia', paper presented at the Institute of Family Studies, Australian Family Research Conference, Canberra, 23–5 Nov. 1983.

[11] Commission of the European Communities, *The Young Europeans: An Exploratory Study of 15–24 Year Olds in EEC Countries*, (Brussels, 1982).

[12] Belgium, Denmark, France, Federal Republic of Germany, Greece, Ireland, Italy, Luxemburg, Netherlands, and the UK.

Table 7.1 Living arrangements of young people in Europe by age, 1982 (per cent)

Age	With parents	With wife/ husband	Alone	Cohabiting	Other[a] No reply	Total
Men						
15–16 yrs.	97	—	—	—	3	100
17–18	95	—	2	1	2	100
19–20	83	4	7	2	4	100
21–2	63	15	6	8	8	100
23–4	42	24	12	13	9	100
Total men	78	8	5	4	5	100
Women						
15–16 yrs.	93	1	2	1	3	100
17–18	89	3	2	2	4	100
19–20	64	15	8	6	7	100
21–2	52	29	7	7	5	100
23–4	21	47	12	8	12	100
Total women	64	19	6	5	6	100
TOTAL	70	13	5	5	7[b]	100

[a] 'Other' refers to sharing accommodation with another person or persons.
[b] This 7% is divided into 3% 'other' and 4% 'no reply'.

Source: Commission of the European Communities, op. cit. (n. 11).

Table 7.2 Living arrangements of young people in Europe by age and type of activity, 1982 (per cent)

Type of activity	Type of household					
	With parents	With wife/ husband	Alone	Cohabiting	Other	Total
Studying (44%)						
15–19 yrs.	94	—	2	1	3	100
20–4 yrs.	64	3	13	9	11	100
Working (31%)						
15–19 yrs.	83	5	4	4	4	100
20–4 yrs.	50	25	10	9	6	100
Unemployed (11%)						
15–19 yrs.	86	1	3	—	10	100
20–4 yrs.	62	21	5	5	7	100
Others (14%)						
15–19 yrs.	—	—	—	—	—	100
20–4 yrs.	19	64	3	6	8	100
TOTAL	70	13	5	5	7	100

Source: as for Table 7.1.

young men (42 per cent), were still living with their parents. About half of the young women and nearly one-quarter of the young men were married. An interesting feature is the greater heterogeneity in the living arrangements of those aged 23–4. Members of this oldest group were less likely to be living in families (with parents or a spouse) than those aged 21–2 years. The young women were more likely to be living alone or sharing with others, and the young men more likely to be living alone or cohabiting, than those at younger ages. Possible explanations for this heterogeneity at older ages is that within the set of nations included in this survey, or within sub-groups within these nations, or both, marriage and leaving home are more coincident at younger ages, but amongst those who defer marriage the coincidence of leaving home and marriage is less marked.

Table 7.2 provides some interesting information on the living arrangements of young people according to whether they were students, working, unemployed, etc. Ideally one would have liked these data separately for each sex and in more finely calibrated age groups. The table shows that students aged 15–19 years, most of whom will be at school, mainly live with their parents. Fewer, but still a majority, of the students in their 20s live with their parents. It is noteworthy that amongst young Europeans it is rare for students to be married. This is in marked contrast to the situation in the USA, where married students are not uncommon.[13] A substantial proportion of young people in employment live with their parents: over 80 per cent of employed teenagers and half those between the ages of 20 and 24 who are working do so. It appears that a substantial proportion of financially independent young people live with their parents, at least for a time, and are therefore potential contributors to the family income. Eleven per cent of these young Europeans were unemployed. There is some evidence that unemployed young people in their early twenties are slightly more likely that those who are working to be living with their parents. The 'other' group, 14 per cent, includes those on job training schemes (6 per cent), those on national service (1 per cent), and those without paid employment (7 per cent). The majority of those not in paid employment were women (6 of the 7 per cent). These are likely to be young mothers, and this is probably the reason why the proportion married is high for this residual group.

These tables raise a host of questions and bring to mind others that could only be answered from detailed retrospective enquiries, or by more expensive prospective longitudinal studies, in which leaving home could be set in the context of other events, such as age at completion of full-time education, age at entry into the labour force, and age at marriage. It would be fruitful to know how the timing of leaving home was related to these other events. It would also be interesting to know the answers to such questions as: how long do

[13] D. P. Hogan, *Transitions and Social Change: The Early Lives of American Men* (New York, 1981); J. Modell, F. F. Furstenberg, Jr., and T. Hershberg, 'Social Change and Transitions to Adulthood in Historical Perspective', *Journal of Family History*, 1 (1976).

economically independent young adults live with their parents and do they contribute to the household income? Do young people in some occupations leave home sooner and for different reasons than those in other occupations? Do unemployed young people stay at home longer and are they a financial burden on their parents? What proportion of students go away to study? Do parents have to finance their studies? Do a significant proportion of students return home after completing their studies? Are young women more likely to leave home at marriage than young men? Are young men more likely to live at home longer not merely because they marry later? What proportion leave home for other reasons? Do the reasons for leaving home vary with age? To what extent is variation in age at leaving home related to the availability and range of jobs and the opportunities for pursuing further education in the home locality?

The aggregate European experience portrayed in Tables 7.1 and 7.2 obviously disguises differences between countries. The only clue relating to the variability between a substantial number of these countries comes from data on the distribution of single-member households by age derived from the 1977 European Labour Force Surveys.[14] A table on the proportion of young persons living in single-person households would obviously have been more pertinent. Table 7.3 shows that young persons are a minority of all single-member households. In all countries the elderly predominate. However, the proportions of young single-member households differ in different countries. In Italy, the UK, and Belgium, between 1 and 3 per cent of those living on their own are aged between 18 and 24 years. The figure is slightly higher in Ireland (5 per cent) higher still in France and Germany (7 per cent) and highest of all in the Netherlands (11 per cent). In these last three countries it is noticeable that greater proportions of the young people who lived on their own were students. This was true of nearly one-half of the Dutch, just over one-third of the Germans, and just under one-quarter of the French. In most of the other countries, living alone was more closely associated with being in a job. It seems that living alone for a time between leaving the parental home and setting up home with a partner is more common in some countries than in others.

International Comparisons: Denmark, Great Britain, and the USA

Leaving-home patterns are very different for young people in each of these countries. Danish young people appear to leave home at a rapid rate during the post-adolescent years, and the vast majority have done so by their 21st birthday. In Britain, the pace appears more gradual during the teens, increases during the 20s; the great majority have only made the transition from living

[14] Eurostat, *Economic and Social Features of Households in the Member States of the European Community* (Luxemburg, 1982).

Table 7.3 Single-member households

	D	F	I	NL	B	L	UK	IRL
No. of single-member households	6,873	4,272	2,583	878	504	23	3,850	135
Proportion of all households (%)	29.3	23.1	14.1	19.0	15.5	18.5	19.6	16.1
Age of single-member households:								
18–24	7.4	7.7	1.2	11.8	3.0	3.6	1.5	5.2
25–34	11.3	11.5	5.8	14.4	7.7	9.9	4.9	9.2
35–49	11.9	10.6	10.1	10.8	10.9	11.7	6.9	12.1
50–59	11.4	11.8	14.4	10.4	12.2	13.9	12.5	16.9
60+	58.0	58.4	68.0	52.5	66.3	70.8	74.3	56.5
Single-member households aged 18–24 according to activity of head:								
Persons with a principal occupation	59.7	70.5	70.0	45.8	75.2	94.1	78.5	81.4
Unemployed persons	2.3	3.5	8.3	4.5	11.4	0.0	5.3	4.3
of whom seeking their first job	0.6	0.6	7.0	1.0	2.7	0.0	0.9	0.0
Not economically active	38.0	26.0	21.7	49.7	13.4	6.0	16.2	14.3
of whom students	36.1	24.1	8.0	47.4	10.1	5.8	12.0	5.7

Note: D = Federal Republic of Germany; F = France; I = Italy; NL = Netherlands; B = Belgium; L = Luxemburg; UK = United Kingdom; IRL = Ireland.

Source: Eurostat, *European Labour Forces, 1977* (Luxemburg, 1982).

with their parents to living independently by the time they are about 25 years old. In the USA the pattern is again different. The rate of leaving home seems to peak during the year or so following high school and, thereafter, changes more slowly; again the great majority have left home by their 25th birthday.

Variations across space and time in the proportions of young people who live independently of their parents may be due to a wide variety of factors, including the extent to which young people go on to higher education, which varies markedly between countries. For example, in the USA 'higher-education enrolment ratios' are substantially greater than in other countries. In 1975[15] the number of young people enrolled in colleges of higher education

[15] This year has been quoted as the comparison to be made between Denmark and Great Britain refers to 1975.

as a proportion of those aged 20 to 24 years was 63.5 per cent for men and 52.7 for women.[16] Denmark has one of the highest enrolment ratios in Western Europe; the ratios in 1975 were 32 per cent for men and 26.7 per women, whilst the equivalent ratios for the UK (Great Britain plus Northern Ireland) were 23.6 per cent for men and 13.9 per cent for women.

Variation between countries may also depend on the availability of cheap accommodation to rent, for students and young workers. The ease with which young people can set up an independent household either on their own, with a friend or friends, with a cohabitant, or with a spouse may well depend on the incomes of young people relative to the costs of housing in a particular country or at a specific time. It would seem plausible that in countries with a plentiful supply of inexpensive housing to rent, *ceteris paribus* more young people would be living independently of their parents and begin doing so at an earlier age than in countries where housing is relatively expensive or difficult to acquire. The housing markets in Denmark and Great Britain differ substantially. In Denmark there is a plentiful supply of cheap accommodation to rent[17] whilst in Britain private accommodation to rent is scarce, and has formed a shrinking component of the housing market during the 1970s. The majority of young people in Britain are faced with two options; to buy a home of their own on mortgage, or to rent from a public authority. To become a tenant of a public authority is difficult; accommodation is generally reserved for married couples with children or unmarried mothers. To become an owner-occupier it is necessary to have access to mortgage funds, to be able to afford the repayments and interest, and to have sufficient savings to put down as a deposit.

The difference between the housing markets of these two countries may account, to some degree, for the marked variation between the proportions of young people still living with their parents at different ages. Table 7.4 shows the living arrangements of young people in Denmark in 1975, by single years of age from 18 to 25 years. In Table 7.5 similar, but not exactly comparable, data are given for young men and women in Britain, for the same year.[18] Over half the Danish young people had already left home by their 19th birthday, and of those who had left home a substantial proportion were either cohabiting or living alone. It would appear that young people in Denmark leave home at a rapid rate during their late teens, and fewer than 10 per cent are still living with their parents by the time they are 21. There is little evidence that leaving home and marriage are coincident in Denmark, although the picture is distorted by the tendency to cohabit before marriage. For Denmark, we were only able to locate data for both sexes combined, which would

[16] UNESCO, op. cit. (n. 9).

[17] O. Bertelsen, *The Young Family in the 1970s* (Copenhagen, 1980).

[18] The Danish data come from L. Roussel, 'Démographie et mode de vie conjugale au Danemark', *Population*, 1977 (2) and the British data from Central Statistical Office, *Social Trends*, 8 (London, 1979).

disguise differences (if any) between the behaviour of young Danish men and women. In Britain, there are certainly noticeable differences between the sexes. At every age a greater proportion of men than of women are still living with their parents. It is noticeable that a far greater proportion of British young people are still living with their parents (child of head of household) in their late teens, and substantial proportions are doing so at age 21, 43 per cent of the women and 63 per cent of the men. The pace at which young people in Britain leave home is much slower than in Denmark. Moreover, the trend in the proportion of British women who live at home at different ages mirrors to a large extent the trend in the proportion of women who are married (wife of head of household). We cannot readily discern a similar situation for the men, but the increase in the number of heads of household with age is likely to be associated with marriage. This suggests that a substantial proportion of young adults in Britain transfer directly from living with their parents to setting up a new household with a spouse. The great majority of young people in Britain have left home by their mid-20s. An analysis based on the residential histories of a British cohort born in 1946, who were contacted 21 times between birth and their 26th birthday[19] showed that only 7 per cent of the women and 16 per cent of the men did not record a move after their 16th birthday.

Table 7.4 Living arrangements of young people in Denmark by age, 1975

Age	Single living with parents	Living alone	Cohabiting[a]	Married[a]	Other	Total
18	53.7	11.6	22.6	4.2	7.9	100
19	44.2	16.7	23.0	9.2	6.9	100
20	23.4	20.5	28.7	20.4	7.0	100
21	9.7	17.3	39.3	28.2	5.5	100
22	6.8	17.4	40.5	32.3	3.0	100
23	2.3	14.6	26.2	51.1	5.8	100
24	4.7	16.5	16.5	59.3	1.2	100
25	3.3	11.7	14.5	67.7	2.8	100

[a] 1% of the cohabiting group and fewer than 0.5% of the married group were living with their parents.

Source: Danish National Institute of Social Research 1975 Survey given by Roussel, op. cit. (n. 18).

Like young people in Denmark, those in the USA appear to leave home at a rapid rate during their late teens. Data from the National Longitudinal Study, in which a sample of the high-school class of 1972 has been followed up, showed that during an 18-month period from the initial contact, when the vast

[19] K. E. Kiernan, 'Characteristics of Young People who Move Inter-regionally: A Longitudinal Study', in J. Hobcraft and P. Rees (eds.), *Regional Demographic Development* (London, 1980).

Table 7.5 Relationship to head of household by sex and age: young people in Great Britain, 1975 (per cent)

Age	Men				Women				
	Son	Head of household	Other	Total	Daughter	Wife of head of household	Head of household	Other	Total
16	97.7	—	2.3	100	93.2	0.4	—	6.4	100
17	97.0	0.9	2.1	100	92.3	2.7	0.9	4.1	100
18	91.8	1.6	6.6	100	78.3	10.6	2.3	8.8	10
19	83.1	8.9	8.0	100	68.0	19.0	3.0	10.0	100
20	74.4	16.4	9.2	100	48.1	31.2	9.0	11.7	100
21	62.8	27.5	9.7	100	42.5	45.7	5.9	5.9	100
22	45.8	43.0	11.2	100	32.4	54.3	3.3	10.0	100
23	36.9	56.2	6.9	100	19.1	69.3	5.0	6.6	100
24	26.3	68.2	5.5	100	14.3	70.9	10.3	4.5	100

Source: General Household Survey of Great Britain, 1975 from General Statistical Office, op. cit. (n. 18).

majority were living at home, to the date of the first follow-up, about half the young people had left home.[20] During this period the average age of members of the sample increased from 17.5 to 19 years. This suggests that many young people in the USA make their initial break from home in the year following graduation from high school, when many go on to college and others enter the labour force. The leaving-home patterns of young people in Denmark and the USA then diverge. After their 19th birthday young Americans leave home at a much more gradual pace than do those in Denmark. For example, at about age 22, over 30 per cent of the men and just over 25 per cent of the women were currently living at home,[21] and when the average sample member was aged 25, 14 per cent of the men and 10 per cent of the women were living at home. Kobrin and DaVanzo also report that, overall, marriage was the most powerful influence on the leaving-home behaviour of these young people.

The norms relating to the ages when children are expected to have left home appear to be different in Denmark, Great Britain, and the USA. One has the impression from these data that young people in Denmark expect to leave home during their late teens, whilst in Britain young people as yet are most likely to associate leaving home with marriage. In the USA the situation is more complex. Young people appear to fall into two broad groups—those who expect to make the break with home on leaving school (in many instances this may be when they go on to college) and another group where marriage is associated with leaving home. These three case-studies show how much the timing of leaving home can vary between countries. It is clear that any attempt to construct a model of this stage of the life cycle would have to try to take this variability into account.

Detailed Studies of Leaving-home Patterns

The most comprehensive information to date on the leaving-home patterns of young adults comes from Christabel Young's analyses of data collected in 1971 in Melbourne and from a more recent analysis based on national Australian data collected in 1982.[22] How far these findings are generalizable must await detailed studies from other countries. The Survey of 1982 was, as far as I can ascertain, the first nation-wide survey in which questions were asked on age at leaving home and reasons for doing so. Life-table analyses of

[20] F. E. Kobrin and J. DaVanzo, 'Leaving Home and the Transition to Adulthood', revised version of a paper presented at the 1983 Annual Meeting of the Population Association of America, Pitsburgh, Pa., 1983. Data from the US Bureau of the Census also showed that in 1970 50% of young women were no longer living in their parental home by the time they were 18.8 years old and 90% had left by age 24.5 years. The analogous figures for young men were 19.2 years and 27.9 years respectively. In P. Glick, 'Updating the Life Cycle of the Family', *Journal of Marriage and the Family*, 39(1) (1977) p. 8 n.

[21] These figures were read off a graph.

[22] C. Young, *The Family Life Cycle: Literature Review and Studies of Families in Melbourne, Australia* (Canberra, 1977) and Young, op. cit. (n. 10).

these data showed that fewer than 10% of young men and women had never left home by their 26th birthday, and the median age at leaving home was 20.0 years for women and 21.2 years for men. These data and the fragmentary evidence from other countries suggest that by the time young men and women reach their mid-20s the great majority have made the transition from living with their parents to living independently, and that young women make this transition sooner than young men.

Some of the main findings from the 1982 survey were that greater proportions of young women (45 per cent) than of young men (31 per cent) made their initial break with home in conjunction with marriage. It is also surprising how relatively low these proportions are. Next in importance for the men were independence (18 per cent), job opportunities (12 per cent), travel (7 per cent) (travel may be an antipodean idiosyncracy) study, and entry into the armed forces (each with 6 per cent). The remainder (20 per cent) left for a variety of reasons including migration, conflict with parents, to cohabit, or to live with others. Amongst the women the other reasons for making the initial break with home were, in order of magnitude, independence (10 per cent) study, job opportunity, and conflict with parents (each with 9 per cent); and the remaining 18 per cent left either to travel, to live with others, to cohabit, or to emigrate. Young people who left home for reasons other than marriage did so, on average, at a younger age. They were also much more likely to return home.

The frequency with which young people return to live with their parents and then leave again is the most striking aspect of Young's recent analysis.[23] Around 50 per cent of the men and 40 per cent of the women who had left home returned to live with their parents. This usually occurred during the first few years after departure, and those who returned had, in the main, left home for reasons other than marriage. However, most of this movement to and fro was completed by the time the women were 22 and the men were 24. Many of those who first left home for 'other' reasons subsequently left home at marriage. Kobrin and DaVanzo report similar comings and goings in the leaving-home patterns of young Americans.[24] Whether this fluidity in the leaving-home behaviour occurs to the same extent in other countries remains to be investigated.

The lesser importance of marriage as a reason for leaving home among young Australians appears to be a recent development. Statistics from the Melbourne Survey in 1971 showed that 80 per cent of the women and 70 per cent of the men left home at marriage. The difference between the surveys of 1971 and 1982 may be smaller than appears. There were important differences between these surveys that have a more general bearing on the study of leaving home. In the earlier survey it was left to the respondent to determine what was

[23] Young, op. cit. (n. 10).
[24] Kobrin and DaVanzo, op. cit. (n. 20).

meant by leaving home, so we do not know whether the respondents were referring to first or last departure. Young's pioneering work has shown how essential it is that surveys now include a clear definition of leaving home; ideally, as a minimum, information on first leaving and on final departure should be obtained. In the earlier Australian survey, the description of the leaving-home patterns of young adults was based on information collected from their mothers, whilst in the later survey it was based on the respondents' own experiences. The views of mothers and those of their children on the timing and reasons for leaving home may well differ. Mothers may well regard marriage as a definite indication of having left home, but may look on other moves as temporary absences, especially if children later return home.

I have not been able to find any detailed retrospective enquiries on the leaving-home patterns of young adults in other countries. Consequently we do not know whether the Australian pattern is unique, or whether it is similar to that in other Western countries. The fragmentary evidence for other countries comes from cross-sectional current-status studies that may disguise the complexities of the leaving-home process; but it suggests that there is a great deal of cultural variability in the leaving-home patterns of young adults. But if there is a general trend for fewer young adults to make the initial break with home in conjunction with marriage and, therefore, to leave home at an earlier age, and if the probability of returning home is greater amongst those who leave for reasons other than marriage, this has implications for the later phases of the family life cycle of parents. The launching stage may begin sooner and the post-parental phase may in its early stages be punctuated by children returning home for a time. It is to these phases of the parental life cycle to which we now turn our attention.

The Emergence of the Post-parental Phase

During the twentieth century, the post-parental phase of the family life cycle of the 'empty-nest' phase, as it has come to be known in American popular culture, has changed from being a relatively short period experienced by a minority of parents to a longer period experienced by the majority. Studies from several countries based on different estimation procedures and a variety of assumptions have shown similar results.[25]

The American experience will serve as an example. In a study based on

[25] For the USA see P. Glick and R. Parke, 'New Approaches in Studying the Life Cycle of the Family', *Demography*, 2 (1965); P. Glick, op. cit. (n. 20); P. Uhlenberg, 'The Study of Cohort Life Cycles: Cohorts of Native-born Massachusetts Women, 1830–1920', *Population Studies* 23(3) (1969); 'Changing Configurations of the Life Course', in T. Hareven (ed.), *Transitions: The Family and Life Course in Historical Perspective* (New York, 1978); 'Death and the Family', *Journal of Family History*, 5 (1980). For Australia see Young, op. cit. (n. 22). For Italy see M. Livi-Bacci, 'Social and Biological Aging: Contradictions of Development', *Population and Development Review* 8(4) (1982). For England and Wales see M. Anderson, 'What is New about the Modern Family: An Historical Perspective', in *The Family*, (op. cit., n. 2).

census records for Providence, Rhode Island[26] it was shown that during the closing decades of the nineteenth century, only a minority of parents experienced a post-parental phase. The proportion of men and women aged 40 who had a child living at home was not less than 60 per cent. Uhlenberg's analysis, based on the experiences of cohorts of women born in Massachusetts between 1830 and 1920, clearly demonstrates the improvement in the chances of women surviving to ages when all their children are likely to have left home.[27] The estimated proportions of women who married, bore and reared children, and survived jointly with their husband to age 55 (their assumed age when the last child left home) were 63 per cent for the cohort born in 1890 and 82 per cent for the cohort born in 1920. It was estimated that 18 per cent of the women born in 1890 would have died by their 55th birthday and 19 per cent would have lost their husband through death. The analogous estimates for the cohort of 1920 were 6 per cent dead and 12 per cent widowed. If these estimates accurately reflect the general experiences of women in these cohorts then, even as late as the 1940s (1890 plus 55 years), a substantial proportion of families did not survive intact long enough for parents to make the transition to the post-parental phase of their life cycle and for children to leave from a home in which both natural parents were present. Glick has provided us with estimates of the duration of the 'empty-nest' stage based on the median experiences of cohorts of women born between the 1880s and 1950s.[28] The 'empty-nest' stage in this instance consisted of the period from the marriage of the last-born child to the death of a spouse. The estimated duration of the 'empty-next' phase for women born during the 1880s, who would have reached this stage in their life cycle in about the 1930s,[29] was 1.6 years. The analogous estimates for women born between 1900 and 1909 and 1930 and 1939 were 9.3 and 11.5 years respectively. This significant increase in the length of the post-parental phase of the life cycle is mainly due to the improved chances of both parents surviving to older ages. The reduction in family size and the cessation of childbearing at younger ages have only made a minor contribution to this development.

Studies of this type provide us with guidelines to the ways that life-cycle patterns have changed over time, but they have severe drawbacks for studying the contemporary situation. As we shall see, the ages at which parents reach this stage of their life cycle varies considerably, in part because of the cumulative differences in their childbearing patterns. Consequently, the average experience may not be an accurate indicator of the duration of the 'empty-nest' stage for a substantial proportion of parents.

[26] H. P. Chudacoff and T. F. Hareven, 'From the Empty Net to Family Dissolution: Life Course Transitions into Old Age', *Journal of Family History*, 4 (1979).

[27] Uhlenberg, op. cit., 1969 (n. 25).

[28] Glick, op. cit. (n. 25).

[29] The mother's median age at marriage of the last-born child was estimated to be 55 years for women born during the 1880s and 53 years for those born between 1900 and 1909 and 1930 and 1939.

Timing of the Transition to the Post-parental Phase: A Review of the Evidence

Our review of the leaving-home patterns of young adults indicates that the great majority of parents will have entered the post-parental phase of their life cycle by the time their children reach their mid-twenties. How old are the parents? Needless to say, there is little direct information on the age distribution of parents whose children have all left home. A simple question whether children were present or absent from the household, cross-tabulated by the ages of the mother/father, would provide some useful information. More detailed questions, the answers to which provided information on the ages of parents when their first child left home and when their last child left home for the last time, would provide the necessary data for studying the duration of the launching-stage and the spread of ages at which parents made the transition to the post-parental stage of their life cycle. Until this information is available we have to make do with clues from disparate sources.

Cursory insights into the timing of this transition can be gleaned from the way average household size varies with age. Table 7.6 shows this information for a selection of European countries that participated in the 1977 round of the EEC Labour Force Survey.[30] The majority of households in these countries consist of married couples (between 60 and 70 per cent). The trends in household size are similar in all these countries. The average household size increases with the age of the head of household up to the age group 35–49, and subsequently decreases. Notwithstanding changes in reproductive behaviour, this movement probably reflects the growth in the size of households as children are born, and the subsequent decline to some extent caused by the movement of grown-up children out of the home. In all these countries the average size of households in which the head is between 50 and 59 years old exceeds two. This may indicate the presence of grown-up children. If this were so (and the presence of other individuals and the contribution of non-family households to these averages should not be ignored), it would suggest that parents were relatively old before all their children had left home.[31] Data from the German Census of 1970 also showed that parents were relatively old when all their children had left home and that the median age at this transition varied with family size.[32] The median age at which mothers had no children living at home was 51 for those mothers who had only borne one child, and the

[30] Eurostat, op. cit. (n. 14).

[31] The figures in Table 6 also show that in some countries, the Federal Republic of Germany, the Netherlands, and, to a lesser extent, France, the average size of households at ages 18 to 24 years is less than two. This provides additional evidence for our inference that there is a more marked tendency for young people in these countries to live alone for a time before marriage.

[32] K. Schwarz, 'Ehen in April 1977 nach dem Einkommen des Mannes', *Wirtschaft und Statistik*, 3 (1979), quoted in C. Höhn, 'The Family Life Cycle: On the Necessity to Enlarge the Concept', paper presented at IUSSP Workshop on Family Demography and its Applications, New York, 12–14 Dec. 1983.

analogous figures for those who had borne two, three, and four children were 55, 58, and 60 years respectively.

We know that, as each family unit ages, the chances that it will contain children change. To illustrate this, we have used some British data derived from the General Household Survey of 1980. The family categories shown in Table 7.7 represent 67 per cent of the population living in private households. In those families where the husband is less than 30 years old, 60 per cent of couples have dependent children present, the remainder being childless. In families where the husband is aged 30 to 44 years, 90 per cent of married couples have co-residing children. In families where the husband is between 45 and 59 years old there is greater heterogeneity: some couples have already launched their children, perhaps some 25 per cent (if we assume 10 per cent of couples to have been childless), nearly 40 per cent of couples have dependent children residing with them and just over one-quarter have non-dependent children living with them.[33] In families in which the husband is over 60, the majority have launched their children, but about one-sixth still have children living with them. These statistics suggest that the family stage reached by couples in later middle age is quite varied; a reflection of the cumulative impact of differences in the age at which people become parents, the number of children they had, and the spacing of their children.

It was difficult to assemble comparable statistics for other countries because of problems relating to the classification of families, but mainly because of variations in the definition of children. Frequently children over a certain age were excluded from the analyses of families in censuses and surveys.[34] The inclusion of co-resident children regardless of age in the analysis of family data would enhance our knowledge of the family structures of parents with grown-up children.

It was also difficult to find studies in which the ages at which parents made the transition to the post-parental phase of their life cycle were specifically investigated. One French study was located.[35] In a survey of a sample of wage-earners, who worked in the private sector of the economy and were aged 64 in 1980, information was collected on the length of time that had elapsed since the last child had left home. This sample is probably not representative of this age cohort of French people. However, given the rarity of direct information in this area it is worth quoting the findings.[36] In the sub-group of the sample who were parents, 75 per cent had no children living at home. Thus,

[33] A dependent child is one who is aged 16 or younger, or aged 19 or younger if in full-time education. All other children are classified as non-dependent.

[34] Glick, op. cit. (n. 2); Organization for Economic Co-operation and Development, *Child and Family: Demographic Developments in the OECD Countries* (Paris, 1978).

[35] P. Paillat, 'La Famille des salariés du secteur privé à la veille de la retraite', i, *Population*, (38(3)); C. Delbès, 'La Famille des salariés du secteur privé à la veille de la retraite', ii: 'Les Relations familiales', *Population*, 1983 (38(6)).

[36] However, the papers prepared for the Berlin seminar included more information on this topic. See the chapters by Young and by Schwarz and Mayer in this volume.

Table 7.6 Average size of households according to head of household's age group

Age	D	F	I	NL	B	L	UK	IRL
All	2.52	2.76	3.12	2.92	2.92	2.88	2.80	3.69
18–24	1.65	1.95	2.66	1.69	2.31	2.15	2.79	2.50
25–34	2.65	3.05	3.22	2.94	3.15	2.94	3.28	3.59
35–49	3.49	3.81	3.92	3.95	3.86	3.71	3.89	5.01
50–59	2.66	2.86	3.29	3.24	3.01	3.03	2.80	4.12
60+	1.69	1.81	2.23	1.93	1.96	2.03	1.83	2.59

Note: D = Federal Republic of Germany; F = France; I = Italy; NL = Netherlands; B = Belgium; L = Luxemburg; UK = United Kingdom; IRL = Ireland.

Source: Eurostat, *European Labour Forces, 1977* (Luxemburg, 1982).

Table 7.7 Family type by age of head of household, Great Britain, 1980

Family type Under 30	Age of head of household 30–44	45–59	60+	
Married couple only	38.3	10.2	36.4	82.5
Married couple with dependent children	61.4	87.2	38.0	3.8
Married couple with independent children only	0.2	2.6	25.6	13.7
TOTAL	100.0	100.0	100.0	100.0

Source: General Household Survey (unpublished data), 1980.

even on the eve of retirement a substantial minority of parents had children still living at home. Delbès presents a table on the length of time elapsed since the last child left home. I have reclassified these durations to approximate the ages of the parents when the last child left home, and these figures are given in Table 7.8. Amongst the parents whose children had already left home, over half had entered the post-parental phase during their 50s. As might be expected, mothers in the sample were younger than the fathers when their last children left home; at this stage about one-third of the women were less than 50 years old, compared with 18 per cent of the men. These statistics for the women are unlikely to be an accurate reflection of the experiences of all French women aged 64. A substantial proportion (28 per cent) of the women in the sample had never had children. Women who are mothers are less likely to be economically active than childless women. Also, there is some evidence from the Australian data that children of economically active mothers tend to leave home sooner than those whose mothers do not work.[37] Whether this is true of other Western countries remains to be seen. If the data for all parents are pro-rated

[37] Young, op. cit. (n. 10).

to include those who still had co-resident children, then only 18 per cent of all the parents included in the sample were less than 50 years old when their last child left home, and one-half had entered the post-parental phase of their life cycle in their late 50s. It would appear that members of this cohort only spent a relatively short time in this child-free stage before another major transition loomed—retirement of one or both spouses from the labour force.

Table 7.8 Age distribution of parents when their last child left home, France, 1980 (per cent)

Age[a]	Men[b] (N=768)	Women[b] (N=455)	Total[b] (N=1,223	Total[c] (N=1,634)
64+	—	—	—	25.2
60–4	21.5	12.3	18.0	13.5
55–9	31.4	24.2	28.8	21.5
50–4	27.0	27.8	27.2	20.4
Under 50	18.5	34.3	24.4	18.2
Unknown	1.6	1.4	1.6	1.2

[a] Age is approximate.
[b] Sample includes those whose children have left home.
[c] Sample includes those whose children are still living at home.
Source: Delbès, op. cit. (n. 35).

One might query whether age is the most appropriate indexing variable for studying family transitions, especially as parents/spouses are normally of different ages. When studying relationships rather than individuals, duration is the more obvious and manageable indexing variable, and duration of either marriage or parenthood is probably more relevant for the study of the determinants of family stages. However, age is probably more relevant for studying the consequences. For example, the characteristics, life-chances, and life-styles of couples who reach the 'empty-nest' stage during their forties are likely to be substantially different from those who do not reach this stage until their late fifties or later. Elucidation of these differences should form part of the research agenda for this topic. In detailed analyses of a particular phase of the family life cycle, an appropriate solution would be to index by the age of a specified marker (for example, husband/father, wife/mother, chief economic supporter) and to control for age at marriage or parenthood. In studies concerned with changes over the family life cycle, the time elapsed since a particular starting-point is probably more appropriate. Analyses by marriage duration, but more particularly by time elapsed since first birth, should reduce the extent of the variability in the timing of transitions during the later phases of the family life cycle.

Examples of studies in which the timing of transitions over the family life cycle have been considered by marriage duration include Hill's classic study of three generations of American families[38] and Young's analysis of the Melbourne data.[39] Hill, who deals with the experiences of parents born some time ago, found that, of all stages of the life cycle, the launching-stage (defined as the time when one child has left home, but not all children) and the post-parental stage (all children have left home)[40] were the most variable. Among parents who had been married for 20 years, 35 per cent were in the launching-stage and 1 per cent in the post-parental phase, the remainder being in earlier stages, whereas amongst those parents who had been married for between 26 and 30 years, the great majority, 82 per cent, were in the launching-stage and only 15 per cent were in the post-parental phase. After 31–5, 36–40, and 41–5 years of marriage the proportions in the post-parental phase were respectively 36, 67, and 88 per cent. It is noteworthy that for a substantial proportion of this generation of parents the post-parental phase did not begin until the fourth decade of their marriage.

Hill's study and Young's analysis showed that the rate of entry into the launching-stage was a good deal faster than that into the post-parental phase. In the Melbourne survey the cohort of women which had progressed furthest along their life course were those married between 1930 and 1939. It was noticeable that by about the 20th year of marriage children began to leave home and the rate at which the first child left home increased rapidly, so that by the 25th year of marriage nearly 70 per cent of this cohort had launched their first child. However, after approximately 33 years of marriage only half the mothers had seen all their children leave home.

Young also presented an interesting graph which showed the cumulative proportions of those married during the 1930s who had, at a given marriage duration, respectively commenced childbearing, completed childbearing, seen one child leave home, or seen all their children leave home. Such information for larger samples (the sample size in this case was 139), later cohorts, and other countries would enable us to assess the extent to which the childbearing period approximates the launching-stage, and whether the start of the launching-stage and its completion resemble the curves of entry into and completion of childbearing. If the span of the childbearing period and the span of the launching-stage were found to approximate each other in some way, we may have a basis for modelling the ways that families grow and shrink over time. The relationship is unlikely to be straightforward. If all children left home in chronological order and at the same age, our task would be simple. But the leaving-home patterns within families may not be independent of

[38] Hill, op. cit. (n. 1).

[39] Young, op. cit. (n. 22).

[40] In fact, Hill subdivides this phase into two stages: the post-parental stage—defined as all children having left home up to the retirement of the breadwinner—and the post-retirement years—from retirement to the death of a spouse. We have amalgamated the two groups.

either sex or parity.[41] Daughters may leave home sooner than sons and younger children may leave home before older children, and when children do leave home in chronological order the pace at which they leave home may not be in accord with the rate at which they were born. However, until detailed empirical results on the dynamics of leaving home, along with childbearing histories, become available, we are unlikely to make any reliable advances in this field.

Heterogeneity and Change

There is little doubt that during the life cycles of families the timing of the launching-stage and the timing of the transition to the post-parental phase are highly variable. This reflects the cumulative impact of differences in the timing of the first birth and the last birth, as well as differences in the leaving-home patterns of the younger generation. Given this heterogeneity, the average experience is unlikely to be an accurate index of the duration and timing of these phases. When appropriate data become available for studying these stages of the life cycle we should endeavour to incorporate spread into our analyses by, for example, quantifying the length of time it takes for a given proportion of parents or children to pass through or into different phases of their life courses.

Other factors which we will have to contend with at the aggregate level are changes over time in reproductive behaviour and in the leaving-home patterns of young people. Much of the information currently available relates to parents whose children left home before or about 1970. These data suggest that parents may have been well into their fifties before they entered the post-parental phase of their life cycle. There may have been changes recently. If young people are leaving home at younger ages and subsequent cohorts of parents have had fewer children and completed their childbearing younger, then we would probably find that these more recent cohorts of parents, who are currently at the beginning or on the threshold of the 'empty-nest' stage, are younger. How much younger remains to be investigated.

Generally speaking, fertility trends have been similar in many contemporary Western societies. But we noted earlier the marked variation between countries in the leaving-home patterns of young adults. One might speculate that recent cohorts of parents in a country like Denmark are likely to be in their 40s at the beginning of the 'empty-nest' stage, given that their children leave home so rapidly during their teens. In countries like Denmark, where the variation in the ages at which children leave home is small, we may well find

[41] Young, op. cit. (n. 22) provides evidence from her analysis of the Melbourne data that daughters tend to leave home sooner than sons. The chances that a second-born child leaves home first is greatest when the second-born child is a daughter and the first-born is a son. Also, the longer the birth interval between the first and second child the greater the probability that the first-born will leave before the second-born.

that there is a closer correspondence between reproductive behaviour and the launching-stage of the parents' life cycle. Also, the variability in the timing of the transition to the 'empty-nest' stage will be less marked in a country like Denmark than in countries where the leaving-home stage of young adults is more protracted.

The USA presents an interesting case. The evidence suggests that the population of young people falls into two broad groups—those who make the initial break with home at ages 18/19, and another group with a more protracted leaving-home pattern. If the moves away from home at ages 18/19 are associated to a large extent with going to college, then the parents of children who go on to higher education are likely to enter the 'empty-nest' stage sooner than parents of children who do not. But this may be counterbalanced by the fact that parents of children who go on to college are more likely to have begun childbearing later. Such counterbalancing effects can lead to a lower variance in the timing of the transition to the 'empty-nest' stage than if fertility and the ages at which children left home were independent. Conversely, in societies where age at leaving home and reproductive behaviour are positively correlated, as may be the case in Great Britain, this would lead to an increased variance. In micro-studies of these parent–child transitions it may well be found that the relationships between the timing of these events and socio-economic characteristics are complex, subtle, and non-linear.

Up to now we have implictly assumed that families survive intact to make these transitions. How realistic is this assumption? The chances that children will survive to their teens are extremely high, given the low mortality rates in childhood and adolescence. The chances that both parents survive to age 50, are also high. Beyond age 50 the impact of death on men, in particular, becomes more important. This may be of some consequence if a significant proportion of parents do not reach the 'empty-nest' stage of their life cycle until their late 50s or later.

An attrition factor that is increasingly likely to make inroads into marriage before children leave home is divorce. If we assume, for the sake of argument, that children start to leave home after their parents have been married for 20 years, the extent of divorce experienced by members of marriage cohorts at this duration will provide us with a guide to the disruptive influence of divorce. Data for England and Wales can serve as an example. Divorce rates there are amongst the highest in western Europe, but are lower than in the USA. Of couples married in 1951, who would have started to launch their children by about 1971, only 7 per cent had been divorced by their 20th wedding anniversary. For those married in 1960 the proportion who were divorced at this stage of their marriage was 16 per cent, more than double the figure for the cohort of 1951. If the rates of 1980 were to prevail, then about 26 per cent of members of the marriage cohort of 1970 would have divorced after 20 years of marriage.[42] These statistics include childless marriages in which the risk of breakdown is greater,[43] so that the proportions will overestimate the impact of divorce on families with children. But the trend is clear. An increasing proportion of parents, in the main fathers, are experiencing an 'empty-nest' phase even before their children have grown up, and an increasing minority of children are likely to be launched from one-parent families. In countries where remarriage rates are high, as in England and Wales and the USA, many children will depart from a home containing a natural parent plus a step-parent, typically the mother and stepfather. This raises the question whether the leaving-home patterns of children who leave from their natural parents' home are different from those who leave from other situations. For example, are children who live with a lone mother (either divorced or widowed) likely to stay at home longer? The increasing tendency for marriages to break down has other implications. Do young adults whose marriage breaks down return home, at least for a time? The work of Young and of Kobrin and DaVanzo suggests that some of the returns at young ages are associated with marital breakdown.[44]

In this section we have highlighted some of the complexities that may arise in studying the later phases of the family life cycle. The variability between and within populations suggests that we should be cautious about making broad generalizations, especially as it is still not clear which are the typical ages covered by the post-parental phase of the life cycle.

A Demographic Irony

It is one of those demographic ironies that factors that have led to the emergence of the post-parental phase and the possibility of spouses having a period of time together after completing their primary parental obligations have also led to the increased likelihood of couples in their middle years having responsibilities for aged parents.

Le Bras has estimated that the modal age at which an individual would lose his or her father was between 30 and 50 and his or her mother between 40 and 60, and that by age 55 one out of two people would have lost both parents, if mortality and fertility rates prevailing in France in 1972 were to continue in the long run.[45] These estimates derived from stable-population theory provide us with insights into what might happen if present trends were to continue. As yet we do not know what is currently happening. Yet simple

[42] K. E. Kiernan, 'The Structure of Families Today: Continuity or Change?' in *The Family* (op. cit., n. 2).

[43] M. Murphy, 'Fertility and Birth Timing and Marital Breakdown: A Reinterpretation of the Evidence', *Journal of Biosocial Science*, 16 (1984).

[44] Young, op. cit. (n. 10); Kobrin and DaVanzo, op. cit. (n. 20).

[45] H. LeBras, 'Living Forebears in Stable Populations', in K. E. Wachter, E. A. Hammel, and P. Laslett, *Statistical Studies of Historical Social Structure* (New York, 1978).

questions such as 'Is your mother/father still alive?' and 'How old is your mother/father?' would enable us to pin-point the typical ages at which grown-up children may have responsibilities for parents. As yet we do not know to what extent parents have simultaneous responsibilities for their children and their own parents during their middle years, nor to what extent parents have generally launched their children before having to cope with the needs of their own elderly parents.

Increased longevity has certainly increased the chances of being a member of a multi-generation family, and the middle generation may well be caught between the older and younger generations because both need assistance. There is evidence that the middle generation tend to be 'high givers' of goods, services, and emotional support and 'modest receivers' in both directions.[46] In the next section we briefly consider some of the social and psychological aspects of the post-parental phase of the life cycle.

The Post-parental Phase: Social and Psychological Aspects

During the 1950s and 1960s a good deal of attention was given to the post-parental stage of the life cycle.[47] The transition to the post-parental phase was regarded as being a stressful period for women in particular, partly because the role in which they had made a heavy investment was now over.[48] It was also suggested that this was a difficult transition for middle-aged spouses, partly because the post-parental phase was a relatively new phenomenon and consequently parents were often without a role model from the previous generation to assist them in adjusting to this stage.[49] Despite these expectations, the limited empirical evidence showed that most couples made this transition relatively easily.[50] However, the ease with which parents, particularly mothers, adjusted to the post-parental phase was found to be related to their degree of involvement in other areas such as paid employment, social organizations, and leisure activities. Given the upsurge in women's employment rates during the 1970s, which was more marked in some countries than in others,[51] women today may find this transition less traumatic than did mothers in times past, whose roles were less diversified. It is also worth emphasizing that women are increasingly going out to work long before they reach the 'empty-nest' stage, as there is an implicit assumption in

[46] Hill, op. cit. (n. 1).

[47] See R. Chester, 'Family and Marriage in the Postparental Years', *Marriage Guidance*, 14 (11) (1973) and Young, op. cit. (n. 22) for reviews of the literature.

[48] J. H. S. Bossard and E. S. Boll, 'Marital Unhappiness in the Life Cycle of Marriage', *Marriage and Family Living*, 17 (1955).

[49] I. Deutscher, 'Socialisation for Postparental Life', in A. Rose (ed.), *Human Behavior and Social Process* (Boston, Mass., 1962).

[50] Ibid. and I. Deutscher, 'The Quality of Postparental Life', *Journal of Marriage and the Family*, 26 (1964).

[51] Eurostat, *Economic and Social Position of Women in the Community* (Luxemburg, 1981).

some of the literature that women enter the world of paid work only at that stage.[52]

An issue that has received a great deal of attention, especially in the USA, is how the quality of marriage varies over time. Results from studies spanning the last three decades are by no means conclusive.[53] Some show a continual decline in marital satisfaction after an initial period of high satisfaction, and others show a curvilinear relationship, a high point at the beginning of marriage followed by a decline during the childbearing years and a subsequent rise when children have left home. A recent study[54] showed that changes in satisfaction at different stages of the family life cycle were slight up to the launching-stage, but there was a noticeable increase in marital and family satisfaction, for husbands and wives, between those in the launching and those in the 'empty-nest' stages. All these studies were based on cross-sectional data, and it is noteworthy that studies based on longitudinal data[55] showed no change in marital satisfaction over time. Where levels of marital satisfaction were high at earlier stages of the marriage, this was true also at later stages, and, similarly, low levels of satisfaction at earlier stages were associated with low levels of satisfaction later. Whether marital breakdown is more or less prevalent at this stage of the life cycle is a complex problem. Nowadays divorce is more common than it was in the past at all marriage durations, and long-standing marriages are selected for survival and stability.

Although members of different generations may reside in separate households there is ample evidence that parents and children are not socially isolated from one another. The nature of the relationship between parents and children may change over time, but the relationship itself remains intact.[56] There is a good deal of evidence that parents and children live near each other, but this may be less marked in some social groups, for example, among those in professional and managerial occupations, and in societies where long-distance mobility is more common. It is also possible that residential proximity varies at different stages of the lives of parents and grown-up children. For example, families may be geographically scattered when the children are young adults, but later, when the young establish their own families or parents retire, families may move closer together again. As yet we have little information on this topic, but it would be useful to attempt a residential mapping of generations within a family, given that for many

[52] E.g. Glick, op. cit. (n. 2) and B. B. Hess and J. M. Waring, 'Parent and Child in Later Life: Rethinking the Relationship', in R. M. Lerner and G. B. Spanier (eds.), *Child Influences on Marital and Family Interaction: A Life-Span Perspective* (New York, 1978).

[53] L. Ade-Ridder and T. H. Brubaker, 'The Quality of Long-term Marriages?', in T. H. Brubaker (ed.), *Family Relationships in Later Life* (London, 1983).

[54] D. H. Olson and H. I. McCubbin, *Families: What Makes Them Work* (London, 1983).

[55] A. L. Clark and P. Wallin, 'Women's Sexual Responsiveness and the Duration and Quality of their Marriage', *American Journal of Sociology*, 71(2) (1965).

[56] L. E. Troll, *Early and Middle Adulthood* (Monterey, Calif., 1975) provides a review of the evidence.

people, particularly the elderly, the family is a primary source of support and care. It has been shown in many studies[57] that social interaction between parents and grown-up children is extensive, and that mutual aid between the generations is common.

An important event in the lives of couples in the post-parental stage is becoming a grandparent. The distribution of ages at which parents become grandparents and the role of grandparents in the family system is another topic on which relatively little work has been done. Couples in the post-parental stage may not be isolated in their 'empty nest' but may be enmeshed in extensive social and material interchange with their children, grandchildren, and parents.

Conclusion

This chapter has largely dwelt on the timing elements of the departure of children within the life courses of parents and children. It is clear that there is a dearth of information on this most basic and crucial aspect. This situation could be rectified by including relatively simple questions in general-purpose national surveys. But more detailed information on the dynamics of family life, embracing the family in the broader sense of multi-generational units, requires more detailed surveys, as has already been recognized in some countries, notably Australia and the USA. The paucity of demographic studies of families to date may be largely due to the lack of relevant census and survey data.

Research on the overlapping phases of the life courses of parents and children and the interaction between parents and grown-up children over their life-span is still in its infancy. During recent years there has been a growth of interest in this area across the spectrum of the social sciences, but the demographic underpinnings to such studies still remain elusive. Therein lies our challenge.

[57] Ibid.

8 The Process of Leaving the Parental Home: Some German Data

KARL ULRICH MAYER *Max Planck Institute, Berlin*

and KARL SCHWARZ *formerly of the Federal German Statistical Office, Wiesbaden*

Introduction

The process of leaving the parental home is of interest both to those who are concerned with the later phases of the parental life cycle and to those who study individual life courses. For the parents, the departure of their children marks the transition to the 'empty-nest' phase of the family life cycle. For the children, their departure generally represents the first independent event of their life course. Three issues need to be considered in looking at the process of leaving the parental home: the timing of the transition in the life cycles of both children and parents, the institutional forms which shape this process, and an assessment of the causal factors that underlie it.

Historically, the timing and pattern of the departure of children were closely related to the exigencies of the family economy and the regulation of succession between the generations. Children tended to remain on the parental farm for as long as they were productive; frequently they did not leave until they married. If they were destined to take over the farm they might not leave at all.[1] However, at a time when families tended to be large, not all adolescent children could be supported at home, and some were therefore sent away to serve as farm-hands or domestic servants in other households.[2] In trades and handicrafts it was common for young people to serve their apprenticeships with a master outside their parental home. A period of migrant work was also not unusual. In the medieval family, children—especially boys—frequently left home by the time they were ten years old to become servants in another household.[3] Economic pressures to meet the needs of marriage and establishing one's own household must have been an incentive to take up employment as a wage-earner outside the parental home.

[1] A. E. Imhof, *Die verlorenen Welten* (Munich, 1984), pp. 27–55.

[2] U. Bräker, *Der arme Mann im Tockenburg* (Berlin, 1978 (first published 1789)).

[3] P. Aries, *Centuries of Childhood* (New York, 1970); P. Laslett, *The World We Have Lost* (London, 1972); M. Mitterauer and R. Sieder, *Vom Patriarchat zur Partnerschaft* (Munich, 1977).

However, at least one daughter was often kept at home, in order that she might care for her parents in their old age.

All these considerations suggest that during the pre-industrial period there was no standard pattern or time for the emancipation of children from their parents' home.[4] By contrast, in contemporary industrial societies these factors are only partially interdependent. In the first place, the introduction of universal education and occupational training has probably resulted in raising the age when young people leave their parents' home. Universal formal education has also tended to institutionalize the age when children leave home as an expected element in their educational career (e.g. age at entry to college or university). Military service is another state-controlled mechanism which 'forces' young people to leave home. Secondly, there appears to have been a secular trend towards a reduction of the age at which young people form an independent household or family of their own (at least this was the case until the 1970s), whether by marriage or by cohabitation, indicating a weakening of control over sexual behaviour. If the medieval rule of not more than one cohabiting couple per household were to apply,[5] this secular trend would also lead to a reduction in the age at which children leave home. Thirdly, if leaving home depends on economic resources being allocated to the child, and if economic independence fosters the formation of new households (with or without marriage), increasing affluence should have a similar effect. The availability of scholarships and bursaries, or of the wage income of partners or spouses, could also reduce the age at departure. Conditions in the housing market, too, are likely to be of some importance.

During recent years, there has been an important debate concerning societal trends that govern the individual life course. Some writers have claimed that there has been increasing individualization, in the sense that an individual's life course has become more independent of that of his or her siblings, parental family, spouse, or children.[6] Another issue which has been discussed is the degree to which individual life histories are socially constrained and institutionally regulated.[7] The process of leaving the parental home is germane to both these issues. Whilst increasing affluence provides the young person with the opportunity to leave his or her parental home, the decision whether and when to use this opportunity depends on values and preferences. The question arises whether conditions in the parental family (e.g. size of dwelling) affect the probability of leaving home. We would expect that upward inter-generational mobility, which creates educational and occupational status differences between parents and their children, will lead to an increased

[4] R. Wall, 'The Age at Leaving Home', *Journal of Family History*, 3(2) (1978).

[5] Laslett, op. cit. (n. 3), p. 94.

[6] T. Held, 'Institutionalization and Deinstitutionalization of the Life Course', *Human Development*, 29 (1986).

[7] K. U. Mayer, 'Structural Constraints on the Life Course', *Human Development*, 29(3) (1986), pp. 163–70.

preference for leaving home in order to avoid conflicts within the family which might result from cognitive dissonances of orientations and life styles, as well as from differences between the values and norms of different generations. We must also consider the effect of norms relating to the minimum age at leaving the parental home—an age below which leaving home is considered exceptional, deviant, and stressful, whereas it is normal, expected, and desirable for those who have attained that age. In the Federal Republic of Germany, the age at which young persons attain their legal majority was reduced from 21 to 18 years in 1970. This change may have triggered changes in the process of leaving home. Recent public and academic discussions suggest that the age at which young people leave home is very low in the Federal Republic of Germany, in comparison to other countries, and that it is decreasing dramatically.[8]

Previous Research

In the Federal Republic of Germany, previous research on the process of leaving home has generally been conducted by economists and statisticians who were engaged in demographic simulation studies.[9] Thus, Steger used information from the micro-censuses of 1965 to 1969 relating to synthetic cohorts to construct age-specific probabilities of children leaving their parents' home. She observed that a higher proportion of men than of women remained in the parental home between the ages of 18 and 40, and suggested that the explanation for this phenomenon lay in the earlier age of marriage for women. In support of her view, she showed that the probability of a man leaving home decreased steadily with age; among women this figure decreased rapidly up to the age of 25, there followed a slight decrease between the ages of 25 and 29 and near-constancy between the ages 29 and 35. She also compared the curves showing the proportions leaving home in synthetic cohorts between 1965 and 1969. The age at legal majority (21 years) seemed to mark a significant turning-point for women. The probability of remaining home after the age of 21 continued to fall; it decreased by 10 per cent for women aged 24, and by 15 per cent at the age of 26, whereas no such changes were observed for men. Steger concluded that changes between different cohorts were minimal: the probability of leaving home was fairly stable over time, and largely age-specific.

Children who married left the parental home shortly after marriage in almost all instances. Co-residence with parents or parents-in-law was typical

[8] In a survey of young people conducted in 1981, 49% of the respondents expected to have left their parents' home by the age of 20. Cf. Shell Jugendstudie, *Jugend '81: Lebensentwürfe, Alltagskulture, Zukunftsbilder*, i. *Jugendwerk der Deutschen Shell*, (Hamburg, 1981), pp. 157–60.

[9] Cf. e.g. A. Steger, *Übergänge zwischen privaten Haushalten: Eine mikroanalytische Untersuchung* (Frankfurt/Mannheim, 1979); K. P. Möller, 'Der Einfluss demographischer Strukturveränderungen auf die Entwicklung der Wirtschaft', in H. Birg (ed.), *Demographische Entwicklung und Gesellschaftliche Planung* (Frankfurt, 1983).

of early rather than of late marriages. Twenty per cent of all 16-year old married women who were enumerated in the micro-census of 1969 lived with their parents; this figure fell to 2 per cent or less after the age of 22. Among men, the corresponding proportion was highest at the age of 20 (15 per cent), and decreased less rapidly to less than 4 per cent at the age of 24. In the synthetic cohorts studied, the annual probability of leaving home was between 0.7 and 0.8 up to the age of 26. It then fell rapidly to 0.18 for women aged 38 and men aged 42. The proportion of married children of these ages who lived in their parents' home fell to about 1 per cent.

Steger's study shows some of the problems of much previous empirical research on this topic:

a causal analysis of the process of leaving home is almost impossible, when only aggregate census data are available;

an aggregate analysis of synthetic cohorts confounds time-dependency of age with differences that may exist between cohorts;

the departure of children from the parental home is a reversible event and may, therefore, occur several times during the life course of the same child;

leaving the parental home is neither subjectively nor objectively a clear-cut event, since multiple residence is possible and probably even typical for some sections of the population, e.g. university students;

the increasing frequency of cohabitation has resulted in marriage being no longer the sole precondition for setting up a new household with a partner;

leaving home is only a crude measure of the quality of exchange and support relations between children and parents. Such relations may be close and intensive even though parents and children do not live together any longer, and, conversely, they may be very weak even though co-residence continues.

Some of these problems are studied more adequately by using information about cohorts, the residential, educational, and family histories of whose members are continuously observed. Some of the statistics in this chapter relate to such cohorts.

Data

The data presented here come from two different sources. The first set is taken from the so-called annual micro-censuses which are representative samples of 1 per cent of the population of the Federal Republic of Germany. The second set comes from a nationally representative, retrospective life-history study which was conducted between 1981 and 1983.

There are some important differences between these two sources. The information from the micro-census relates to the composition and characteristics of persons living in different households, whereas the life history data are recollections of continuous residential histories. The sizes of the samples are also very different. The sample in the micro-census contains about half a million cases, and a single-year age group may consist of between 7,000 and 10,000 persons, depending on cohort size. The life-history study contained altogether 2,171 respondents, and the size of a single-year cohort was of the order of 250 persons. The method of sampling used in the two studies was also slightly different. In spite of these differences, a comparison of the percentage of respondents who were still living in their parents' home at different ages showed very similar results (see Table 8.1). The only major difference was found for men in the older birth cohorts. We cannot provide any immediate explanation for this difference.

Table 8.1 Departure of children from the parental home: comparison of West German data from the micro-census and a retrospective life-history survey

		Micro-census: % in parental home	Life-history survey: % who had never left parental home after age 14
		Birth cohorts 1947–51	*Birth cohorts 1949–51*
20–4	Men	63.4	62.6
	Women	34.4	35.9
25–9	Men	23.3	23.8
	Women	10.0	8.9
30–4	Men	11.8	13.4
	Women	6.6	5.3
		Birth cohorts 1937œ41	*Birth cohorts 1939œ41*
30–4	Men	13.5	18.4
	Women	9.5	9.2
35–9	Men	8.4	13.8
	Women	6.1	7.0

Sources: West German Micro-censuses 1972, 1977, and 1982; West German life-history study 1983.

The data from the micro-census relate to the years 1972, 1977, and 1982, spanning a period of rapid social change, when nuptiality rates were falling and the number of consensual unions, particularly among young people, was increasing rapidly. The statistics we have collected relate to individuals born in successive quinquennia between 1937 and 1961, although the period of observation extends over a full ten years only for those born between 1942 and 1956. Table 8.2 shows the basic distribution of the proportions of men and women in these cohorts who, at different stages of their lives, were living in different types of household.

The figures demonstrate clearly that women leave their parents' home at an earlier age than men. In every cohort and in every age group, the proportion of women who live in their parents' household is lower than the corresponding proportion of men. In part this is due to earlier marriage, but in the more

Table 8.2(*a*) Living arrangements by type of household (per 1,000)

Age	Birth cohort																								
	1937–41					1942–6					1947–51					1952–6					1957–61				
	1	2	3	4	5	1	2	3	4	5	1	2	3	4	5	1	2	3	4	5	1	2	3	4	5
Men																									
15–9	—	—	—	—	—	—	—	—	—	—	—	—	—	—	—	6	964	8	2	20	10	968	3	4	15
20–4	—	—	—	—	—	—	—	—	—	—	264	617	8	9	102	197	641	8	34	120	143	658	7	55	137
25–9	—	—	—	—	—	694	196	6	8	96	635	213	6	29	117	526	240	6	66	162	—	—	—	—	—
30–4	855	89	3	3	50	843	76	3	9	69	783	93	2	27	95	—	—	—	—	—	—	—	—	—	—
35–9	896	52	3	5	44	879	50	2	11	58	—	—	—	—	—	—	—	—	—	—	—	—	—	—	—
Women																									
15–9	—	—	—	—	—	—	—	—	—	—	—	—	—	—	—	77	890	11	5	17	52	904	4	13	27
20–4	—	—	—	—	—	—	—	—	—	—	585	312	5	11	87	472	362	5	41	120	348	410	5	85	152
25–9	—	—	—	—	—	877	69	3	4	47	834	74	2	18	72	750	94	3	44	109	—	—	—	—	—
30–4	928	38	2	3	29	926	32	2	6	34	902	35	2	13	48	—	—	—	—	—	—	—	—	—	—
35–9	947	23	1	4	25	941	22	1	5	31	—	—	—	—	—	—	—	—	—	—	—	—	—	—	—

1 = married; 2 = single with parent(s); 3 = single with relatives other than parents; 4 = single with non-relatives; 5 = alone.

Table 8.2(*b*) Percentage of married children living with parents

Age	Birth cohort									
	1937–41		1942–6		1947–51		1952–6		1957–61	
	Men	Women	Men	Women	Men	Women	Men	Women	Men	Women
15–9	—	—	—	—	—	—	0	6	20	8
20–4	—	—	—	—	6	5	5	4	9	7
25–9	—	—	4	5	3	3	4	4	—	—
30–4	5	6	3	3	3	3	—	—	—	—
35–9	4	4	4	4	—	—	—	—	—	—

recent cohorts a higher proportion of women than of men live in households with non-relatives. Ninety per cent of such households consist of unmarried couples living together without children, i.e. in consensual unions. The decline in nuptiality rates is evident in Table 8.2: in every age group the proportion married of both sexes is lower in the later cohorts. (The only exception to this rule relates to the very small proportion of men married as teenagers, where among those born in 1957–61 the proportion married was higher than among those born five years earlier). The decline in the proportion married has resulted in a higher proportion of single men below the age of 30 continuing to live in their parents' households. The proportion for men aged 20–4 has increased from 617 per 1,000 among those born between 1947 and 1951 to 658 per 1,000 among those born 10 years later. There has been a similar, though smaller, increase for women from 312 to 348 per 1,000. This is not, however, the whole story. Table 8.3 shows the proportions of unmarried persons living in different types of household. In this table we have combined into one category those who live with their parents and the small number who live in households with other relatives. The figures show that the proportion of both unmarried men and unmarried women who live in their parental household has steadily fallen between the earlier and the later cohorts. In particular, the proportion living with non-relatives, the vast majority of whom are living in consensual unions, has increased considerably for those aged less than 30 years. Thus the tendency to leave home for reasons other than marriage has increased, and the rising proportion of those remaining in the parental home shown in Table 8.2 merely reflects the fall in nuptiality.

It is possible to demonstrate the tendency to leave home for reasons other than marriage by calculating separately the probabilities of leaving home and those of marrying. It must however be borne in mind that the movement between different types of household shown in Table 8.1 does not take account of temporary changes, i.e. the departure of children who leave their parents' household temporarily and later return. However, we thought it justified to calculate the probabilities shown in Table 8.4. If it is assumed that all those who marry leave the parental home (and the figures in Table 8.2 show that the vast majority of them do so), then the difference $p_1 - p_2$ will give us an indication of the probability of children leaving home for reasons other than marriage. We have shown these figures in Table 8.5, and they confirm that there is an increasing tendency for both men and women to set up a home independently for reasons other than marriage.

The decline in nuptiality, therefore, has a double effect. The proportion of men and women who continue to live with their parents has increased, but so have the proportions who live in consensual unions and one-person households. Even when the children did not marry they became more independent of their parents, and tried to leave their parents' home during their early 20s. The increase in the probability of leaving the parental home between the ages of 15–19 and 20–24 for reasons other than marriage is

Table 8.3 Proportions of unmarried persons (per 1,000) living in different types of household

Age	Birth cohort														
	1937–41			1942–6			1947–51			1952–6			1957–61		
	1	2	3	1	2	3	1	2	3	1	2	3	1	2	3
Men															
15–9	—	—	—	—	—	—	—	—	—	978	2	20	981	4	15
20–4	—	—	—	—	—	—	849	12	139	808	42	149	766	64	160
25–9	—	—	—	660	26	314	600	79	321	519	139	342	—	—	—
30–4	634	21	345	503	57	439	438	124	438	—	—	—	—	—	—
35–9	529	48	423	429	91	479	—	—	—	—	—	—	—	—	—
Women															
15–9	—	—	—	—	—	—	—	—	—	976	5	18	958	14	28
20–4	—	—	—	—	—	—	764	27	209	695	78	227	637	130	233
25–9	—	—	—	585	33	382	458	108	433	388	176	436	—	—	—
30–4	556	42	403	459	81	459	378	133	490	—	—	—	—	—	—
35–9	452	75	472	390	85	525	—	—	—	—	—	—	—	—	—

Note: 1=living with parents or other relatives; 2=living with non-relatives; 3=living alone.

particularly striking for women, though the figure for men is also high. We therefore conclude that there were two overlapping trends during the last ten years: declining nuptiality and an increased desire for independence. Because the first tendency was stronger than the second, the proportion of men and women who live in the parental household between the ages of 20 and 30 has increased slightly over the value in 1971. This has surprised some observers. However, the situation may well change, and the pressures for change seem extremely strong.

Information about the ages at which men and women left their parents' household may also be obtained from the life-history study. Three indicators were used in this study. The first of them relates to the first occasion on which an individual changed residence after his or her 14th birthday. The second refers to the last change of residence between the 14th birthday and the date of interview. (Compulsory military service was not considered to be a change of residence, provided the respondent returned to the parental household after his period of duty.) The third indicator was the respondent's subjective statement relating to the date (and, therefore, to the age) when he or she established a separate household. These three events may occur simultaneously in the lives of some individuals; for others they may be separated by as much as ten years. Individuals may leave their parents' household and return on several occasions, or they may live in temporary accommodation before settling in a situation which they perceive to be their first independent household.

Table 8.4 Quinquennial probabilities of leaving home (p_1) and of marrying (p_2)

Age		Birth cohort									
		p_1					p_2				
		1937–41	1942–6	1947–51	1952–6	1957–61	1937–41	1942–6	1947–51	1952–6	1957–61
15–9	M	—	—	—	0.332	0.315	—	—	—	0.192	0.134
	F	—	—	—	0.593	0.508	—	—	—	0.428	0.312
20–4	M	—	—	0.650	0.621	—	—	—	0.504	0.409	—
	F	—	—	0.760	0.736	—	—	—	0.600	0.527	—
25–9	M	—	0.609	0.566	—	—	—	0.513	0.405	—	—
	F	—	0.528	0.513	—	—	—	0.398	0.409	—	—
30–4	M	0.402	0.342	—	—	—	0.282	0.229	—	—	—
	F	0.400	0.324	—	—	—	0.263	0.202	—	—	—

Table 8.5 Values of $p_1 - p_2$ (i.e. quinquennial probabilities for leaving the parental household for reasons other than marriage)

Age	Males					Females				
	1937–41	1942–6	1947–51	1952–6	1957–61	1937–41	1942–6	1947–51	1952–6	1957–61
15–9	—	—	—	0.140	0.181	—	—	—	0.165	0.236
20–4	—	—	0.146	0.212	—	—	—	0.160	0.209	—
25–9	—	0.096	0.161	—	—	—	0.130	0.104	—	—
30–4	0.120	0.113	—	—	—	0.037	0.122	—	—	—

The cohorts used in the life-history study differ slightly from those used in the micro-census, and include an older cohort, those born between 1929 and 1931. However, the figures shown in Table 8.6 confirm the results that were obtained from the microcensus. Sons left their parents' homes at an older age than did daughters, and the difference between the median age at leaving home for the two sexes has increased in the later cohorts. Moreover, the dispersion of the distribution has become smaller, indicating that the process of leaving home has become more homogeneous. The reduction in the dispersion (as measured by the interquartile range, the period during which 50 per cent of the respondents left home) has been particularly pronounced for women, where its value in the birth cohort 1949–51 was less than half that found for the oldest cohort, those born in 1929–31. In the last cohort the median age at which women left home (21.3 years) was close to the age at which women in this cohort attained their legal majority. If the ages at which children left home for the first time are compared with those when they finally left home, it is clear from the table that members of the older cohorts left home for the first time at an earlier age than their final separation from their parents. But in the youngest cohort the values are very nearly the same. We may infer from these figures that residence in the parental home has become more continuous, but that it came to an end earlier during the 1970s than during the 1950s. However, about one in 10 of the men for whom life histories were available had not left the parental home at the time of interview. We can only speculate about the reasons for this. It is possible that some men may have remained on the parental farm, or at least regarded it as their residence, even though they had moved out of agriculture.

Table 8.7 contains information similar to that contained in Table 8.6, but relates to the age when individuals established their own independent households. The interquartile range of this distribution for men is lower than that of the distribution of ages when they left home, i.e. this process occurs during a shorter span in an individual's life. For women, however, the two figures are nearly identical for the last cohort. Generally speaking, women tended to set up an independent household much earlier than men, and it is noteworthy that one-quarter of the female respondents had set up independent households before their 20th birthday. The proportion of women without an independent household at the age of 29 was very low indeed, but an appreciable proportion of men were still not living in independent households at that period of their lives.

Respondents in the life-history study were also asked the reasons for their leaving the parental home, the distance they had moved, and the type of accommodation that they moved into. In Table 8.8 we show the percentages of respondents in different birth cohorts who gave different replies. There are a number of interesting features in the table. For women, marriage is the most important factor associated with leaving home. More than half the female respondents in each cohort gave marriage as the main reason for leaving home

Table 8.6 Ages at which specified proportions of respondents had left their parents' homes (i) for the first time after their fourteenth birthday, and (ii) on the last occasion before interview (per cent)

Percentage who had left		Birth cohort					
		Men			Women		
		1929–31	1939–41	1949–51	1929–31	1939–41	1949–51
10	(i)	15.2	18.7	19.7	15.2	16.2	18.1
	(ii)	19.0	20.3	20.0	18.3	18.4	18.3
25	(i)	19.9	21.8	21.5	19.3	19.4	19.6
	(ii)	22.0	22.5	21.8	20.7	20.1	19.7
50	(i)	24.7	24.8	23.9	22.6	22.3	21.2
	(ii)	25.6	25.3	24.2	24.0	22.6	21.3
75	(i)	29.3	29.0	27.0	27.4	25.2	23.4
	(ii)	29.0	29.0	27.5	28.1	25.7	23.5
90	(i)	[a]	[a]	[a]	48.5	32.5	26.7
	(ii)	49.8	[a]	[a]	48.1	32.3	26.8
Interquartile range							
	(i)	9.4	7.2	5.5	8.2	5.8	3.8
		7.0	6.5	5.7	7.4	5.6	3.8

[a] More than 10% were still living at home at the time of interview.

Table 8.7 Ages at which specified proportions of respondents had set up independent households (per cent)

Percentage with independent household	Birth cohort					
	Men			Women		
	1929–31	1939–41	1949–51	1929–31	1939–41	1949–51
25	23.8	23.3	22.4	21.8	20.9	19.9
50	26.2	25.7	24.6	24.2	22.7	21.5
75	29.2	28.3	27.3	27.3	25.2	23.6
Interquartile range	5.4	5.0	4.9	5.5	4.3	3.7
% without own household at age 29	21.5	17.1	14.0	13.9	5.7	3.5

finally, and this proportion was highest in the last cohort. Even among women who left home for the first time, at least 40 per cent gave marriage as the reason, and in the youngest cohort the proportion was as high as 50 per cent. The proportion of men in this category was consistently lower than that of women. By contrast, the proportion of men who left for residential reasons, i.e. because they had acquired a house or a flat, was consistently greater than among

Table 8.8 Percentages of respondents leaving their parental home for the first time after the age of fourteen (F) and leaving finally (L), by reason for move, distance moved, and type of accommodation after move.

		Birth cohort					
		Men			Women		
		1929–31	1939–41	1949–51	1929–31	1939–41	1949–51
Reasons for moving							
Marriage	F	29	39	39	42	40	50
	L	42	51	41	54	53	58
Other private	F	5	6	6	5	6	5
	L	3	4	5	4	5	4
Occupational	F	20	17	21	19	19	19
	L	18	16	18	17	16	17
Political[a]	F	29	17	4	21	20	1
	L	11	5	4	8	4	3
Residential	F	15	17	27	10	18	18
	L	23	22	30	14	22	20
Other	F	3	4	4	4	2	1
	L	3	4	4	3	1	2
Distance moved							
Less than 5 km.	F	35	40	45	37	31	43
	L	49	50	48	46	38	45
6–30 km.	F	17	22	24	19	25	31
	L	21	25	26	21	31	32
30–300 km.	F	17	19	25	18	20	20
	L	16	18	21	17	19	30
More than 300 km.	F	31	19	6	26	21	6
	L	14	8	6	15	12	3
Type of accommodation after move							
Own home	F	21	26	19	22	25	21
	L	26	32	20	27	29	22
Rented flat	F	35	42	59	41	40	60
	L	50	51	64	51	54	63
Lodger	F	9	7	10	8	9	6
	L	11	8	8	8	8	6
Institution, etc.	F	35	25	12	29	29	11
	L	13	9	8	14	8	9

[a] Sequelae of war, resettlement, etc.

women. Political reasons, i.e. those connected with the aftermath of war and resettlement, mainly affected members of the oldest cohort. Occupational or professional reasons appeared to be equally important for both sexes. Similar findings have been reported from a survey on household mobility taken during 1980.[10]

[10] N. Ott, 'Analyse der Haushaltsmobilität', unpublished manuscript (1980).

The figures also show that the proportion of respondents who finally moved for a distance of less than 30 km. from their parental home was never less than two-thirds, and that a proportion which generally exceeded 40 per cent moved over distances of less than 5 km. This means that close relations between the parental household and that of the child remained possible, even though there was no actual co-residence. Even in the oldest cohort, only 14 per cent of the men and 15 per cent of the women moved more than 300 km. away from their parental home, and the proportions were much smaller in the most recent cohort.

Most of the respondents who moved out of their parents' home either moved into their own home or into a rented flat. The proportions of both men and women who moved into rented accommodation on the first occasion when they left home increased considerably in the youngest cohort.

The Parents' Viewpoint

So far we have considered the process of leaving home from the point of view of the children only. In this section we shall look at the process from the opposite point of view, that of the parents.

We begin once again with information from the micro-census. Table 8.9 shows the situation as it was in 1970, classifying ever-married women by age and number of children born and showing the percentages of women who continued to have unmarried children living in their households. As is to be expected, the lower the number of children a woman has had during her lifetime, the larger will be the proportion of those of any age who have no unmarried children living in their household. The median and the two quartiles of the distribution are shown below:

Number of children born	1	2	3	4
Lower quartile	46	50	52	54
Median	51	56	58	60
Upper quartile	57	63	64	67

The figures show that 50 per cent of ever-married women with children enter the 'empty-nest' phase within a period of about 12 years, and this figure does not vary greatly with the number of children they have borne. However, the more children a woman has borne, the later in her life will that phase occur. The difference between women who have borne only one child and those who have borne three children is approximately seven years. Unfortunately, we have no information on the ages of the children who continued to live in their mothers' households. Clearly, the children of mothers who are over 55 years old will in general have passed their 15th birthday, and many of them will be over 18 years old, so that their presence will not have prevented the mother from taking work on outside the home. But it is of interest to note that at the age of 55 over one-quarter of the mothers who had borne three children and as many as 40 per cent of those with four children continued to have more than two unmarried children living at home.

There is no information about parents who live with married, widowed, or divorced children. We do however have information on the total numbers of men and women who were living with children or grandchildren irrespective of the latter's marital status. We have only considered those aged 70 and over in this context, as many of them will be in need of care. In 1980, 16 per cent of men and 17 per cent of women aged 70 and over were living with children or grandchildren, but this proportion is declining rapidly.

The figures in Table 8.10, which are taken from the micro-censuses of 1981 and 1982, make it possible to calculate estimates of the age-specific probabilities of parents entering the 'empty-nest' stage of the family life cycle. The figures include childless couples, so that the proportion of couples who had had children of whom one or more were still living in the parental household would be even higher, by a factor of the order of 5–10%.

Although the procedure is not completely accurate, we can estimate the probabilities of entering the 'empty-nest' phase by looking at the diagonals in Table 8.10. For instance the proportion of couples with unmarried children living in their household in which the mother was 40–4 years old in 1972 was 86 per cent. Ten years later, in 1982, the proportion had been reduced to 58 per cent. Thus the probability of a woman aged 40–4 in 1972 entering the 'empty-nest' phase within the next ten years would be 28/86=0.33. These probabilities, calculated over five-year as well as over ten-year periods, are shown in Table 8.11. The figures show that the chance of men entering the 'empty-nest' stage within the next ten years exceeds one-half from the age of about 50 onwards; women tend to reach that stage of their life course some five years earlier.

The situation of women who had unmarried children living with them in 1981 can also be shown by the marital status of the mother (see Table 8.12). The noteworthy feature is the high proportion of divorced women between the ages of 35 and 44 who had children living in their household. This amounted to 68 per cent, though only about half the marriages which end in divorce are those of couples with children, and some 10 per cent of the children of divorced couples live with the father. The high proportion is likely to have been caused by the lower frequency of remarriage among divorced women with children, compared with that of divorced childless women.[11] At ages 55–64, 25 per cent of separated women, 22 per cent of those who were widowed, and 17 per cent of those who were divorced had children living in their households, who would all have been at least 15 years old.

[11] We estimate that 90% of childless women who are divorced remarry, but only between 40% and 45% of divorced women with children. Cf. K. Schwarz 'Eltern und Kinder in unvollständigen Familien', *Zeitschrift für Bevölkerungswissenschaft*, 1 (1984).

Table 8.9 Proportion of ever-married women with unmarried children living in their households, 1970 (per cent)

Mother's age	No. of live-born children	No. of children living in mother's household				
		0	1	2	3	4
40	1	6	94			
	2	1	8	91		
	3	1	2	12	85	
	4	—	1	3	16	80
45	1	20	80			
	2	6	23	72		
	3	2	10	25	63	
	4	1	4	13	26	50
50	1	45	55			
	2	25	37	38		
	3	14	29	30	27	
	4	7	18	27	23	25
55	1	65	35			
	2	52	33	15		
	3	36	37	18	9	
	4	28	32	23	11	6
60	1	80	20			
	2	71	23	6		
	3	61	29	8	2	
	4	50	33	12	4	1
65	1	87	13			
	2	83	15	2		
	3	78	18	3	1	
	4	71	22	5	2	2
70	1	91	9			
	2	89	10	1		
	3	85	13	2	—	
	4	82	16	2	—	—

Source: K. Schwarz, 'Ehen im April 1977 nach dem Einkommen der Männer', *Wirtschaft und Statistik*, 3 (1979).

Summary and Conclusion

There have been some noticeable changes in the process of departure from the parental home in the Federal Republic of Germany. In the three birth cohorts 1929–31, 1939–41, and 1949–51, this process is increasingly concentrated in the beginning of the third decade of life. The variance of the distribution of ages at this significant step in an individual's life cycle has diminished, and in this respect at least the life cycle has become more homogeneous. On the other

Table 8.10 Percentage of couples with unmarried children living in their household

Age of parent	% living with unmarried children in household					
	Men			Women		
	1972	1977	1982	1972	1977	1982
35–9	90	88	86	91	91	89
40–4	88	89	85	86	88	87
45–9	82	82	84	75	76	78
50–4	72	69	68	59	59	58
55–9	53	53	51	40	39	39
60–4	38	34	35	26	21	23
65–9	27	22	21	18	14	12
70–4	20	16	14	16	11	9
75+	18	13	12	15	12	11

Table 8.11 Probability of entering the 'empty-nest' phase within five and ten years for individuals of different ages

Age of parent	Probability of entering the empty-nest stage within					
	5 yrs.				10 yrs.	
	Men		Women		Men	Women
	1972	1977	1972	1977	1972	1972
35–9	0.01	0.03	0.03	0.04	0.07	0.14
40–4	0.07	0.06	0.12	0.11	0.23	0.33
45–9	0.16	0.17	0.21	0.24	0.38	0.48
50–4	0.26	0.26	0.34	0.34	0.51	0.61
55–9	0.36	0.34	0.48	0.41	0.60	0.70
60–4	0.42	0.38	0.46	0.43	0.63	0.65
65–9	0.41	0.36	0.39	0.36	0.56	0.39

hand, the difference between the distribution for the two sexes has increased: women leave their parental home at a considerably younger age than men. It should be borne in mind, however, that in the great majority of cases young people tend to live near their parents' home, and that the distance between the parental and the child's home has been decreasing in successive cohorts. The departure from the parental home does not, therefore, imply an abrupt reduction in contact between the generations.

Among those born between 1952 and 1956 and 1957 and 1961, the rise in the age at marriage has resulted in an increase in the proportion of children who remain in their parents' homes until the age of 30. However, the proportion of

Table 8.12 Percentage of women with unmarried children living in their household by marital status of mother

Age of Women	% of women with unmarried children in their household									
	All children					Children under fifteen				
	Married	Never married	Separated	Widowed	Divorced	Married	Never married	Separated	Widowed	Divorced
15–24	54	1	33	—	48	54	1	33	—	48
25–34	80	7	54	74	60	80	7	53	74	59
35–44	88	11	63	82	68	66	6	44	52	43
45–54	67	28	44	54	46	23	2	16	14	16
55–64	30	3	25	22	17	2	—	—	1	—
65+	8	1	—	7	6	—	—	—	—	—

those who found an independent household whilst still unmarried has clearly increased. Thus, during the last ten years the departure from the parental home has become less closely connected with marriage. But up to the mid-1970s marriage remained the dominant reason for departure, particularly for women. Other events in the life cycle also affect this process however: for instance, nearly 20 per cent of those who left the parental home gave professional reasons for their move.

Information from the micro-census does not make it possible to date the beginning of the post-parental phase exactly. This will depend on the age at marriage of the parents, the number of their children, and the intervals between successive births. There is therefore considerable variability in the age distribution of mothers at the time when their last child leaves home, and it is difficult to speak of a 'typical' age at the beginning of the post-parental phase. Fifty per cent of ever-married mothers experience this event within a range of 12 years.

In 1972, 1977, and 1982 the age-specific proportions of women who live with their unmarried children changed little. Mothers tend to be relatively old at the beginning of the post-parental phase. Those women who have interrupted their participation in the labour force because of the birth of a child and who wish to resume their work can hardly afford to wait to do so until all children have left.

The two types of data used in this chapter yield consistent results. Retrospective surveys have the great advantage of including questions relating to motives. They are expensive, however, and sample sizes must be small. Official enquiries, on the other hand, relate to much larger groups. In this case no additional costs were incurred, as the results could be obtained as a by-product of annual representative surveys which form part of regular household and family statistics.

9 The Effect of Children Returning Home on the Precision of the Timing of the Leaving-Home Stage

CHRISTABEL M. YOUNG

Department of Sociology, Australian National University

Introduction

Until recently, the approach to the analysis of the process of children leaving the parental home was very simple. It was assumed that all children left home at marriage, and accordingly the average age at leaving home was taken to be equivalent to the average age at marriage. In the family life course of the parents, the leaving-home stage was assumed to begin with the marriage of the first-born child and to be completed at the date of marriage of the last-born child. This was a simple and useful approach, in that basically all the information needed to determine the timing of different stages in the family life cycle in any society was the average age at marriage, the average age of mothers at the births of their first and last children, and estimates of the average age at widowhood and the average age at death of the surviving spouse.

However, during the last decade or so, data have been produced which show that a significant proportion of young adults in Western countries live away from their parental home before they marry, and that this proportion is increasing.[1] The average age at marriage, therefore, is no longer a good indicator of the timing of the leaving-home stage, nor is the proportion of young adults who are married at a given age a suitable indicator of the proportion of young adults who have left their parental home.

A first step towards refining measurement of the timing of the leaving-home stage, therefore, is to collect data which provide an estimate of the average age of young adults leaving home for all reasons.

There have been three surveys in Australia in which information about the

[1] See e.g. O. B. Di Iulio, *Household Formation 1911–2001*, Research Report no. 10, National Population Inquiry (Canberra, 1981); European Community, *Economic and Social Features of Member States of the European Community* (Luxemburg, 1982); R. Harrison, *Living Alone in Canada: Demographic and Economic Perspectives 1951–1976* (Ottawa, 1981); F. Kobrin, 'The Fall in Household Size and the Rise of the Primary Individual in the United States', *Demography*, 13(1) (1976); A. Monnier, 'Composition de la population', in *La Population de la France* (*Population*, special issue, June 1974); OECD, *Child and Family Demographic Developments in the OECD Countries* (Paris, 1979).

ages at leaving home of young adults has been collected. The first was conducted in 1971 in Melbourne, the second largest city in Australia, in which information on the time of leaving home was collected from approximately 500 young adults.[2] The second, in 1977, was also conducted in Melbourne and covered a group of unmarried young adults between the ages of 18 and 25 years and a group of young married women.[3] Both these surveys were carried out by members of the Department of Demography of the Australian National University. The third survey was conducted by the Australian Institute of Family Studies in 1982 and covered all Australia. During this survey over 2,500 young adults aged between 18 and 34 years were interviewed, and information about the time they left home was collected. This last survey has provided a unique opportunity to study the characteristics of leaving home among young adults. In particular, the large sample size has permitted a wide range of investigation of the leaving-home process.[4]

There is also evidence of a decline in the proportion leaving home in order to marry among members of more recent cohorts within the 1982 sample, as shown in Table 9.2. A maximum of only 29 per cent of men between the ages of 25 and 29 years at the time of the survey can ultimately leave home to marry (i.e. 6 per cent who have not yet left home, added to the 23 per cent who had already left home to marry) and this is less than the 36 per cent of the 30–4-year-old men who have left to marry. Similarly, a maximum of only 44 per cent of women aged 20–4 and 41 per cent of women aged 25–9 years at the time of the survey can ultimately leave home to marry, compared with the 51 per cent of those aged 30–4 years, thus continuing the trend observed between 1971 and 1982. In contrast, higher proportions of the younger cohorts have already left home to live independently, to cohabit outside marriage, or because of conflict. The young adults who are most likely to continue to leave to marry are those with a strong attachment to religion, with southern European parents, with strong traditional family values, those who come from a large family, who left school whilst young, and who are happy living at home.

Evidence that those who leave home for reasons other than marriage leave at younger ages than those who leave to marry is provided by the information in Table 9.3. Note that in the 1982 survey the average ages at leaving home for marriage, 23.1 years for men and 20.6 years for women, are

[2] C. M. Young, 'Ages, Reasons and Sex Differences for Children Leaving Home', *Journal of Marriage and the Family*, 36 (1974); 'Factors Associated with the Timing and Duration of the Leaving Home Stage of the Family Life Cycle', *Population Studies*, 29(1) (1975).

[3] C. M. Young, 'Leaving Home and Life Style: A Survey Analysis of Young Adults', in Centre for Continuing Education, *Living Together: Family Patterns and Lifestyles: A Book of Readings*, (Canberra, 1980).

[4] A full report of the analysis from the 1982 study of children leaving home is contained in C. M. Young, *Children Leaving Home: Reasons, Dynamics and Conflict* (Melbourne, 1985). See also C. M. Young, 'Leaving Home and Returning Home: A Demographic Study of Young Adults in Australia', Australian Family Research Conference, Canberra, 23–5 Nov. 1983. The research reported herein was funded as a contract by the Institute of Family Studies, Melbourne, Australia. The Institute holds the data which are available on request for further analysis by researchers.

Table 9.1 Median ages at leaving home in relation to median ages at marriage for Australia, 1971, 1982

Date of survey and age	Age at leaving home (yrs.)[a]		Birth year of cohort	Age at marriage (yrs.)[b]
	First departure	Final departure		
Men				
1971[c]				
20–32	23.1		1945	24.1
1982				
30–4	21.5 }	22.9	1950	23.9
25–9	21.0 }		1955	25.3
20–4	21.0	—	1959	26.5
All	21.2	—		
Women				
1971[c]				
20–32		20.8	1945	21.6
1982				
30–4	20.2	—	1950	21.4
25–9	20.1	—	1955	21.6
20–4	19.7	21.3	1959	23.2
All	20.0	—		

[a] Derived from survival analysis.

[b] Derived from official data from Australia by P. F. McDonald, 'Marriage and Divorce in Australia' in United Nations Economic and Social Commission for Asia and the Pacific, *The Population of Australia* (New York, 1982); and G. Carmichael, 'The Transition to Marriage: Trends in Age at First Marriage and Proportions Marrying in Australia', Australian Family Research Conference, Australian National University, 23–5 Nov. 1983. However, it should be noted that part of the increase in the median age at marriage is due to the fact that an increasing proportion of young adults are not marrying.

[c] Estimate for all geographical areas in Australia.

very similar to the average ages found in the 1971 survey of those leaving home for all reasons (given in Table 9.1). Apart from women who leave home to cohabit with a man (average age 20.5 years) or to travel (average age 20.7 years), all the other ages at leaving home are considerably lower than the average age at leaving to marry. In particular, those leaving home to study (18.4 years for men and 18.3 for women) or because of conflict (19.0 and 18.0 respectively) tend to be youngest. Those who leave home for the increasingly important reason, independence, average 20.8 years for men and 19.4 for women. Table 9.3 also shows the stability in the pattern of average ages at leaving home for different reasons found for women in the surveys of 1977 and 1982.

Two other research papers presented at the Berlin seminar enabled ages at leaving home in Australia to be compared with those in other countries, and

Table 9.2 Distribution of reasons for first leaving home according to age at the time of the survey, 1982 (per cent)

Reason for leaving	Age at time of survey (yrs.)			
	18–19	20–4	25–9	30–4
Men				
Not yet left home	70	34	6	6
Marriage	1	7	23	34
Independence[a]	8	16	24	15
Cohabitation	1	5	3	3
Travel, migration	—	6	9	11
Study	3	5	9	5
Job[b]	7	13	14	19
Conflict	5	7	4	4
Other	5	7	8	7
Total	100	100	100	100
N	159	379	338	365
Women				
Not yet left home	62	21	2	3
Marriage	6	23	39	48
Independence[a]	6	16	13	11
Cohabitation	3	7	3	1
Travel, migration	—	6	6	7
Study	6	8	7	9
Job[b]	5	6	11	8
Conflict	10	7	11	8
Other	2	6	8	5
Total	100	100	100	100
N	156	369	350	346

[a] Includes 'live with others'.
[b] Includes 'joined armed forces'.

the results of this comparison are given in Table 9.4.[5] The main difference between the various countries is the increase in the age at leaving home found in Britain among those born since the 1950s, in contrast to the relatively steady level suggested by the Australian figures. In addition, Schwarz and Mayer presented an analysis at the same seminar which showed an increase in the proportion of children living in their parents' home in the Federal Republic of Germany at census dates 1972, 1977, and 1982 (or among cohorts with birth years centered around 1948–52, 1953–7, and 1958–62) which corresponds with the British pattern. The fact that Brass's and Mayer and Schwarz's figures

[5] W. Brass, 'A Note on the Estimation of Family Transition Rates from Census or Survey Data' and K. Schwarz, 'When Do Children Leave the Home of Parents? An Analysis of Cohort Data in the Federal Republic of Germany for the Years 1972–1982', papers presented at the Seminar on the Later Phases of the Family Life Cycle, Berlin, 3–7 Sept, 1984.

Table 9.3 Average ages at leaving home according to reason for leaving, 1977 and 1982

Reason for leaving home	Men, 1982, 26–34 (yrs.)	Women, 1982, 26–34 (yrs.)	Women, 1977, 18–25 (yrs.)
Marriage	23.1	20.6	20.3
Independence	20.8	19.4	19.1
Living with others	20.4	20.5	—[a]
Cohabitation	21.8	20.7	19.4[b]
Travel	19.6	20.4	20.4
Study	18.4	18.3	18.1
Job	19.4	18.7	18.4
Conflict	19.0	18.0	18.5[c]

[a] Not recorded separately in 1977.
[b] Recorded as 'to live near boy friend' in 1977.
[c] Recorded as 'domestic difficulties' in 1977.

are based on the proportions of children living at home (rather than the proportions of children who have ever left home) may explain some, but not all, of the difference from the Australian trend. Other figures in their analysis refer to cohorts born before the 1950s, and the steep decline in the age at leaving home appears consistent with the earlier decline in age at marriage. As regards the actual ages at which children born around 1950 leave home, the differences between the Australian figures and those for Britain and the Federal Republic of Germany are quite small for daughters, and the Australian figures differ most with regard to the younger ages of sons on their departure from home (see Table 9.4).

Characteristics of Those Returning Home

Apart from the information provided by the surveys of 1971, 1977, and 1982 relating to the decline in the proportion of young adults leaving home to marry, a new phenomenon became apparent in the 1982 survey—the widespread practice of young adults returning home after leaving. Whether or not this practice existed before 1971 or 1977 is not known, as no questions were asked about this topic in those surveys. Nor are there any data from other countries which indicate the extent to which children return home.

The incidence of returning home has been analysed with data from the 1982 survey through the technique of survival analysis, which is similar to a life-table analysis.[6] Using this technique on the entire sample it is found that 51

[6] In this context the initial population consists of those who have left home, and instead of a death, as in conventional life-table analysis, the decrement is a return home. Accordingly it is possible to derive a life-table showing the cumulative proportions of leavers who have never returned home in relation to each interval since leaving home. The value of this approach is that it takes into account 'censored' cases, i.e. those who have left home but not yet returned.

Table 9.4 Comparison of ages at leaving home in Australia, Federal Republic of Germany, and Britain

Country and birth cohort	Age at leaving home (yrs.)	
	Men	Women
Australia—first departure[a]		
1948–52	21.5	20.2
1953–7	21.0	20.1
1958–62	21.0	19.7
Australia—final departure		
1939–53[b]	23.1	20.8
1948–56[a]	22.9	21.1
Federal Republic of Germany[c]		
1929–31 birth cohort	25.5	23.6
1939–41	25.1	22.5
1949–51	24.1	21.0
Britain[d]		
Period 1971–76 (or centred around the 1947–56 birth cohort)	22.6	20.6
Period 1976–81 (or centred around the 1952–61 birth cohort)	23.2	21.2

Sources:
[a] 1982 Survey of the Institute of Family Studies.
[b] 1971 Melbourne Family Survey. These values would include some first departures, but relate mostly to final departures from home.
[c] Mayer and Schwarz (this volume).
[d] Brass, op. cit. (n. 5).

per cent of men and 40 per cent of women return home at least once, and that 48 and 39 per cent return within ten years (see Table 9.5 and Fig. 9.1). In addition, it was also found that the proportion of leavers who returned was associated with the reason for originally leaving home. In particular, a small proportion who left to marry returned home within ten years (12 per cent of men and 16 per cent of women) compared with a much larger proportion of those who left for other reasons (59 per cent of men and 54 per cent of women). Clearly, the implication is that since an increasing proportion of young adults leave home for reasons other than marriage there will be an increasing proportion who return home after leaving. This assumption is confirmed by the data. From Table 9.5 it can be seen that a lower proportion of members of the older cohort in the sample have returned home than in the total sample, and this relationship holds at whatever age children originally left home.[7]

[7] This latter qualification is necessary because the probability of returning home is greatest among those who left home at a young age. Without this finding, therefore, the greater incidence of returning home among the younger cohorts could have been attributed to their necessarily younger age at leaving home.

Other characteristics of returning home are that it is more common among men than women, partly but not entirely because more women than men leave home to marry. The incidence of returning home peaks between one and two years after leaving home, and returning home is more common among those who left at a young age.

Table 9.5 Proportions who returned home at least once within 10 years after leaving according to age when leaving, 1982 (per cent)

Age at leaving home (yrs.)	Sub-group aged 26–34 yrs.		Total sample 18–34 yrs.	
	Men[a]	Women	Men	Women
All reasons for leaving home				
15–17	62	41	63	50
18–19	48	32	53	39
20–1	40	30	48	32
22–4	21	20	22	20
Total[b]	41	33	48	39
All reasons except marriage				
15–17	62	45	63	53
18–19	52	47	57	55
20–1	61	49	68	55
22–4	38	49	39	49
Total[b]	53	46	59	54

[a] Derived from a survival analysis.
[b] Including a small number who left at age 25 or older.

The majority of young people return home because it is more convenient and cheaper than living away from home. Some also return because they are lonely, while another important group are those who return because they have completed their education or travel, or because their job has finished. Another reason, being requested to return home by the parents, is usually indicative of a 'stormy' departure from home, and/or returning home to a stressful family situation. Those who left home to marry return because of the breakdown of the marriage, the parents' need, or, occasionally, because it is more convenient to live with the parents.

Leaving Home for the First and Last Time

Not only does the fact that some children return home indicate that their first departure may be only temporary, but it also implies that there will be another departure from home at a later date. Accordingly, many young adults now follow a pattern of leaving home, returning, and leaving again. As is shown in Figs. 9.2 and 9.3, at any given age there are differences between the

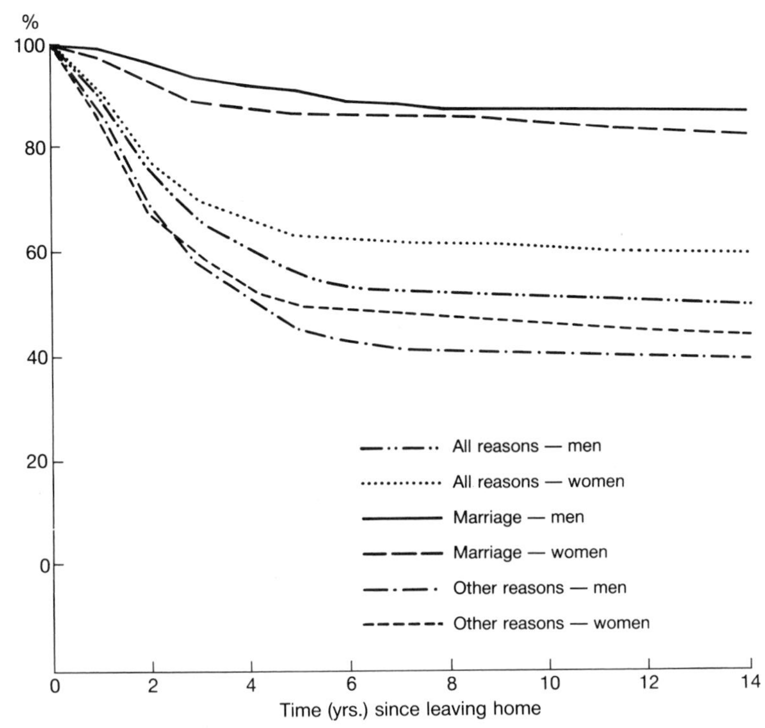

Fig. 9.1 Cumulative proportions who have never returned home, according to whether they left home to marry or for other reasons (1982 survey).

proportions of young adults who have ever left home and the proportions who are now living away from home, because of the relatively high rate of return. This means that information about the proportion of young adults at each age who are living away from home obtained from census or survey results may greatly understate the proportion who have ever left home, particularly at the younger ages. As may be seen from Fig. 9.3, most will have left home by the time they are between 25 and 29 years old, so that after this age has been reached living away from home becomes virtually equivalent to 'ever left home'.

A relatively high proportion of those who left home and returned subsequently left home to marry, thus augmenting the total proportion who ultimately left home for this reason. This is illustrated in Table 9.6 from the experience of the sub-group of young adults aged 26 years or older, when the process of leaving home is virtually complete. Thirty-one per cent of men and 45 per cent of women at their first departure from home left to marry, and 33 per cent and 36 per cent respectively of the departures of returners occurred for this reason, thus bringing the proportions at their final departure who left in order to marry to 41 and 50 per cent, respectively. A further calculation can be made to determine the proportion who *ever* leave home for marriage, since

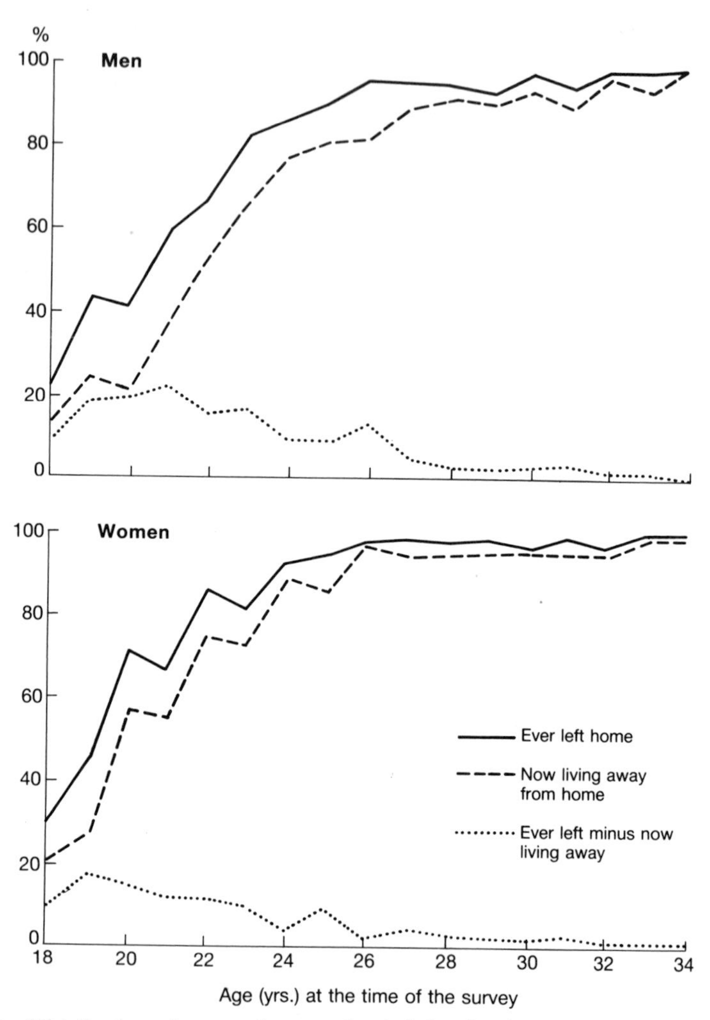

Fig. 9.2 Distribution of men and women by their leaving-home status (1982 survey).

some of those who first leave for this reason subsequently return and leave for some other reason. This shows that 44 per cent of men and 57 per cent of women *ever* leave home in order to marry (see Table 9.6). Many of the returners leave again for the same or a related reason. For example, those who first left to live independently will again leave for the same reason, those who left because of conflict will again leave because of conflict, and those who left for education will subsequently leave for a job.

With regard to the timing of the first and last departures from home, among those now aged 26 years or older the mean ages of men and women at their last

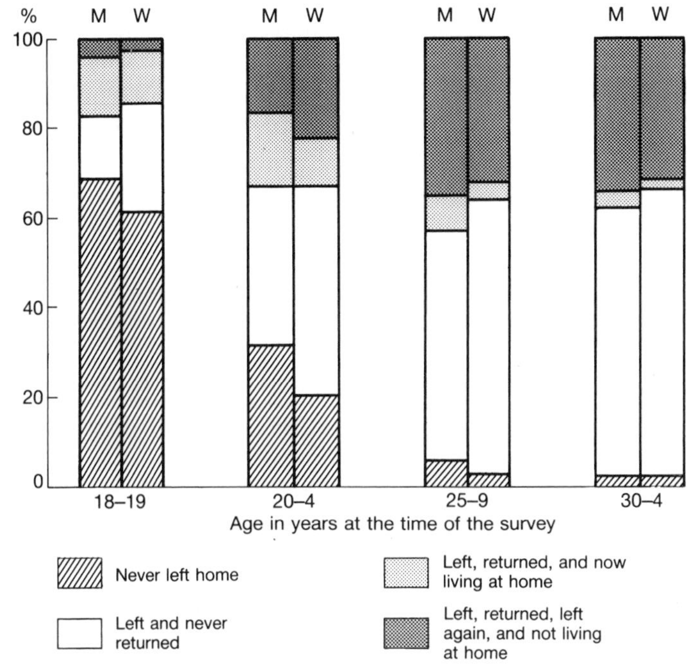

Fig. 9.3 Proportional distribution of young adults according to whether they have never left home, ever left home, ever returned, or stayed at home since returning (1982 survey).

Table 9.6 Proportion who left home to marry on their first or final departure, and the proportion who ever left to marry (persons aged 26 or older at the 1982 survey (per cent)

Proportion who left home to marry	Men	Women
At the first departure	31	45
Among returners on their second departure	33	36
Among all on their final departure[a]	41	50
On either the first or the second departure	44	57
Proportion who ever returned		
Actual values	39	32
Based on survival analysis	41	33

[a] Final departure refers to the first departure of those who left home only once, and the last departure of those who left home more than once.

departure are 22.9 and 21.3 years respectively, compared with 21.3 and 20.1 years at their first departure—a difference of about 1.5 years. The difference is greater for men than for women, since a higher proportion of men return home (see Table 9.7). Therefore, a measure of the age at leaving home based on the age at the first departure would be between one and two years lower than a measure relating to the last departure from home; the choice of which measure to use would depend on the aims of the particular study. The figures in Table 9.7 also demonstrate the similarity between estimates of ages at leaving home derived from median ages from a survival analysis and estimates derived from the arithmetic means for this older age group.

Table 9.7 Median and mean ages at leaving home the first time and finally in relation to whether or not marriage was the reason for leaving, 1982 survey

Reason for and type of departure	Men		Women	
	Age (yrs.)	No.	Age (yrs.)	No.
Total sample, median ages, survival analysis				
First departure: all reasons	21.2	1,234	20.0	1,221
Sub-group aged 26–34, median ages, survival analysis				
First departure				
All reasons	21.3	615	20.1	628
Marriage	23.1	183	20.8	277
Other	19.9	411	19.1	337
Final[a] departure: all reasons	22.9	615	21.3	628
Difference between first and final departures	1.6		1.2	
Sub-group aged 26–34, mean ages				
First departure				
All reasons	20.9	594	19.8	614
Marriage	23.1	183	20.6	277
Other	19.9	411	19.1	337
Final[a] departure: all reasons	22.6	594	21.1	614
Difference between first and final departures	1.7		1.3	

[a] Final departure refers to the first departure of those who left home only once, and the last departure of those who left home more than once. Note that the means differ from the medians because the means are based on the experience only of those who have left home, whereas the medians also include the few who have not left home.

However, it is more interesting to examine separately those who never return and those who ever return after leaving. As shown in Table 9.8, in the cohort aged 26 years or older, the mean age at leaving home of non-returners is 21.8 years for men and 20.0 for women, ages which are 1.4 and 1.2 years higher than the corresponding ages at first leaving home among returners (19.2 years for men and 18.8 for women). However, the mean ages at leaving home on the last occasion among the returners are considerably higher than those at leaving home on the last occasion among non-returners—23.8 for men and 23.3 for women compared with 21.8 and 20.0 respectively. As regards the timing of returning and leaving among those who ever return, it is found that on average the interval between the first departure and the first return is about two years, and the interval between the first return and the last departure is about 2.5 years, giving an overall average duration between the first and last departure of about 4.5 years (see Table 9.8).

Table 9.8 Mean ages at leaving home on the first and last departures from home, among non-returners and returners aged 26–34, 1982 survey

Type of departure	Men		Women	
	(yrs.)	No.	(yrs.)	No.
All[a]				
First departure: all reasons	20.9	594	19.8	614
Non-returners		362		414
First and final departure				
All reasons	21.8		20.0	
Marriage	23.2		20.7	
Other	20.6		19.2	
Returners		204		189
First departure: all reasons	19.2		18.8	
First return home	21.4		20.8	
Last departure				
All reasons	23.8		23.3	
Marriage	23.9		22.7	
Other	23.6		23.6	
Intervals between events: returners				
First departure–first return	2.2		2.0	
First return–last departure	2.4		2.5	
First departure–last departure	4.6		4.5	

[a] This group also includes a small number of men and women who left home at least once, have returned, and are still at home.

This brings us to a further consideration of the trend in the age at leaving home obtained from the data for 1971 and those for 1982, discussed in relation to Table 9.1. From Fig. 9.4 it is evident that the differences between the proportions who have left home by a given age according to data from the two surveys are relatively large when the 1982 figure is based on the proportion who have ever left, but are quite small when the 1982 proportion is based on the proportion who are currently living away from home. It seems, therefore, that, although there may have been in increase between 1971 and 1982 in the proportion who have ever left home by a given age, the increase in the proportion who have remained away from home shown in the two surveys is quite small, although greater for men than for women.

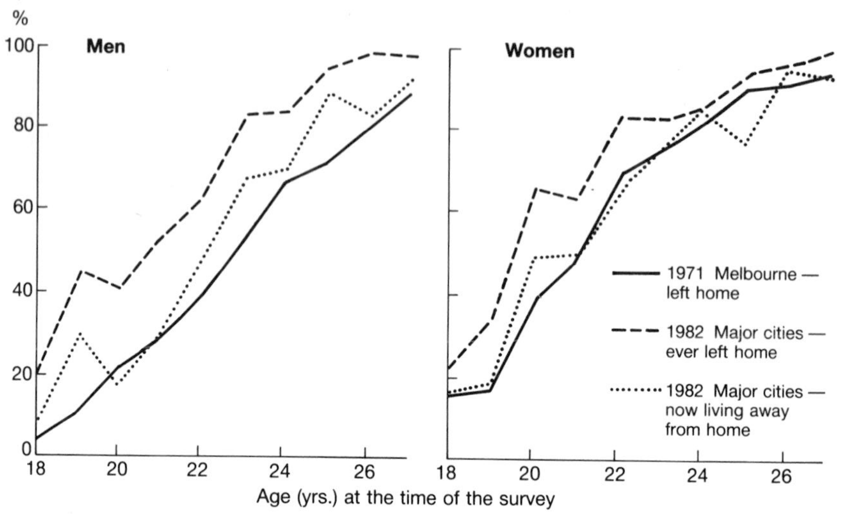

Fig. 9.4 Comparison of the proportions who have left home in relation to major cities in Australia (1971 and 1982 surveys).

Parents' Experience during the Leaving-home Stage

The current definition of the timing and duration of the leaving-home stage during the parents' life cycle is that the leaving-home stage extends from the departure of the first to that of the last child. Therefore, from the demographic information which is normally available regarding the family, the point when the leaving-home stage begins would be the mother's age (or duration of marriage) at which the first child was born added to the average age at which young adults left home, while the point of completion would be obtained similarly from the date of birth of the last child. Alternatively, survey data for mothers may be available which include information about their ages when the first and last children in the family left home. The advantage of this second method is that it takes into account the 'cross-over' effect.[8] This term is used to describe the fact that the first-born child is not always the first, nor the last-born child always the last, to leave home. 'Cross-over' is a possibility in all families with two or more children, but its incidence is greater when the age gap between the first and second child or between the last and penultimate child is small, and when the eldest of the first two and the last two children is a son and the younger a daughter.

In the 1982 survey information was obtained about the ages of the mother and father at the time the first-born and the last-born child left home, for parents with children aged 18–34 years at the time of the survey. From this information it was found that mothers were on average 46.1 years old when the

[8] Young, op. cit. (1975) (n. 2).

first child left home and 53.5 years when the last child left. The corresponding figures for fathers were 49.3 and 55.6 years respectively.

Obviously, the ages of the parents when the first- and last-born children left home also depend on the sex of the children in the family. Accordingly, the mother's average age when the first-born child first leaves home may be as low as 43.4 years when the first child is a daughter, or as high as 46.7 years when it is a son. Similarly, the mother's average age when the last child first leaves home may be as low as 52.9 years or as high as 54.1. Similar differences also occur in the average ages of the father when the first and last children first leave home. However, these figures refer to the mother's (and fathers') age when the children leave home for the first time. As was pointed out earlier, a high proportion of children return after the first departure and leave again later. Accordingly, from the parents' point of view, while the leaving-home stage commences with the first departure from home of the first-born child, it is not complete until the last departure from home of the last-born child. Therefore, instead of extending from an age of 46.1 to 53.5 years, the leaving-home stage extends on average from the time when the mother is 46.1 years old until she is 54.8, that is, an additional 1.3 years, giving a total of 8.7. Again, there are further differences depending on the sex of the children in the family, and these are illustrated for two-child families in Fig. 9.5.

In addition to the overall effect of returning home in lengthening the leaving-home stage, families can be separated depending on whether or not any of the children return home after leaving. In families in which the children leave home and never return, the leaving-home stage is relatively short, with an average of only 7.5 years. In contrast, in families in which both the first-born and last-born children return home before their final departure, the average duration of the leaving-home stage in the parents' family life cycle becomes 11.1 years. Moreover, while parents in the first category with two children would experience two major events during the leaving-home stage—the beginning and the end—parents in the second category would experience a total of six events during the leaving-home stage—the first departure, first return, and final departure of the first-born child, followed by the first departure, first return, and final departure of the last-born child (see Fig. 9.6). Note that there is no evidence that the departure of the youngest child results in more stress for the parents than departure of the other children. On the contrary, a first-born child is more likely than a middle or youngest child to leave home amidst conflict.

Summary and Implications

Leaving home is no longer simply a case of a departure from the household at marriage. More than one-half of young adults in Australia now leave home for the first time before they marry (with the number of sons exceeding that of daughters), and about one-half of these return home before leaving finally,

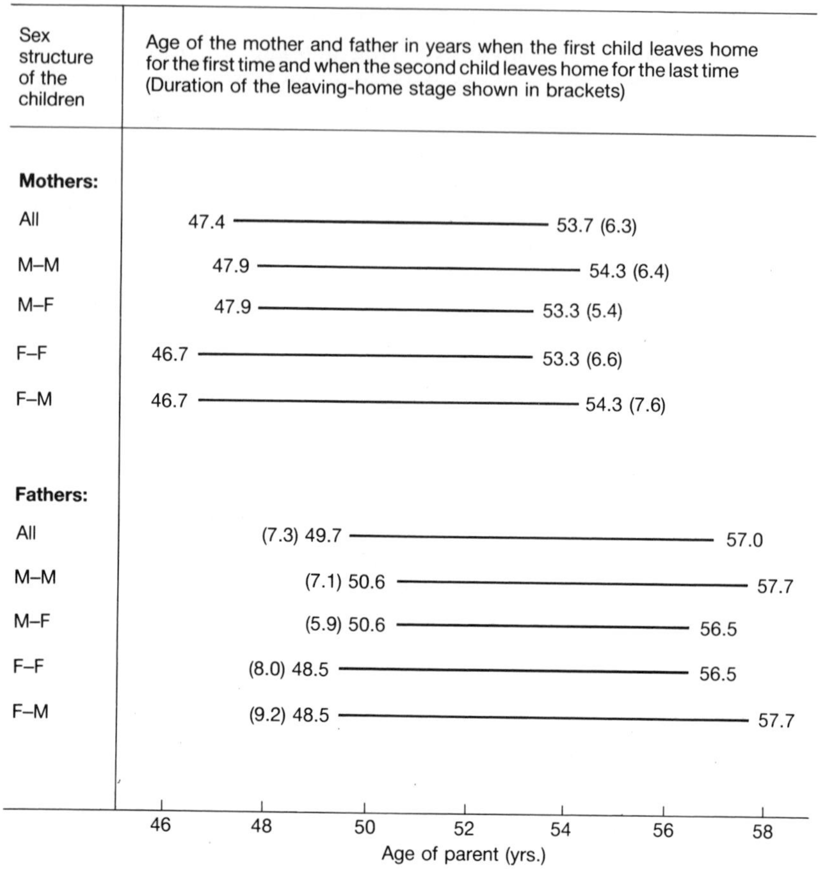

Sex structure of the children	Age of the mother and father in years when the first child leaves home for the first time and when the second child leaves home for the last time (Duration of the leaving-home stage shown in brackets)
Mothers:	
All	47.4 —— 53.7 (6.3)
M–M	47.9 —— 54.3 (6.4)
M–F	47.9 —— 53.3 (5.4)
F–F	46.7 —— 53.3 (6.6)
F–M	46.7 —— 54.3 (7.6)
Fathers:	
All	(7.3) 49.7 —— 57.0
M–M	(7.1) 50.6 —— 57.7
M–F	(5.9) 50.6 —— 56.5
F–F	(8.0) 48.5 —— 56.5
F–M	(9.2) 48.5 —— 57.7

46 48 50 52 54 56 58
Age of parent (yrs.)

Fig. 9.5 Timing and duration of the leaving-home stage of the family life cycle in two-child families, according to the age of the parents and the sex structure of the children (1982 survey).

again with more men than women returning. Virtually none remain at home after marrying. About one-third of those who return subsequently leave home in order to marry, thereby slightly increasing the proportion who eventually leave for this reason. Even so, the proportion of men and women who ever leave to marry only reaches 44 and 57 per cent respectively.

Increasingly, independence and conflict are becoming important reasons for leaving home, and these contrast with the more acceptable reasons from the parents' point of view—marriage, study, and job opportunity. Leaving home for reasons other than marriage also represents a different sort of independence from that associated with leaving home to marry. Although young adults who leave home for other reasons retain less contact with their parents, they are also more likely to return home. It is worth noting that those

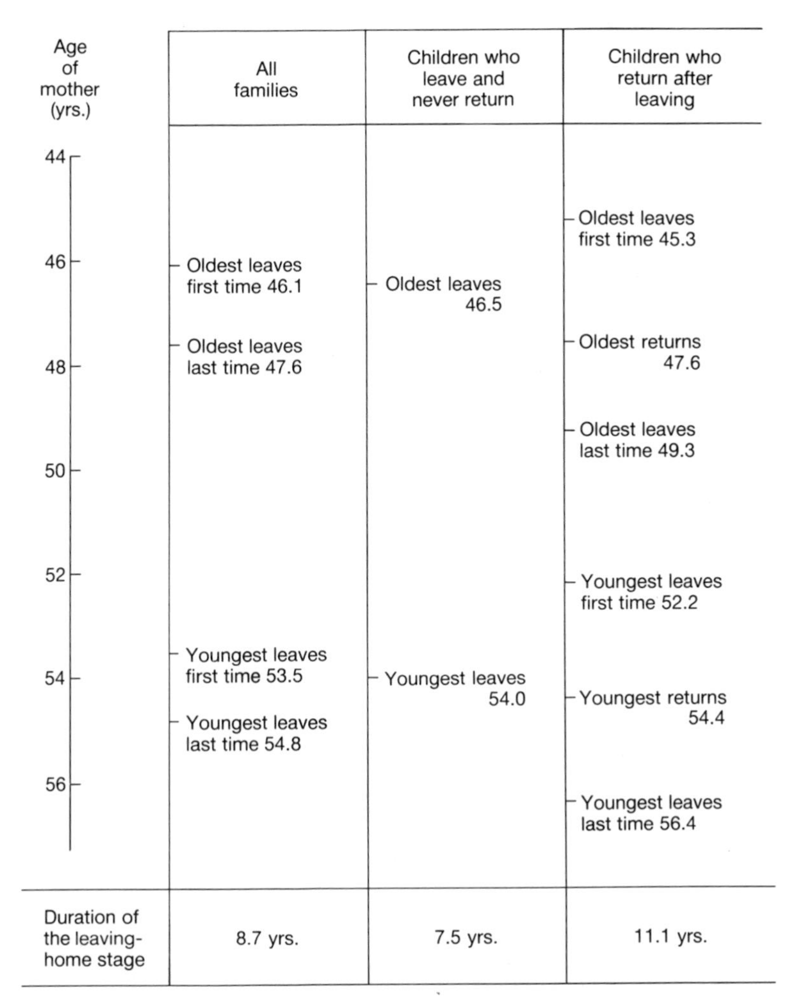

Fig. 9.6 Leaving-home experience of mothers according to whether or not the oldest and youngest children return home after leaving: families of two or more children (1982 survey).

who leave home because of conflict are most likely to return, and these returners also stay away from home for the shortest period. Study and travel appear to be reasons for leaving home associated with the more privileged groups, while conflict and job opportunities are relatively more often the reasons for leaving home among the disadvantaged.

In addition, leaving home no longer depends on the young adult first completing his or her education. Among those studied in the 1982 survey, just over one-half of men and almost one-third of women left home before they completed studying. Financial dependence also no longer seems as strong a barrier to leaving home as it was in the past, while being unemployed actually seems to increase the probability of a young adult leaving home, although at the same time it also greatly increases the probability that he or she will return. Therefore, leaving home is no longer the final step in the sequence of events: completing study–starting work–marrying and leaving home; it now seems to be linked more often with the achievement of independence and social development.

Returners, on average, leave home for the first time at younger ages than non-returners, but their average age when they finally leave home is considerably greater. Although on average returners stay away from home for two years following their first departure, they then remain at home for an average of 2.5 years before finally leaving. Overall, women who return home live independently of their parents for a slightly shorter time than those who do not return, whereas among men the number of years of independence is virtually the same for each group. This raises the question about the timing of the achievement of independence from the parents: do those who leave earlier but subsequently return and leave at an older age achieve independence sooner or later than those who only leave once and at an age intermediate between leaving for the first and second time?

The implications for the precision of the timing of leaving home among young adults and the timing of the leaving-home stage during the family life cycle of the parents are fourfold:

(i) The average age at marriage is no longer a suitable proxy for the timing of the leaving-home stage, except in societies where marriage is virtually the only reason for leaving home.

(ii) The proportion of young adults who are currently living away from home understates the proportion who have ever left home.

(iii) The average age of young adults when leaving home for the first time is between one and two years lower than the average age at leaving home for the last time. The choice of which measure is used depends on the researcher's assessment of the relative importance of the first and the last departure from home. While the first departure marks the first break from home and the first attempt of the young adult to live independently, the last departure from home marks the permanent break from the parents' household. In any case, the researcher should specify which measure is used in any presentation of data.

(iv) Following the previous item, it would seem that the most satisfactory description of the timing and duration of the leaving-home stage in the family life cycle of the parents is from the point at which the oldest child leaves home for the first time to the point at which the youngest child leaves home for the last time.

It is possible that part of the decline in the age at leaving home, the increase in the proportion leaving home because of conflict, and the greater extent of returning home among the younger cohorts compared with the older cohorts in the 1982 survey may result from higher unemployment levels in the younger group. A sharp upturn in the level of unemployment in Australia began during the mid-1970s, rather later than in Western countries. This resulted in a relatively high proportion of those aged 18–24 in the Survey of 1982 experiencing unemployment—22 per cent of men and 25 per cent of women compared with only 12 and 7 per cent respectively among those aged 25–34 at the time of the survey.

Characteristics of the ever-unemployed include a young age at leaving home (20.2 years for men and 19.3 years for women compared with 21.3 and 20.1 years respectively for those who had never been unemployed), and a very high rate of return home (72 per cent of men leavers and 49 per cent of women leavers, compared with 44 and 38 per cent respectively of those who had never been unemployed). In addition, much higher proportions of the ever-unemployed left home because of conflict, and slightly higher proportions left home for a job, or to cohabit (more common for women than for men), while relatively lower proportions left home to study or to marry (especially among women) in comparison with the never-unemployed.

This raises the question about the origins of the recent trend away from marriage as the only reason for leaving home. Is this a response to, or a cause of, the recent increase in the median age at marriage? In other words, has the postponement of marriage occurred because young adults have discovered that they can achieve independence without marriage as a means of leaving home, or has the prospect of an early marriage receded by reason of the high level of youth unemployment and economic insecurity, and so forced many to seek the independence normally achieved through marriage through other reasons for leaving home? Alternatively, the impact of unemployment may have played only a minor role, and the trend towards leaving home at a young age, with the option of returning if the venture proves too difficult, may simply reflect an increasing desire among young people to experience a period of independence from their parents before they begin their own family. This view of an increasing wish for independence and separateness from the family is also reflected in the living arrangements of the elderly, and their apparent preference for living alone. It is also interesting to note that, according to the Survey of 1982, those young adults whose parents did *not* encourage them to be independent were most likely to leave home for independence.

The information from the Survey of 1982 also raises the question whether a return home is an indication of an unsuccessful venture at living independently. An examination of the characteristics of leavers who are most likely to return home places them into two widely divergent groups. On the one hand, returning home is more common among those who left because of conflict, among those who had ever been unemployed, among those with the lowest level of schooling, and among women whose parents strongly disapproved of their original departure. On the other hand, returning home and remaining home after returning is also more common among those who are emotionally very close to their parents, and (among men) those who have a very strong positive attitude to living at home, or whose activities as a teenager were mostly with the family.

Therefore, while in the first group returning home has often come about because the young adult from a difficult family situation has insufficient emotional or scholastic resources to establish long-term living arrangements, in the second group returning home reflects an inability to cope independently outside the home because of too close emotional bonds with the parents. Nevertheless, there also appears to be a large group between these two extremes for whom neither leaving home nor returning home was overly stressful. In particular, this middle group includes the returners who left for a specific short-term purpose, such as a course of study or an overseas trip, or who are merely returning home because it is cheaper, friendlier, and more comfortable.

10 Kinship Networks and Informal Support in the Later Years

ALICE T. DAY
Australian National University

Introduction

Of all the areas within family demography, that of kinship networks is the most complex and the least developed. If the demography of families and households can be described as 'immature',[1] the demography of kinship must be seen as still in its infancy. Underdevelopment of research on kinship applies particularly to work on family systems in Western industrial societies,[2] and extends beyond demography to the other social sciences. In a review of American studies of kinship over the last decade[3] Lee concludes: 'The process of explaining how and why individuals associate with kin, and how kin relationships affect individuals and families, has just begun.'

Within family demography, study of kin relations during the later years has been especially meagre. What interest there has been in the demography of families and households has focused on the earlier and middle years of the family life cycle.[4] Until the 1980s, in the demographic study of life-cycle events the effects of family formation and fertility on family structure were emphasized[5] in preference to the study of major transitions during the later years, e.g. children leaving home, retirement, death of spouse, moving in with family, or institutionalization. Yet, at a time when the proportion of people in the oldest age groups is rapidly increasing, when the association of impairment

I am grateful to Lincoln H. Day for substantial help in preparing the paper on which this chapter is based. Space and time to make the necessary revisions were made possible by the Mellon Visiting Scholar Program, Population Reference Bureau, Inc., Washington, DC.

[1] T. K. Burch, 'Households and Family Demography', *Population Index*, 45(2) (1979).

[2] Much demographic research has been conducted on family systems in developing countries, particularly with reference to fertility and family size. Cf. e.g. J. C. Caldwell, 'The Wealth Flows Theory of Fertility Decline', in C. Höhn and R. Mackensen (eds.), *Determinants of Fertility Trends: Theories Re-examined*, (Liège, 1981).

[3] G. R. Lee, 'Kinship in the Seventies: A Decade Review of Research and Theory', *Journal of Marriage and the Family*, 42(4) (1980).

[4] G. B. Spanier and P. C. Glick, 'The Life Cycle of American Families: An Expanded Analysis', *Journal of Family History*, 5 (1980).

[5] Cf. e.g. F. Lorimer, *Culture and Human Fertility* (Paris, 1954); K. Davis, 'Institutional Patterns Favoring High Fertility in Underdeveloped Areas', *Eugenics Quarterly*, 2 (1955).

with advanced years is well established,[6] and when older persons are increasingly likely to reside in one-person households[7] building a demographic base of information about them and their kinship systems is crucial to understanding the issues related to the future needs of ageing populations. This is particularly true now, when the capacity of kin in developed countries to be 'all-purpose' providers[8] of support to their ageing members is becoming a matter of doubt and a major issue of public concern.

Social Support Issues

Survey research on cohorts whose members are now in their 60s and older shows that the bulk of help with health care and daily activities—even among those who are seriously ill or severely impaired—is provided by family members.[9] In an Australian survey in 1981 relating to handicapped persons aged 60 years and over,[10] for example, it was found that among the 15 per cent of the aged who were disabled and dependent on others, two-thirds relied on family and community care, while only one-third were in institutions. Results from another survey in the same year, of 1,050 persons aged 60 years and over who lived in Sydney outside institutions,[11] showed that, apart from spouses, 89 per cent of those providing household and personal care were family members, and 83 per cent of those providing this kind of care were women.[12] The corollary to this, borne out by other survey results in Australia[13] and elsewhere,[14] is that community services play only a very minor role in assisting the aged at home: only 7 per cent of those in the Sydney sample were receiving any formal services. Thus, the low proportion of older people

[6] 1980 Health Interview Survey, in National Center for Health Statistics and US Bureau of the Census, *Projections of the Population of the United States: 1982 to 2050* (Washington, DC, 1982); D. M. Gibson and D. T. Rowland, 'Community vs. Institutional Care: Case of the Australian Aged', *Social Science and Medicine*, 18(11) (1984).

[7] F. E. Kobrin, 'Household Headship and its Changes in the United States, 1940–1960, 1970', *Journal of the American Statistical Association*, 68(344) (1973).

[8] M. B. Sussman, 'The Family Life of Old People', in R. H. Binstock and E. Shanas (eds.), *Handbook of Aging and the Social Sciences* (New York, 1976).

[9] H. L. Kendig, 'The Providers of Community Care', in H. L. Kendig, D. M. Gibson, D. T. Rowland, and J. M. Hemer, *Health Welfare and Family in Later Life* (Sydney, 1983); M. J. Gibson, 'Family Support Patterns, Policies and Programs', in C. Nusberg with M. J. Gibson and S. Peace, *Innovative Aging Programs Abroad: Implications for the US* (Westport, Conn., 1984).

[10] Australian Bureau of Statistics, *Survey of Handicapped Persons 1981*, cited by D. T. Rowland, 'Family Structure', in Kendig *et al.*, op. cit. (n. 9).

[11] *Survey of the Aged in Sydney*, conducted by the Ageing and the Family Project (Australian National University, Canberra, 1981).

[12] Kendig, op. cit. (n. 9), p. 151.

[13] Cf. New South Wales Council for the Ageing and Department of Social Security, *Home Care Services for Aged Persons in New South Wales* (Sydney, 1981); Home Support Services Committee, Council of Social Services of New South Wales, *Rockbottom: A Report on the Developing Crisis for Home Services in New South Wales* (Sydney, 1981).

[14] E. Brody, *Innovative Programs and Services for the Elderly and the Family*, testimony before the Select Committee On Aging, House of Representatives (Washington, DC, 1980).

institutionalized at any one time (e.g. 7 per cent in Australia, 5 per cent in the USA) is a function of help from families. Community services (in their present form and quantity) are not a viable alternative.

But there is growing uncertainty about the resiliency of kin networks to sustain long-term home care of the dependent aged. Increasingly, family researchers and policy-makers are asking: Who will be available to provide care? What services will they be expected to provide? How should care be distributed between public and private resources? What mix of formal and informal support works best for the aged themselves? In a variety of current social and demographic trends, family researchers see barriers to providing care that may jeopardize the flow of support between the generations. Examples cited include the growing acceptance of childlessness and preference among younger couples for the childless state, the increase in the number of adults choosing to remain unmarried and the fall in the average number of children per family, the high incidence of divorce, participation of women in the work-force well into middle age, the increasing tendency for women to outlive their husbands, and the growing imbalance in the sex ratio at the older ages.[15]

The consequences of these trends for the structure of family support in the later years are ambiguous. Some researchers argue that changes in contemporary family patterns will generate new kinship ties that will actually diversify and enlarge the support systems upon whom the aged can call for help.[16] Reconstituted families, for example, may result in a child having two stepgrandparents in addition to four natural ones; parents whose children divorce and remarry may add one or more stepchildren to their pool of third-generation kin.[17] Research is now under way to study the impact of such changing kinship configurations on the norm of filial responsibility that traditionally has bound younger adults to care for older relatives.[18] One fact has clearly emerged from recent American studies: there are marked generational differences in preferences for long-term care arrangements. Younger people express much more willingness to care for their parents than the parents say they want from their children.[19] In an American study in 1984

[15] A. Cherlin, *Marriage, Divorce, Remarriage* (Cambridge, Mass., 1983); F. R. Furstenberg, Jr. and G. S. Spanier, *Remarriage after Divorce* (Beverly Hills, Calif., 1983); W. H. Baldwin and C. W. Nord, 'Delayed Childbearing in the US: Facts and Fictions', *Population Bulletin*, 39(4) (1984).

[16] E. Shanas and P. M. Hauser, 'Zero Population Growth and the Family Life of Old People', *Journal of Social Issues*, 30(4) (1974); B. L. Neugarten, 'The Future and the Young-Old', *Gerontologist* 15 (1975); F. F. Furstenberg, op. cit. (n. 15); J. Blake, 'Demographic Revolution and Family Evolution: Some Implications for American Women', in P. W. Berman and E. R. Ramey (eds.) *Women: A Developmental Perspective* (Washington, DC, 1982); R. W. Riley, 'Implications for the Middle and Later Years', in ibid.

[17] G. O. Hagestad, 'Divorce: The Family Ripple Effect', *Generations* (Winter 1982).

[18] G. O. Hagestad, M. A. Smyer, and K. L. Stierman, 'Parent–Child Relations in Adulthood: The Impact of Divorce in Middle Age', in R. Cohen, S. Weissman and B. Cohler (eds.), *Parenthood: A Psychodynamic Perspective* (Guilford Press, 1984).

[19] (Associated Press), 'Old and Young Differ over Issues of Aging', *New York Times*, 17 Jan. 1985.

of what three generations of women think adult children should do for their parents,[20] it was found that 'adjustment of family schedules and help with costs of professional health care were seen as appropriate for adult children, but adjustment of work schedules and sharing of households were not'. The proportion in favour of receiving financial support or instrumental help from children was smallest in the middle generation of this study: they preferred to bypass family members and seek formal services for such assistance. Such generational differences suggest that expectations about family support among the old in future cohorts may differ markedly from those that have characterized the views of the contemporary aged.

Contribution of Demography to Gerontology

What can demography contribute to these issues? Demographic work bearing on gerontological issues has tended to emphasize 'formal' rather than 'social' dimensions.[21] The latter approach considers the implications of a population's size or structure for economic, political, and social institutions and processes, and how demographic change affects the health and life circumstances of older people. 'Formal' demography concentrates more on describing the present and estimated future characteristics of the aged population: projecting future trends; analysing mortality, migration, marital, and household dynamics as they affect the old; and estimating the impact of different models of fertility, mortality, migration, and marital regimes for 'the stock' of elderly kin.

This chapter will present a case that such 'formal' approaches, while clearly filling a vital information need, present a partial, sometimes even misleading view of the aged and their support potential. In supporting this claim, I look first at reasons why study of kinship in later life has lagged behind other areas of demographic research, then at major developments in research in this area, and finally at fresh approaches demographers might take to generate new data and enrich the fund of knowledge relevant to informal support of the aged.

Reasons for Underdevelopment of Demographic Research on Kinship in Later Life

A review of the literature on demographic approaches to kinship in later life reveals a number of obstacles to developing a strong research base. They include problems of conceptualization, beliefs about the nuclear family, technical difficulties of description and measurement, and subjective dimen-

[20] E. M. Brody, P. T. Johnson and M. C. Fulcomer, 'What Should Adult Children Do for Elderly Parents? Opinions and Preferences of Three Generations of Women', *Journal of Gerontology*, 39(6) (1984).

[21] S. De Vos, 'Where Demography and Gerontology Meet', CDE Working Paper 84–7 (Madison, Wis., 1984).

sions of kinship phenomena themselves. These can be seen as both cause and effect—that is, they have both deterred demographers from undertaking research in this area and impeded progress in developing new approaches.

Problems of Conceptualization

Lack of conceptual precision has been a prime deterrent to demographers from initiating research on some of the more subtle and difficult aspects of family phenomena, of which kinship is a prime example. Progress in developing the field has been impeded by lack of common standards, both nationally and internationally, of terminology, of appropriate models for analysis, and of techniques of measurement.[22] Practitioners have been unable to reach a consensus about how to define and measure the major units of family study (i.e. conjugal pair, nuclear family, household, kinship networks).[23] Hence these core concepts continue to be used in different ways in scholarly works and in the official statistics of different countries.

Conceptual uncertainty has figured as well in the question of how to delineate the scope of phenomena for study and how to distinguish between various units of analysis within the field. What should 'kin' include, and where should the boundaries be drawn between families, households, and kinship networks? Defined as ties between persons related by blood or marriage, but not necessarily sharing a dwelling or living in the same household, kinship networks include the members of both families and households and extend beyond these to more distant, widely dispersed relations. Ball,[24] for example, distinguishes between 'conventional kin'—those tied by blood or marriage —and two other types: 'discretionary kin', 'those distant relatives with whom one develops close and intimate relationships, not normally expected because of their location in the kin network, e.g., a spouse's sister-in-law or cousin', and 'fictive kin', 'those non-kin, usually friends, whose relationships with members of the conjugal unit are "as family". They are adopted members who take on obligations, instrumental and affectional ties similar to those of conventional kin.'

Demographic trends over the past two decades have made the definition of kinship even more complex than in the past. Cherlin[25] has described the multiple definitions that can arise when both partners remarry after divorce and both remarriages include children and in-laws from the new partners' previous marriages:

[22] J. Bongaarts, 'The Formal Demography of Families and Households: An Overview', *IUSSP Newsletter*, 17 (1983); J. A. Sweet and L. Bumpass, 'Families and Households', paper presented at the Annual Meeting of the Population Association of America, Minneapolis, 1984.

[23] Ibid.

[24] D. W. Ball, 'The Family as a Sociological Problem: Conceptualisation of the "Taken-for-granted" as Prologue to Social Problem Analysis', *Social Problems*, 19 (1972).

[25] Cherlin, op. cit. (n. 15), p. 86.

In these kinds of post-divorce families there is no invariant definition of the immediate family that we can apply to all parties. Instead, a household formed by a divorce or remarriage that involves children from a previous marriage becomes the intersection of an overlapping set of relationships, each of which constitutes an immediate family for one or more members of the household. There are no fixed rules as to who should be included as members of each of these families.

Defining the place of more distant kin can be even more complex. People in different households formed by broken marriages, whose only formal tie was through the now defunct marriage, may still continue to interact. The anthropologist Paul Bohannan[26] has labelled these linked households, 'divorce chains' and the persons related by ties of broken marriages 'quasi-kin'. But if we include 'discretionary', 'fictive', and 'quasi-kin', who is left out? Although a number of writers[27] have argued for a less restrictive definition of kin as a means of providing care-giving incentives to a more diverse support network, too inclusive a definition loses conceptual meaning.

Beliefs about the Nuclear Family

A possible explanation for the relatively slow development of demographic research in developed countries on kinship in later life is that in these societies the concept of 'family' has tended to be associated with the idea of a separate, nuclear family consisting of the conjugal pair and their children, usually excluding lateral kin and more distant relatives. Nydegger[28] has attributed this convention to the belief that the nuclear family is strong 'naturally', and that it is the primary form found in 'the state of nature'. Such a belief, in turn, is likely to foster the view that other family types are aberrant or anachronistic, somehow less worthy of concerted scholarly attention. Researchers investigating family systems in cultures outside their own may have felt less restricted by preconceptions about the 'natural' order and hence more at liberty to examine a spectrum of family types. In any case, while a number of demographers have applied anthropological and sociological techniques in studying family structure and inter-generational relations in developing countries,[29] these techniques have been used less in demographic research on kinship systems in modern, industrial societies.

[26] P. Bohannan, 'Divorces', in P. Bohannan (ed.), *Divorce and After* (New York, 1970).

[27] Sussman, loc. cit. (n. 8); P. L. Berger and R. J. Neuhaus, *To Empower People: The Role of Mediating Structures in Public Policy* (Washington, DC, 1979); M. A. Smyer and B. F. Hofland, 'Divorce and Family Support in Later Life', *Journal of Family Issues*, 3 (1982).

[28] C. N. Nydegger, 'Family Ties of the Aged in Cross-cultural Perspective', *Gerontologist*, 23(1) (1983).

[29] J. C. Caldwell, 'A Theory of Fertility: From High Plateau to Destabilization', *Population and Development Review*, 4(4) (1978); D. Lauro, 'The Demography of a Thai Village: Methodological Considerations and Substantive Conclusions from Field Study in a Central Plains Community', Ph.D. thesis, Australian National University, 1980.

Technical Difficulties: Description and Measurement

A more direct reason for the underdevelopment of demographic research on kinship in industrial societies may be the technical difficulties associated with description and measurement. Absence of a physical locus defining the boundaries of kinship makes family networks difficult to study by conventional census and sample survey techniques. In fact, all American and Canadian census data are based on the 'residential unit', and therefore relationships extending beyond the dwelling (in which the household resides) cannot be studied with census data. In family demography there is currently much interest in the quantitative analysis of households, largely because of 'the growing theoretical focus on the household as the key decision-making unit in demographic behavior'.[30] However, family researchers are also becoming increasingly aware of the need to develop a definition of 'family' that extends beyond relationships tied to dwellings or households.

Dramatic changes in household headship and composition are highlighting the limitations of household statistics as indicators of trends in family life. From American studies of changes in household headship over the past three decades, and of cohort changes in family structure and household composition, massive evidence is accumulating of the loosening of social ties that bind family members to a common place of residence. Kobrin[31] concluded her analysis of trends in headship with the observation that 'increases in headship which have been so broad in their incidence have broken the close tie which formerly existed between household and family.' Similarly Price,[32] analysing data from the censuses of 1940 to 1970 on each individual's relationship to the head of household, showed that the incidence of two-family households and households containing 'other relatives' and non-kin has declined; while one-person households and households with children headed by a single parent have increased. Looking at these trends, Cherlin[33] concluded: 'the increased tendency for people to move in and out of households—marry, divorce, and re-marry—means that "families" are increasingly extending across boundaries of households, so that statistics about households are becoming less useful as a guide to the situation of families'.

Subjective Aspects of Kinship Phenomena

A further deterrent to research development in the demography of kinship is the voluntary, fluid nature of kinship ties. As Sussman[34] noted,

[30] Burch, op. cit. (n. 1).
[31] Kobrin, op. cit. (n. 7).
[32] D. O. Price, 'Changing Family Structure: A Cohort Analysis', mimeograph (1981).
[33] Cherlin, op. cit. (n. 15), p. 75).
[34] Sussman, op. cit. (n. 8).

There are no legal statutes, common laws, or cultural prescriptions to obligate oneself to be connected with relatives . . . Moreover, one can opt out of the network, but if one remains a member then in time there develop expectations of interpersonal exchange, emotional support, and forms of aid and assistance under various conditions.

As noted earlier, definition of kinship is all the more elusive in an era in which the 'pace of recoupling' is quickening.[35] More couples are getting divorces, the interval between marriage and divorce is dropping, and the interval between divorce and remarriage has shortened. These trends are not only increasing the number and variety of households through which an individual may pass in his/her life course; they are also increasing the number and complexity of the average individual's kinship ties.[36]

The fluid, voluntary nature of kinship ties makes it important to supplement the usual indicators of observed contacts between members of kinship networks—such as type and frequency of contact (e.g. visiting and telephoning), inter-generational wealth transfers,[37] and the exchange of instrumental assistance (house-cleaning, home maintenance, yard work, etc.)[38]—with measures of self-definition and self-report so as to establish the individual's assessment of the quality of the kinship tie. However, these latter—perceptual—measures lend themselves more readily to traditional sociological techniques of data collection than to those typically employed by demographers. Indeed, the bulk of research on kinship networks, and the most innovative ideas about how to study and analyse kinship relations, have so far come from sociologists and social gerontologists.

Demographic Approaches to Kinship in Later Life: What Has Been Done

Demographic approaches to the study of kinship have been of two main types: (i) simulation research in which models are used to establish the parameters of size and composition of family units under various demographic conditions, and (ii) empirical research with census and survey data to describe the present situation of families, households, and kin groups, and to forecast what may happen in the future. Cutting across these approaches have been three major perspectives on the aged and their families: the family life cycle, the life course, and historical investigation of families in particular social and economic

[35] F. F. Furstenberg, G. Spanier, and N. Rothschild, 'Patterns of Parenting in the Transition from Divorce to Remarriage', in Berman and Ramey, op. cit. (n. 16).

[36] Furstenberg *et al.*, op. cit. (n. 35); P. McDonald, 'Can the Family Survive?' *Australian Society*, 1 Dec. 1983; M. W. Riley, 'The Family in an Aging Society: A Matrix of Latent Relationships', *Journal of Social Issues* (1983).

[37] J. C. Caldwell, 'Toward a Restatement of Demographic Transition Theory', *Population and Development Review*, 2(3–4) (1976); M. Moon, 'The Role of the Family in the Economic Well-being of the Elderly', *Gerontologist*, 23(1) (1983).

[38] H. L. Kendig, 'Blood Ties and Gender Roles: Adult Children who Care for Aged Parents', paper presented at the Australian Family Research Conference, Canberra, 1983.

contexts. A review of these approaches and perspectives lays the groundwork for understanding past deficiencies, and demonstrating why new directions are necessary to advance demographic research on this topic.

Main Approaches

Simulation

Simulation was particularly prominent during the 1970s. Its major aim is to study the demographic factors (e.g. nuptiality, fertility, adoption, mortality) that directly determine the size and characteristics of family units. Its means are akin to those of a controlled experiment.

While it is relatively easy to outline the possible factors that influence the structure and composition of families and households, it is difficult to quantify these factors and their likely effects. Three methods are possible, at least theoretically:[39] (i) observation of actual historical events (e.g. the demographic transition), (ii) controlled experimentation with actual events, and (iii) model-building.

While some cohort analyses have been made of the effects of the demographic transition on the potential 'stock of relatives' in old age,[40] the growing literature disclaiming this transition as an explanatory theory[41] illustrates the type of problem encountered in trying to use a particular historical event or process as a general explanation for social change. Given this uncertainty about the use of earlier events, and the fact that controlled experimentation with real populations is clearly not feasible, demographers have turned to model-building as the principal method to estimate what will happen to families and householders when one factor is varied and others held constant.

Simulation, as applied to kin, has two general purposes. The first is to demonstrate what would be the consequences of demographic change for different kin relationships of various kinds: for example, what effect a particular change in mortality would have on the proportions of the aged whose spouses are alive, or what effect a change in age at birth of last child would have on the timing and duration of the 'empty-nest' phase.

The second of these purposes is to establish parameters, to demonstrate the extent of variation that is theoretically possible. For example, Ryder[42] used computer simulations to develop a set of three demographic ideal types with

[39] Bongaarts, op. cit. (n. 22), p. 32.

[40] D. T. Rowland 'Old Age and the Demographic Transition', *Population Studies*, 38(1) (1984).

[41] K. Davis, 'Theory of Change and Response in Modern Demographic History', *Population Index*, 29(4) (1963); Caldwell, op. cit. (n. 37).

[42] N. B. Ryder, 'Reproductive Behaviour and the Family Life Cycle' in United Nations, *The Population Debate: Dimensions and Perspectives. Papers of the World Population Conference, Bucharest, 1974*, vol. ii (New York, 1975).

markedly different patterns of fertility and mortality (two of which—those at the extremes—were designed to be at an equilibrium state with a net reproduction ratio equal to unity) in order to determine the limits of possibility for such kinship relations as the proportion of fathers who would not have a male heir, the length of joint married life, the length of time a child would live within the family setting, and the length of a child's period of family life during which only one parent would be alive. As in other simulations of kin groups[43] the concern was with assessing the availability of kin through looking at the formal kinship structures that might be expected under different hypothetical conditions of fertility and mortality.

A particularly good illustration both of the central focus of family demography on the availability of kin and of the importance of the demographic perspective to issues related to family support in later life is provided by Pullum's[44] model for estimating the frequencies of kin in a stable population with low mortality. Assuming fertility to be at replacement level, he calculates, for example, that eventually about 11 per cent will have no children, 7 per cent will have no siblings, 13 per cent will have no grandchildren, and 12 per cent will have no nieces or nephews. Yet from the standpoint of more extended kin such a population will be rather well covered: more than 98 per cent will have at least one first cousin (with fully one-quarter having ten or more), and virtually no one will be without an aunt or uncle. Nevertheless Pullum, taking migration probabilities into account, conjectured that 'in a stationary population a very large proportion of persons will have no or very few locally available kin in the categories which have traditionally been most important socially'. In terms of social support for the aged, however, what Pullum's model makes clear is the importance of determining to what extent the functions traditionally performed by close kin (spouses, children) may be performed instead by more distant kin, or even non-kin. Sociological studies suggest that a hierarchy of supports operate, depending on available kin and the type and comprehensiveness of the services required.[45] When comprehensive care is needed, spouses are turned to first, then children, siblings, and finally other relatives. But we still have little information about what older people do who have no close or even distant kin.

Empirical research

However intriguing simulations may be, they are, as Ryder himself acknowledges, 'crude over-simplifications'. What is needed are 'hard data

[43] H. Le Bras, 'Parents, grandparents, bisaïeux', *Population*, 28(1) (1973); L. Goodman, N. Keyfitz, and T. W. Pullum, 'Family Formation and Frequency of Various Kinship Relationships', *Theoretical Population Biology*, 5 (1974); T. W. Pullum, 'The Eventual Frequencies of Kin in a Stable Population', *Demography*, 19(4) (1982); N. Goldman, 'Fertility, Mortality, and Kinship', paper presented at the Annual Meeting of the Population Association of America, Minneapolis, 1984.

[44] Pullum, op. cit. (n. 43).

[45] Kendig, op. cit. (n. 9).

concerning real families'.[46] This is what the second demographic approach has sought to provide. To the extent that they have dealt with kinship in the later years, demographers, using empirical approaches, have sought to describe the quantitative aspects of family structure and household composition. They have concerned themselves with, for example, rates of household headship (including the incidence of one-person households), the social and economic characteristics of household heads, and the relationships between heads and other members of the household (i.e. whether that of spouse, child, parent, other kin or non-kin). They have dealt with the incidence and timing of marriage and divorce, and with changes in the composition of the aged population (number, rural–urban status, schooling, nativity, income).[47] The data for these studies have come from censuses, and sometimes from sample surveys.

As with the simulations, there has been no attempt to consider the character of the network relations themselves. These studies are descriptions of present conditions, often with consideration as well of how present conditions differ from those of some previous period, and what they portend for some future period. But, unlike the simulations, such studies present real data on real populations. They are based on actual conditions, not on arbitrary assumptions.

Influential Perspectives

The family life cycle

The family life-cycle perspective dates from at least the mid-1930s, but received a particularly systematic presentation in an article by Glick, published in 1947,[48] which provides a framework for analysis of 'the succession of critical stages' through which the 'typical' family passes during its existence. So far as kin relations in the later years are concerned, the life-cycle perspective has been used mainly by sociologists, who have employed it to explore changing patterns of kinship and their implications for support in old age. Sociologists have, for example, employed the life-cycle perspective to examine the role of the mother–daughter bond in maintaining the flow of support between

[46] Ryder, op. cit. (n. 42).

[47] Cf. e.g. Kobrin, op. cit. (n. 7); P. Uhlenberg, 'Changing Structure of the Older Population', *Gerontologist*, 17 (1977); 'Changing Configurations of the Life Course', in T. K. Hareven (ed.), *Transitions: The Family and the Life Course in Historical Perspective* (New York, 1978); C. Gokalp, 'Le Réseau familial', *Population*, 33(6) (1978); C. H. Mindel, 'Multigenerational Family Households: Recent Trends and Implications for the Future', *Gerontologist*, 19(5) (1979); D. T. Rowland, 'The Vulnerability of the Aged in Sydney', *Australian and New Zealand Journal of Sociology*, 18 (1982).

[48] C. P. Loomis, 'The Study of the Life Cycle of Families', *Rural Sociology*, 1 (1936); P. C. Glick 'The Family Cycle', *American Sociological Review*, 12 (1947); Spanier and Glick, op. cit. (n. 4).

families in separate households, the role of grandparents in the provision of child care, and the effect of the death of a parent or 'other connecting relative' on the strength of ties between siblings.[49]

In a landmark study conducted in the 1960s, Rosenmayr and colleagues[50] used a life-cycle perspective with Austrian families to replicate earlier research which showed that the living arrangement most favoured by the aged and their adult children could be described as 'intimacy—but at a distance'—that is, living in separate households but maintaining frequent contact and exchanging mutual help. Their data indicated that over the life course, while kin move in and out of joint households depending on their circumstances, close relatives tend to stay in touch, and the extended family in industrial societies can be said to maintain flexibility and persistence as a support group performing subsidiary functions for its ageing members. The results of this early Austrian study bears out the findings of surveys before and since[51] that the dominant family structure of the aged today is 'the modified extended family (with its women members as the main binding force), affording the main source of emotional rather than material security for the old, who, nevertheless, wish to preserve a state of semi-autonomy towards it as long as possible'.

With demographers, a major use of the life cycle perspective so far as kinship in the later years is concerned has been to trace the acquisition of close kin through marriage and childbearing, and the loss of close kin through children leaving home and the death of a spouse. Additionally, because a major function of families is to provide people at all ages with meaningful roles in and ties to the wider community, living arrangements (whether living with spouse, alone, with relatives or with non-kin) can provide partial indicators of the extent to which older people are integrated or isolated, and the extent to which they may require supplementary outside support. Demographers have, therefore, also employed the life-cycle perspective with both census and survey data to study living arrangements and household size over the life course in

[49] See the review of these studies in C. Young, *The Family Life Cycle* (Canberra, 1977); M. Young and P. Willmott, *Family and Kinship in East London* (London, 1975); M. F. Nimkoff, 'Changing Family Relationships of Older People in the United States during the last 50 years', in *Social and Psychological Aspects of Aging: Proceedings of the Fifth Congress of the International Association for Gerontology, 1962;* C. Rosser and C. Harris, *The Family and Social Change: A Study of Family and Kinship in a South Wales Town* (London, 1965); J. I. Martin, 'Extended Kinship Ties: An Adelaide Study', *Australian and New Zealand Journal of Sociology* 3(1) (1967); C. Robertson, A. Gilmore and F. I. Caird, 'Demography of the Families of the Elderly in Glasgow', *Health Bulletin*, 33 (1975).

[50] L. Rosenmayr, E. Kotkeis, and A. Kaufmann, 'Intergenerational Relations and Living Arrangements in the Course of the Life Cycle', paper presented at the Sixth International Congress of Gerontology, Copenhagen, 1963.

[51] G. H. Beyer, *Economic Aspects of Housing the Aged* (Ithaca, NY, 1961); E. Shanas, *The Health of Older People: A Social Survey* (Cambridge, Mass., 1962); 'The Family as a Social Support System in Old Age', *Gerontologist*, 19(2) (1979); H. L. Kendig and D. T. Rowland, 'Family Support of the Australian Aged: A Comparison with the United States', *Gerontologist*, 23(6) (1983).

order to look at major family events that precipitate change. Rowland,[52] for example, combined life events, presumably experienced by everyone, with family events, presumably experienced only by married persons, to explore the patterns of living arrangements associated with later life-cycles stages. He described these stages as:

(i) child-launching
(ii) childless pre-retirement
(iii) birth of first grandchild
(iv) death of last parent
(v) retirement
(vi) birth of first great-grandchild
(vii) death of spouse
(viii) disability: locality-bound, house-bound, bed-bound

Life-course perspectives

The life-course perspective, which came into prominence during the mid-1970s, developed in part in response to dissatisfaction with family life-cycle approaches. In Rowland's study of transitions in later life, as with others using this approach, the units of analysis were the family events experienced by individuals who lived within separate and distinct households. Owing to difficulties of measurement cited earlier, family life-cycle researchers have not attempted to trace the interlocking life transitions of networks of kin over the course of a family's life history. During the 1970s, however, a growing number of scholars began to urge experimentation with more complex research designs in order to capture the real complexities of family phenomena. Specific concerns with the life-cycle approach included the fact that (i) the typologies developed to describe the phases of the family life-cycle cannot be applied to all families—families differ in the phases they experience and in the sequence, timing, and arrangement of life events; (ii) conventional typologies have not included some events or phenomena (e.g. cohabitation, childlessness) that are currently assuming greater demographic importance; (iii) conventional family life-cycle phases are historically and culturally idiosyncratic—not generally applicable in different time periods or in different societies.

To address these shortcomings, proponents of the life course recommended:

(i) a *continuous, longitudinal* view of individual and family experience, rather than a 'snapshot' view of family events—frozen, as it were, at a particular stage in family history;
(ii) an emphasis on *transitions*, that is, on life changes that are 'socially recognized, socially structured, and shared',[53] such as the death of

[52] D. T. Rowland, 'Living Arrangements and the Later Family Life Cycle in Australia', *Australian Journal on Ageing*, 1(2) (1982).
[53] O. Hagestad and B. L. Neugarten, 'Age and the Life Course', in Binstock and Shanas, op. cit. (n. 8).

children and parents, entry into grandparenthood, and marital disruption;[54]

(iii) differentiation between the *sequence* or relative position and pattern of life events and the *timing* of events or transitions within the life course as a whole;[55]

(iv) going beyond the conventional nuclear definition of 'family' that excludes by implication, the never-married, the divorced, childless, and remarried; and finally,

(v) consideration of broader cohort effects, such as depression, war, and demobilization.[56]

Recent work by Norton,[57] who used data from a US Census Bureau survey of women's marital and fertility histories conducted in 1980, modifies the traditional family life-cycle approach and incorporates some of the above proposals. Extending life-cycle events to include separation, divorce, and remarriage, his study attaches greater importance to monitoring the frequency and timing of marital dissolution and reconstitution in order to meet the specialized needs of persons and families negotiating these transitions. His findings emphasize the fact that the life course of most Americans now involves many more transitions than in the past, that divorce is projected to end nearly one-half of the marriages of today's young adults, and that, consequently, what once was considered exceptional events in the family life cycle are now viewed as nothing out of the ordinary.

There are several ways in which life-course perspectives can be applied to research on families in later life. They can be used to emphasize the interdependence between family histories and the histories of individual members within a total kinship context that, while changing, remains binding from birth through the death of individual members. They can be used to analyse the different family patterns and kinship structures of successive birth cohorts beginning their life courses at different times and entering old age with different configurations of social and demographic experience,[58] and they can be used to trace the impact of social and environmental changes on the life history of a single individual—with ageing seen as a lifelong process of growing up and growing old, and family relations at each stage in a person's life viewed both as building upon the cumulation of past experience and as forming the basis for future life events.[59]

[54] O. Hagestad, 'Twentieth-century Family Patterns: A Guide for the Twenty-first Century?' paper presented at the Annual Meeting of the Eastern Sociological Society, Boston, Mass., 1984.

[55] G. H. Elder, Jr., 'Family History and the Life Course', in Hareven, op. cit. (n. 47).

[56] G. H. Elder, Jr., *Children of the Great Depression* (Chicago, 1974).

[57] A. J. Norton, 'Family Life Cycle, 1980', *Journal of Marriage and the Family*, 45 (1983).

[58] Uhlenberg, op. cit. (n. 47); Price, op. cit. (n. 32).

[59] M. W. Riley (ed.), *Aging from Birth to Death: Interdisciplinary Perspectives* (Boulder, Colo., 1979); A. T. Day, '*We Can Manage*': *Expectations about Care and Varieties of Family Support Among People* 75 *years of Age and Over* (Melbourne, 1984).

Perspectives from Historical Research

Often in conjunction with life-course perspectives, findings from historical research have provided demographers with bench-marks by which to compare the lives of older people and their families in the changing circumstances of today.[60] Since the early 1970s historians, using a variety of techniques, have amassed a substantial body of data relating to colonial America and pre-twentieth-century Europe concerning demographic aspects of family structure—particularly marriage patterns and the size and composition of households. Historians have also, on occasion, done research that illuminates aspects of the quality of ties between older and younger generations in the past. An example is a study of first-generation settlers in 17th-century Andover, Massachusetts[61] which documents the relations between sons' ages at marriage and their fathers' control over the inheritance of property.

A historical issue of quite some significance to demographers has been determination of the size and kin composition of pre-industrial families. Different views have been advanced on the matter.[62] Confining his study to numbers in the residential household, Levy[63] claimed that the extended family was nowhere predominant. Burch,[64] however, looking at household composition, presented data which showed that though, for example, the average Indian or Nicaraguan household was twice as large as the average American household, the number of 'other relatives' in the average household in the two developing countries was six times as high.

A number of family researchers now claim that the three-generation family has never been very common, even where it was ideal. In answer to a question, for example, about who was living with them when they were ten years old (i.e. between 1901 and 1910), barely 9 per cent of the 1,050 persons aged 60 and over interviewed in the Sydney survey of 1981 mentioned a grandmother, grandfather, or other third-generation relative.[65] Yet the evidence is ambiguous. Contemporary data for Japan and Europe—especially eastern Europe—show high rates of co-residence, particularly in rural areas.[66] In Romania, for example, the proportion residing with offspring is 50 per cent

[60] P. Laslett and R. Wall (eds.), *Household and Family in Past Time* (Cambridge, 1972); T. K. Hareven, 'Introduction: The Historical Study of the Life Course', in Hareven, op. cit. (n. 47).

[61] P. J. Greven, Jr., *Four Generations: Population, Land and Family in Colonial Andover, Massachusetts* (Ithaca, NY, 1978).

[62] K. W. Wachter, E. Hammel, and P. Laslett (eds.), *Statistical Studies of Historical Social Structure* (New York and London, 1978).

[63] M. J. Levy, Jr., 'Aspects of the Analysis of Family Structure', in A. J. Coale *et al.* (eds.), *Aspects of the Analysis of Family Structure* (Princeton, NJ, 1965).

[64] T. K. Burch, 'The Size and Structure of Families: A Comparative Analysis of Census Data', *American Sociological Revew*, 32(3) (1967).

[65] D. T. Rowland, 'Family Structure', in Kendig *et al.*, op. cit. (n. 9), pp. 23–4.

[66] United Nations, *Aging in the Context of the Family* (New York, 1982), p. 8.

among the rural elderly, as against between 10 and 30 per cent among the urban elderly.[67] In Austria, the comparable figure is more than 50 per cent in rural areas, compared with 14 per cent in Vienna.[68]

If questions remain about what proportions of the aged in different countries live in joint households, historical research on the family lives of ordinary people has all but banished the myth of a Golden Age when three generations lived together under one roof, enjoying mutually supportive relations. Instead, historical findings suggest that closeness of bonds between the generations and provision of support to older relatives has gained rather than lost with changes accompanying modernization. Cherlin, for example, sees a connection between 'intimacy—but at a distance', the predominant living arrangements of the aged and their families today, and the strength of bonds between parents and children.[69] Increased income security among the aged is seen to foster financial and residential independence, with—as one possible consequence—the opportunity for old and young to maintain a comfortable distance, and to enjoy relative equality in access to economic resources and the power to determine their own affairs. The low incidence of three-generation households in Australia during the early twentieth century may be attributed partly to the separation of relatives through migration, as well as to lower rates of survival to old age. But then as now, the infrequency of inter-generational co-residence is thought to reflect the pervasive preference among the old for separate households, and the desire to avoid setting up joint living arrangements, unless a crisis (usually precipitated by both physical dependency and low income) leaves a family with no other choice.

Deficiencies in Demographic Approaches

I want now to sum up what I see as significant deficiencies in the demographic approach to the study of kinship in later life. My aim is not to devalue past demographic work, but to consider concerns increasingly raised by statisticians and demographers employed by governments about how to make demographic research and findings more relevant to care for the aged. Sylvia Wargon of Statistics Canada, when presiding over a round table discussion organized by the Population Association of America in 1984 on changing definitions of families and households, stated the position concisely:

[67] A. Ciuca, 'The Elderly and the Family', in G. Dooghe and J. Helander (eds.), *Family Life in Old Age* (The Hague, 1979), p. 49.

[68] J. Horl and L. Rosenmayr, 'Assistance to the Elderly as a Common Task of the Family and Social Services Organizations', *Archives of Gerontology and Geriatrics*, 1 (1982).

[69] A. Cherlin, 'A Sense of History: Recent Research on Aging and the Family', in M. W. Riley, B. Hess, and K. Bond (eds.), *Aging in Society: Selected Reviews of Recent Research* (Hillsdale, NJ, 1983).

With increasing proportions of the elderly in contemporary populations, and with growing numbers of the elderly living alone, there is a need to conceptualize the family and family membership in terms of networks, that is, using a definition that goes beyond the classic standard concept of 'residential unit'. A compelling reason for this (to cite only one example) is the need to determine existing, private support systems available to a nation's elderly prior to developing public policy, and estimating or earmarking the resources required for health and housing facilities, nursing and other care for aging populations.

From the standpoint, then, of increasing knowledge about the aged and their sources of informal support (family, friends, and neighbours), three general deficiencies in past approaches can be discerned: first, the concept of kinship has been too narrow; secondly, the focus has been on the aged as a category of need rather than as part of a complex network of interacting relationships; and, thirdly, the research orientation has been largely confined to the more formal quantitative dimensions of kinship structure, with little attention being paid to either the functions kin perform, or the dimensions of family support. These three deficiencies are interrelated and reinforce one another.

If we view kinship as a network, we have to extend our concept of family beyond the household to include a variety of family types apart from the elementary nuclear form. We also have to see relations between the aged and their kin as systems involving exchange of help between two parties—the recipients of care and the providers of care. And if we are interested in kinship networks not just in terms of structural dimensions but in terms of their potential for social support, we need to employ the orientations and techniques that other social scientists have used in their research on families as support systems.

Too Narrow a Concept of 'Family'

Enlarging on the first point, we have claimed that the concept of a nuclear family sharing a common household distorts the realities of today's older families, and is an inappropriate framework with which to study kinship networks in later life. To work with a concept of 'family' defined as persons related by blood and residing in the same household is certainly to simplify the complexity of ties between members of modern kin groups, and to risk creating misconceptions about the kinds of function kinship networks perform in meeting the varied needs of their older members.

This claim is based on two kinds of evidence. The first is the extensive work by sociologists and social gerontologists documenting the fact that in today's industrial societies a dominant form of family organization may be described as 'the modified extended family', consisting of persons related by blood, maintaining separate households, but keeping in close touch and exchanging a variety of informal services.[70] Despite the fact that increasing numbers of persons aged 65 and over live alone rather than in family settings (in the USA, the proportion living alone was 14.4 per cent in 1950 and 30 per cent in 1980), the old are not isolated individuals but members of family networks. It has been shown in surveys we have described here that when an older person needs help to remain living at home, support is provided by family members, usually daughters. Even among the 'oldest-old' (those aged 85 years and over), fewer than one-quarter are in institutions and only 11.3 per cent live with children.[71] Given the modest use of non-family home help services by the aged, paradoxically the trend away from living with children (even among the population aged 85 and older) is a powerful argument for developing a concept of 'family' that extends beyond the household.

A second reason for moving toward a network concept of family is the growing body of research which shows that the nuclear family form is itself undergoing extensive change. Although still the most prominent form, and the form most people in Western industrial societies consider ideal, the nuclear family is for increasing numbers of individuals becoming only one of several possible family types they experience over a lifetime. Other types—cohabitation, childlessness, one-person households, single-parent and reconstituted families, for example— are all becoming more common. Moreover, trends in patterns of family formation and dissolution have increased both the number of life transitions an average individual will experience and the pace at which these take place. Cherlin and Furstenberg,[72] on the basis of data for the USA, estimated that

> about half of the young children alive today will spend some time in a single-parent family before they reach 18; about nine out of ten will eventually marry; about one in two will marry and then divorce, about one in three will marry, divorce, and then remarry. In contrast, only about one in six women born between 1910 and 1914 married and divorced, and only about one in eight married, divorced, and remarried.

This greater variety in family settings has led to more families extending over two or more households, and to more families with kinship ties of greater complexity than is the case with families formed by first marriages only.

Family research has tended to focus on the effect of such changes on parents and children in the early phases of the family life cycle. Yet a 'family ripple

[70] E. Shanas and G. Treib (eds.), *Social Structure of the Family: Generational Relations* (Englewood Cliffs, NJ, 1965); E. Shanas *et al.*, *Old People in Three Industrial Societies* (New York, 1968); J. Treas, 'Family Support Systems for the Aged', *Gerontologist*, 17 (1977); Kendig *et al.*, op. cit. (n. 9); A. Horowitz 'US Public Policy on Family Support of the Aged: Current Trends and Reported Preferences of Family Caregivers', paper presented at the Annual Conference of the National Council on the Aging, Washington, 1984; B. Wellman and A. Hall, 'Social Networks and Social Support: Implications for Later Life', in V. Marshall and T. Harris (eds.), *Later Life: A Microsociology* (Norwood, NJ).

[71] G. Collins, 'First Portrait of the Very Old: Not so Frail', *New York Times*, 3 Jan. 1985.

[72] A. Cherlin and F. F. Furstenberg, Jr., *The Shape of the American Family in the Year 2000* (Washington, DC, 1982), p. 6.

effect' of divorce and remarriage can have implications for kinship structure and family relations in later phases of the life cycle as well, with those who are both the parents of divorcing couples and the grandparents of these couples' children also being affected.[73] Riley[74] observes, in association with extensions in the life span (particularly for women), that such trends as rising rates of divorce and remarriage have transformed the extent and configuration of kinship networks in later life, prolonging linkages between family members and increasing the number and complexity of generations within the family.

Focus on the Aged as Recipients of Care

A second major deficiency in the demographic approach is the tendency to focus on the aged as recipients of care, to the neglect of the wider kin network of care-providers. Trends in mortality leading to an increasing life span have important implications for the health and potential for dependency of the very old, and also for the health and capacity to furnish support by the younger old, those in their late 50s and 60s, who will increasingly have to shoulder responsibility for providing care. Writing about the process by which the aged 'sort themselves among the array of household types available to them', Wolf[75] concluded,

> A major further advance in our understanding of the process would be gained if data were available which provided measures not only of the financial and health circumstances of the elderly, and of the pattern of living arrangements available to them, but of the financial and health circumstances of these available kin as well.

The need to focus on the circumstances of kin in determining potential support is highlighted by studies that explore the impact of increasing life span and of women's labour force participation on the structure of home care. Together these two trends increase the demand for care among potential recipients and lower the capacity to give care among the potential providers. Longer life is resulting in substantial increases in that very category of the population who by reason of age are most vulnerable to disability and to dependence on outside help. A significantly higher proportion of the 'very old' are unable to carry out at least one activity important to self-maintenance without substantial personal assistance: in the USA, for example, 22 per cent of those aged 75 years and over were thus restricted, compared with 15 per cent among those aged 65 to 74, and half that proportion (7 per cent) in the age group 45 to 65.[76]

Intersecting with this increase in the likely need for home care is the

[73] Hagestad, op. cit. (n. 17).
[74] Riley, op. cit. (n. 36).
[75] D. A. Wolf, 'Kin Availability and the Living Arrangements of Older Women', *Social Science Research*, 13 (1984).
[76] US Senate Special Committee on Aging in Conjunction with the American Association of Retired Persons, *Aging America: Trends and Projections* (Washington, DC, 1984), p. 61.

extensive employment of women outside the home in mid-life: in the USA 60 per cent of women between the ages of 45 and 54 now work, and 42 per cent of those aged 55 to 64.[77] The study mentioned earlier of three generations of American women[78] shows, moreover, that a substantial proportion of these women have responsibilities for children as well as for an older parent, thus creating the modern phenomenon of 'women in the middle', that is, women, who traditionally have been the major providers of care for the aged at home, facing competing demands from children and outside employment. Brody *et al.* conclude:[79] 'Although there is no evidence to suggest erosion in family help to elderly parents, these powerful trends could disrupt that flow of assistance.'

Finally, a focus on the aged as recipients of care overlooks the important fact that many of the most important providers of care themselves are 'old'. In the Sydney Survey of 1981 it was shown that most disabled spouses rely primarily on a husband or wife, who takes over more of the household tasks.[80] Due to the greater longevity of women and the fact that men tend to marry women who are younger than themselves, most of those providing primary care to spouses are wives, and most carry the load with little outside help. Apart from spouses, this Australian study found that among the women who provided the bulk of household help and personal care, 28 per cent were already aged over 60 themselves, and 23 per cent were in their 50s.[81] A growing literature testifies to the emotional strain and physical demands of care-giving superimposed on the stresses older women already face in coming to terms with their own ageing and all its attendant changes. Many of these carers need help and support as much as do the spouses and parents they are looking after.[82] The health and quality of life of support-providers is inextricably interwoven with (and hence of equal importance in policy terms to) the health and quality of life of aged support-recipients.

Focus on Formal Structure and Neglect of Actual Behaviour

Closely related to these is a third deficiency in the demographic approach to kinship in the later years: the tendency to overlook what is really going on among members of kinship networks. This can lead to defining the support potential of kin in terms of numbers of close relatives, thereby obscuring both

[77] Brody *et al.*, op. cit. (n. 20).
[78] Ibid.
[79] Ibid, p. 737.
[80] H. L. Kendig, 'The Providers of Care', in Kendig *et al.*, op. cit. (n. 9), p. 134.
[81] Ibid., p. 151.
[82] A. Fengler and N. Goodrich, 'Wives of Elderly Disabled Men: The Hidden Patients', *Gerontologist*, 19 (1979); A. Horowitz and R. Dobrof, 'The Role of Families in Providing Long-term Care to the Frail and Chronically Ill Elderly Living in the Community', Final Report submitted to the Health Care Financing Administration, US Department of Health and Human Services, May 1982; D. Kinnear and C. Rossiter, 'Family Care Policies: Findings from a Survey of Carers', paper presented at the Australian Family Research Conference, Canberra, 23–5 Nov. 1983.

the limits to the care-giving capacities of kin, and the possibility that, under certain circumstances (e.g. when an older person is childless or close kin are not available) important assistance may be provided by more distant kin, or even by non-kin. Having even a close relative available in a demographic sense is no guarantee that help will be forthcoming in the amount and kind necessary to provide long-term care at home. In emphasizing the strictly formal aspects of kinship structure (such as size, composition, and living arrangements) demographers may be overlooking significant questions about the way kinships operate, and the nature of support flows in later life: what functions are being performed, by whom? meeting what kinds of needs? under what circumstances?

Serendipitous Findings about the Aged and their Family Networks

The findings we have presented here reveal a number of anomalies surrounding the exchange of help between the aged and their kin that make the task of assessing support potential much more complex than a simple count of close relatives would imply:

(i) *Living arrangements.* Though the trend (even among the oldest old) is away from parents living with children, emotional bonds and the flow of help between generations seems no less strong.

(ii) *Attitudes toward help—preferences for care.* Members of the younger generation show greater willingness to assume responsibility for care than older parents want from them. The oldest generation is most receptive to formal services, the youngest most in favour of family care.

(iii) *Dual roles of the aged—recipients and providers of care.* Persons aged 60 and older (especially women) are as likely to be providing support as to be on the receiving end.

(vi) *Impact of demographic trends on family support available in later life.* Despite the appearance of instability, the increase in family settings created by higher rates of divorce, re-marriage, and family reconstitution—in combination with lengthening life span—may be increasing the duration and durability of family support of the aged.

These 'anomalies' (as I have called them) represent irregularities in our expectations about the aged and their family support that require deeper probing to find an explanation. All four argue for extending the concept of family as household to a broader concept of family as network, in which persons related by blood live in separate residential units and exchange emotional and practical support.

New Directions

These considerations point to a major research issue for demographers interested in families in later life—how to conceptualize and measure kinship networks as both structures and ties of obligation involving informal exchange of help. In this last section I will offer some suggestions about how to proceed, and the kinds of data needed to move in the directions I have proposed. Many of these recommendations are already in the field or being discussed by demographers or other scholars working in the area of family research. These proposals reflect my view that—at this juncture—the demography of kinship networks in later life will be advanced more by 'social' than by 'formal' approaches.

Use of 'First-class' Fieldwork

In the context of research approaches to fertility decline in developing countries, Caldwell[83] has written that first-class fieldwork is needed to define the extent of kin tied by reciprocal obligations, to identify specific aspects of the inter-generational transfer of resources, and to learn how such transfers are affected by specific demographic trends. By the same token, I would suggest that to avoid moving from models of formal structure to assumptions about the implications of these models for actual behaviour, demographers need to conduct first-class fieldwork with the aged and their families in modern industrial societies.

Fieldwork I have conducted in Australia shows the value of small-scale, intensive studies to fill in the gaps and provide information not likely to be obtained by larger, more quantitative, survey methods.[84] The research design—follow-up interviews with 23 persons aged 75 years and over, selected from the earlier survey of 1,050 persons aged 60 and over living in Sydney—enabled me to integrate qualitative data from in-depth, semi-structured interviews with quantitative data from the larger survey. The detailed life histories of men and women, matched on selected individual and social attributes, provided information about kinship ties and the varieties of support they provide. More than the less probing survey, the follow-up study revealed that relations between support and kin are complex and highly differentiated. Not all family relations were supportive. Some respondents were depending on sporadic help from neighbours and friends, rather than ask for more regular assistance from family and community services. One-third of the persons I interviewed felt that their families were not available to provide help either in the short run for household tasks or in the longer run for more comprehensive personal care. The reasons given were family break-up, children too far away, and the strong belief that children should lead lives of their own. Rather than let their children 'do' for them, these older Australians—almost to a person—declared 'We can manage', and said they preferred to 'battle on' until disability or death overtook them.

[83] Caldwell, op. cit. (n. 37).
[84] Day, op. cit. (n. 59).

The number I interviewed was small, and I did not employ formal network analysis. However, I believe my results show that looking at policy issues for the aged in terms of the stock of available kin (measured in terms of number of surviving relatives), and living arrangements (measured in terms of the older persons' household composition) generates a constricted data base and misconceptions about the real nature of the aged's social support.[85]

Fuller Cross-Tabulation of Data Already Collected

We can improve and extend census data by making fuller, more detailed cross-tabulations of data already collected, especially on (i) the socio-economic characteristics of household heads and (ii) the relationships of household members to household heads. More detailed census information is desirable in order to take account of the great diversity of circumstances among the aged and their families associated with different socio-economic categories (e.g. sex, race, national origin, income, health status, age, and phase of the life cycle). More detailed information is also needed to study the impact of demographic trends on the kinship networks of sub-groups, such as aged blacks in the USA, whose well-documented and marked differences from whites in marital, fertility, and mortality patterns during the earlier phases of the life course would imply marked differences in family patterns during the later phases as well.

Incorporation of Cohort and Life-Course Perspectives

We need to explore the impact of social change on various aspects of inter-generational relations and demands for supplementary social support. For example, since substantial work-force experience is more common among women now entering their 50s than among those now entering their 70s, we would do well to study the likelihood that members of future cohorts of aged women may have had fewer opportunities to forge reciprocal helping arrangements with their daughters, that they may have higher expectations for material comfort in their later years, and that they will expect to do less of the housework themselves, preferring to pay for services rather than rely on the unpaid assistance of their middle-aged daughters, who in all probability will themselves be employed in full-time jobs. Information of this sort about

[85] Wellman and Hall, op. cit. (n. 70). The authors argue for a more detailed study of actual kinship ties and the kinds of support they provide. 'Policy makers can no longer assume that all ties are broadly supportive, or that all community networks are local and solidary. The trick is to recognize the differentiated nature of networks and supportive resources in contemporary societies and to develop ways of utilizing their more specialized and more flexible divisions of labor. Epidemiological studies of social categories—such as gender and occupation—will at best give only proxy measures of access to informal health care resources. It makes a lot more sense to study the social networks themselves and the societal factors which differentially allocate access to resources in social systems.'

differences between aged populations would be an effective check on the tendency to make assumptions about the needs of future aged cohorts—and the availability of close relatives to meet those needs—on the basis of the family circumstances and support systems of the contemporary aged.

Collection of Data on Relationships Pertaining Specifically to the Later Years of Life

Going beyond investigation of a 'family ripple effect' on later life of marital and fertility patterns in earlier phases of the life cycle, we need to gather more information specifically about the important transitions and social relations associated with the post-retirement years. These include:

(i) retirement of spouse and self;
(ii) losses of kin, friends and neighbours through migration and death;
(iii) part-time work, paid and unpaid, for both men and women;
(iv) participation in further education and training;
(v) involvement in voluntary organizations, churches, and social clubs.

We need to view people in the post-retirement years as continuing to be employed and productive members of society, and to study the new ways in which their activities and life-styles put them in touch with a non-kin network. The new relationships older people form and the functions exchanged in these relationships need to be examined in terms of how they influence and intersect with older people's family relationships. Particular note needs to be taken of differences between men and women, and between the young-old and the old-old, in both the balance of kin and non-kin and the impact of the changing health and family circumstances of descendent kin on the support they provide, or might provide, to ascendent kin.

Collaboration with Researchers in Other Disciplines

Finally, cutting across these other four is the need to develop greater collaboration with researchers conducting micro-studies focused on specific aspects of inter-generational relations in specific social contexts. This is necessary to identify ways in which kinship networks both influence and are influenced by specific demographic trends, such as the effect on occupational choice and job mobility of being an only child responsible for care of a frail aged parent, or the effect of caring for an ailing grandparent (or great-grandparent) on one's own expectations about bearing children in order to provide security for oneself in old age.

Overall, the long-range research goal is to develop ways to analyse kinship as a system of interlocking ties instead of treating relations between the generations as matters of simple dyads or aggregates, and in the process losing the concept of family as network. To obtain data appropriate to this more complex sort of analysis we need interdisciplinary collaboration to explore new methods of observation, new techniques of statistical analysis, and a wider variety of research designs. And notwithstanding what we have said earlier about 'formal' demography, new models will be required to estimate the consequences for kinship structure and inter-generational support in later life of such increasingly common family forms as cohabitation, childlessness, second and subsequent marriages, and reconstituted families.

11 Changes in the Life-Space during the Final Stages

MICHEL POULAIN
Université Catholique de Louvain

> The old stay put
> Their faces are wrinkled
> Their world is small
> From bed to window
> Then from bed to armchair
> And in the end from bed to bed.
>
> *Jacques Brel*

Introduction

An individual's life-space, in the spatial and social sense, consists of the places he or she visits and of the persons he or she meets. It describes his field of activity, that part of physical and social space with which he or she interacts. The strength of each of these interactions may be measured in different ways: frequency, duration, strength of the affective bond, etc. The set of life-spaces of different individuals is an enormous network of relationships, a network which has recently attracted the interest of research workers.[1] We shall be particularly interested in the place taken by relations with kin in this network, because such relationships, by reason of their strength, can normally be distinguished from others.

In addition to looking at the life-spaces of individuals, it would also be possible to consider a 'family life-space'. In the narrow sense this would consist of the intersection of the life-spaces of each member of a family. In a larger sense, it would be the union of the set of individual life-spaces. During the later stages of life, an individual's life-space diminishes and relations with other members of the family are also reduced in number, so that the two definitions tend to coincide. During the last stages of life, when the family is often reduced to a single person, the identity between the two definitions becomes trivially true. Changes in the life-space during the later stages of life form the object of this study. Our approach will be strictly exploratory, and we make no claim that our conclusions are generally true.

[1] Cf. the reference given in nn. 2–7, and particularly the work by Courgeau cited in n. 3 and the survey at present being conducted by INSEE (n. 2).

Sources of Data for Studying the Life Space

As we have defined it, a family life-space can only be studied by means of special surveys which must inevitably be complex, so that different approaches—demographic, ethnological and sociological—can be combined. According to François Heran this task has not yet been successfully accomplished.[2]

Limiting ourselves to studies conducted in France, the following may be mentioned:

Courgeau's study of the network of relations between individuals in town and countryside;[3]

Catherine Gokalp's study of families[4] based on a sample of 3075 individuals aged between 45 and 64 years;

a study undertaken by Louis Roussel and Odile Bourguignon[5] dealing with the relationships between different generations of family members after the marriage of members of the younger generation;

a survey of wage-earners in the private sector on the eve of retirement by Paul Paillat and Christiane Delbes;[6]

a study by Daniel Courgeau and Benoît Riandey[7] in which special attention was given to the interactions between family history and geographical and occupational mobility;

a study conducted for INSEE by François Heran which deals with interpersonal contacts. This study was based on a sample consisting of some 8,000 persons interviewed in 1982 and 1983, but its results have not yet been published.

In view of the nature of the problems investigated, it is the last-mentioned study which is of greatest interest to us. The sample was representative, the elderly were not excluded, and the questionnaire sought information on relations with kin, neighbours, and friends. During the later stages of life, relations with neighbours and friends may increasingly take the place of

[2] F. Heran, 'Cycle de vie et cycle des relations de parent', *Les Ages de la vie* (Paris, 1982).

[3] D. Courgeau, 'Les Réseaux de relations entre personnes: Étude d'un milieu rural', *Population*, 4–5 (1972); 'Les Réseaux de relations entre personnes: Étude d'un milieu urbain', *Population*, 1975 (2).

[4] C. Gokalp, 'Le Réseau familial', *Population*, 1978 (6).

[5] L. Roussel (with O. Bourguignon), *La Famille après le mariage des enfants* (Paris, 1976).

[6] P. Paillat, 'La Famille des salariés du secteur privé à la veille de la retraite, I: Le Réseau familial', *Population*, 1983 (3); C. Delbes, La Famille des salariés du secteur privé à la veille de la retraite, II: Les Relations familiales', *Population*, 1983 (6).

[7] B. Riandey, 'L'Enquête biographie familiale, professionnelle et migratoire, *Actes de la Chaire Quetelet, 1983*; D. Courgeau, 'Analysis of French Migration, Family and Occupation History Survey', *Materialien zur Bevölkerungswissenschaft*.

relations within the family. Answers given to the individual questionnaires in which all contacts between the respondent and other persons were noted over a period of one week should provide an indication of the respondent's universe or life space. However, the information collected relates to a single point in time, whereas we would have preferred a longitudinal approach. There are two ways of overcoming this difficulty. First, questions about the past could be included in the questionnaire so that the situations at different points in the family's life could be compared. But answers to such questions may turn out to be biased, because of recall lapse and retrospective rationalization of behaviour; situations and relationships which existed in the past may not be mentioned for a variety of reasons, and at the stages of life in which we are interested, mortality may introduce a distortion. This could only be avoided by a multi-round survey which would have to be taken every five or ten years, if significant changes in the family's life were to be detected. Such surveys are both difficult and costly. Another possibility exists, provided all age groups are represented in the sample. Synthetic cohorts could be constructed which would summarize the experience of different age groups at the same point in time. But this method does not solve the difficulties introduced by mortality, and would give distorted results. A representative longitudinal study of family life space is not yet possible, because not only are individuals removed from observation through mortality at later stages of life but the family life-space of other members of the family is also reduced to a significant degree and so, therefore, is total family life-space.

There are two other sources which can be used to study our problem, but they provide limited results compared with surveys: simulation and vital statistics. They have two major advantages: both are normally based on a large number of observations so that sampling error is reduced. Moreover, both take account of mortality and are not subject to bias because of the mortality factor. The family cycle and transition probabilities between different stages of this cycle can be reconstructed by simulation, on the macro-scale through analytical models and on the micro-scale by Monte Carlo methods. These methods also make it possible to trace changes in the kin available to individuals of different ages.[8] Vital statistics are of two kinds: census data, which yield the structure of the population by age and marital status, and which can also be used to describe family nuclei by their characteristics, and annual statistics, which give numbers of specific events such as deaths or moves.[9] Spanning these two types are continuous registration data, which allow us to look at families at different stages of their life cycle. These last are a valuable source of information, but have been

[8] J. Bongaarts, 'Simulation of the Family Life Cycle', *Proceedings of the International Population Conference, Manila, 1981* (Liège, 1981), vol. iii; H. Le Bras, 'Evolution des liens de famille au cours de l'existence: Une comparaison entre la France actuelle et la France du XVIIIe siècle', *Les Ages de la vie* (n. 2).

[9] They also give figures for divorces and remarriages which we shall not consider here.

relatively little used because they are available only for a relatively small number of countries.

From Theoretical Models of Kinship to Observed Family Relationships

The micro-simulation approach developed by Le Bras[10] makes it possible to reconstitute the kin available to each individual as a function of his or her age. In Table 11.1, which is taken from Le Bras's work, we show the average number of kin up to the second degree of kinship (excluding relatives by marriage) which are available to individuals aged respectively 50, 65, and 80 years in the contemporary French population. The total available kin is reduced by 30 per cent between the ages of 50 and 80; however, less than 10 per cent of this reduction occurs between the ages of 50 and 65. These theoretical figures may be compared with actual figures obtained by Catherine Gokalp (see Table 11.2).[11] We show figures which are comparable: the theoretical value for 50-year-olds is compared with the mean values obtained for the age groups 45–50 and 50–5, that for 65-year-olds with the value observed for the age group 60–5.

Table 11.1 Mean number of kin by degree of kinship and age of individual[a]

Degree of kinship	Individual's age (yrs.)		
	50	65	80
Children	2.05	2.00	1.87
Grandchildren	1.72	4.71	4.94
Siblings	1.87	1.57	0.78
Parents	0.90	0.12	0.00
Grandparents	0.01	0.00	0.00
Uncles/aunts	2.10	0.41	0.01
Nephews/nieces	4.62	4.53	4.25
Cousins	8.00	6.45	3.22
TOTAL	21.47	19.79	15.08

[a] Obtained by simulation—cf. Le Bras, op. cit. (n. 8), p. 35.

The two results are not very different, except as regards the number of grandchildren. Le Bras's simulation approach also yields a distribution of numbers of available kin, and leads him to conclude that 2 per cent of individuals aged 80 will have no available kin. As far as we know this figure has not been empirically verified; however, similarities in the demographic

[10] Op. cit. (n. 8).
[11] Op. cit. (n. 4), p. 1082.

Table 11.2 Available: comparison of numbers obtained by Le Bras by simulation methods and by Gokalp's actual observation

	50 Simulation	45–50/50–5 Survey	65 Simulation	60–5 Survey
Children	2.05	2.45	2.00	2.27
Parents	0.90	0.90	0.12	0.16
Grandchildren	1.72	0.76	4.71	3.14
Siblings	1.87	2.03	1.57	1.82
Nephews/nieces	4.62	4.14	4.53	4.76
TOTAL	11.16	10.28	12.93	12.15

behaviour of different generations of the same family point to the fact that the variance observed may be greater than the theoretical variance, and that the actual proportion may be substantially higher than Le Bras's estimate of 2 per cent.

However, the number of 'available kin' is not necessarily a good indicator of kinship ties. There are many obstacles which reduce the number of contacts between persons who are related, or which may do away with them altogether. Two principal factors which explain this reduction are respectively demographic (differences in age) and spatial (the distance separating the residences of family members).

Most relations with kin are between persons of similar ages who belong to the same generation. Whenever the difference between an individual's age and the average age of his kin increases, the level of contacts is reduced by rather more than the 30 per cent which is suggested by the simulation. The results of the simulation make it possible to compare age differences between individuals and their kin where the individual is 50 and 65 years old respectively. For individuals aged 80 the double peak of the distribution which corresponds to kin of the same generation is even less marked; the figures in Table 11.1 show that the mean number of kin of the same generation is 9.87 for individuals aged 50, 8.02 for those aged 65, and only 4.00 for those aged 80. The proportion that kin of the same generation are of all kin is reduced from 46 per cent for individuals aged 50 to 27 per cent for those aged 80.

The geographical distance between an individual and his or her kin also strongly affects the strength of kinship ties. As an example we can consider the relation between the place of residence of parents and that of their married children, and compare the results obtained by Gokalp[12] with those of Roussel[13] and with those in our own survey at Fosses-la-Ville (see Table 11.3).[14] Even though the distances which separate parents and married

[12] Op. cit. (n. 4), p. 1087.
[13] Op. cit. (n. 5), p. 28.
[14] J. Duchêne and M. Poulain, 'Interaction de la mobilité résidentielle et du cycle de vie des individus et des ménages', in *Les Ages de la vie*, op. cit. (n. 2).

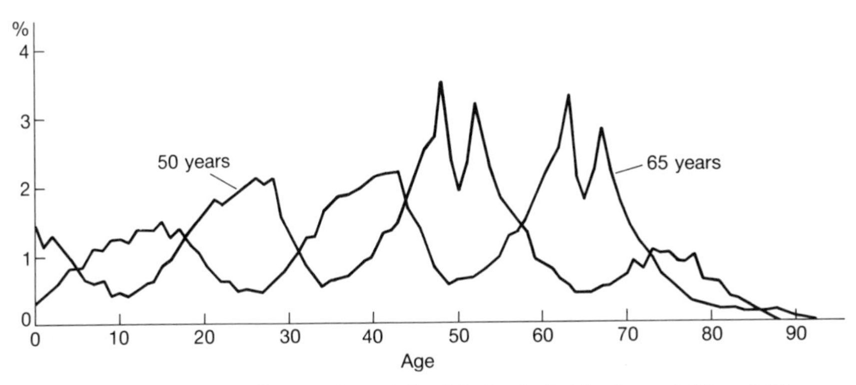

Fig. 11.1 Distribution of ages of surviving kin for individuals aged 50 and 65. *Source:* Le Bras, op. cit. (n. 8).

children appear larger in France than in Belgium, in all three cases between 30 and 40 per cent of married children live near their parents. Roussel has shown that the type of contact varies with distance: where both parties live in the same commune there are short daily visits, where the distance does not exceed 20 km. visits tend to be weekly, and where the distance is greater, short visits or holiday visits tend to be more frequent. As might have been expected, it is not possible to conclude that the strength of relationships is affected by distance, as the criteria are difficult to quantify. Overall, however, because of the impact of the geographical distribution of available kin and the reduction in the number of contacts as distance increases, the distribution of the number of contacts with kin, according to Courgeau,[15] is a decreasing Pareto distribution—a tenfold increase in distance reduced the number of contacts by a factor of 40.

Table 11.3 Distances between place of residence of parents and their married children found in three different surveys (per cent)

Survey	Under the same roof	In the same commune	0–20 km.	20–100 km.	100+ km.
Gokalp	3	24	24	21	27
Roussel	4	26	23	18	28
Duchêne/Poulain	3	39	36	14	4

However, the principal reasons for a reduction in the number of contacts with kin are psychological and social. Tensions between members of different generations, or between members of the same generation, caused by differences in behaviour or temperament or by social or educational mobility,

[15] Op. cit. (1977) (n. 3).

may result in barriers to contacts, even when age differences are small and the parties live near each other. This aspect of family relationships is too vast a subject to be treated here, but we may cite two examples from our own survey which show how great a gap can exist between theoretically available kin and effective relations between them.

The first example relates to two married brothers, one of whom is childless, the other with a married daughter. Both couples are in their seventies and have not had any social contact for a period of nearly forty years because of a dispute about inheritance. The two families completely ignore one another, even though they live in adjoining houses and their front yards are separated only by a low wall and a shrub of lilac. The second case is that of a woman and her daughter who continued to manage the family farm for ten years after the death of the husband. The daughter, who was 40 years old, became friendly with a man from an adjoining parish but, contrary to her mother's wishes, did not wish to marry him. Continuing disagreement between the mother and daughter led to the mother being battered by her daughter and, at the age of 69, forced to enter an old people's home. Since then she has lost contact completely not only with her daughter, but also with her son and her grandchildren.

It should be emphasized that these social and psychological factors are not independent of those that we have mentioned earlier. Louis Roussel has shown[16] that tensions between parents and their married children are reduced the further apart they live from each other. The two examples we have cited show the difference that may exist between simulation results based on theory and effective family relationships in all their variety, about which information can only be obtained through a complete survey, such as the one conducted by INSEE.

A Dynamic View of the Development of Life-space

It seems reasonable to expect that the most valuable results would be obtained by looking at individual and family life-space from a dynamic and longitudinal perspective. Simulation can only provide average values which change slowly with age. Information obtained from surveys relates to a given moment in time, and any attempt to convert this information into a longitudinal form is beset with difficulties, arising mainly from the effects of mortality. Does it, therefore, follow that any attempt to characterize an individual's life-space during the later stages of his or her life is bound to fail? We would not accept this pessimistic point of view, and we have therefore attempted an exploratory investigation in which the data come from three sources: an interview in which questions about an individual's past are included, national population statistics, and local population registers.

[16] Op. cit. (n. 5).

Information about the changes which have occurred in a family's life space may be obtained from answers to questions put in an interview. The first major change occurs with the departure of children. After their move from the parental home to live their own lives, most frequently because of marriage, relations between parents and children change fundamentally. As Roussel and Bourguignon put it: 'One is always at home with one's parents, but never with one's children.' In some cases, the change occurs suddenly and the shock may lead to a complete rupture of relations between the families concerned. If we exclude these cases, we find that there is generally an adjustment, ideally a progressive adjustment, of the life-space with changes in the type and intensity of relationships. The decline in relationships between close kin is often compensated by new friendships, which explicitly replace the former relationships with children and which are facilitated by the activities which are available to the elderly. If no such new relations are formed, this may lead to hardship for the couple and affect their mental and physical health. However, the majority of couples adjust their life-space to the new situation. The death of a spouse, on the other hand, generally leads to much greater disruption. The bond between two spouses cannot be replaced. Even when the network of other relationships with members of the family and with friends is maintained, the emptiness caused by the loss of a spouse cannot be filled. The life-space is now completely different, and in Jacques Brel's words, 'the survivor remains in hell'. Where the survivor lives alone, moral or physical dependency may cause him or her to move residence soon after being widowed; the decision to move may be the survivor's own, or that of his relations. Such a move often leads to a complete change in the survivor's life, both as regards the physical dimensions of his or her life-space and relationships. A third factor which may transform an individual's life-space is the sometimes brutal transition from independence to a state of physical or moral dependency. An illness or a surgical operation may cause such transition for an individual or even a couple from one day to the next. There are generally two alternatives: to move in with one's children or to enter an old people's home. This move, which is often the last move in a person's lifetime, has a very considerable impact on the life-space. Habits which have been formed over a long period must be abandoned, long-standing relationships must be severed because of distance and because the individual has become less mobile. In these final stages of life, the life-space is dramatically reduced.

This qualitative study at individual level is supplemented by a quantitative approach to complete the picture. Unfortunately, the wealth of individual information is in stark contrast to the paucity of aggregative data. Census figures classify individuals in terms of the family nucleus within which they live. In Table 11.4 we show information about the Walloon population of Belgium, taken from the Census of 1981, showing the proportionate distribution of ever-married persons aged 60 and over by type of residence separately for each sex. From data available in the national register (a centralized and computerized register of the whole population) it is possible to obtain information about the moves of people who are 50 years old or older. Replies to questions put in the interview have shown that moves of elderly persons greatly affect their life-space. In Figure 11.2 migration rates between different communes in Belgium are shown for individuals of different ages, and it is evident that moves among the older population have increased significantly, particularly among persons aged 70 and over. These recent data, which relate to the period 1979–82 and cover the whole Belgian population, make it quite clear that there has been an almost linear increase in mobility which, for women between the ages of 70 and 90 years may be put at 150 per cent. The level is virtually the same for men of that age. Mobility rates are lowest throughout life at about the age of 70 years.

Table 11.4 Distribution of the Walloon population, aged 60 and over, at the Census of 1981 by family situation (per 1,000)

Age		Married	Widowed, living alone	Widowed, living with family	Widowed, in old people's homes
60–4	M	936	34	30	1
	F	709	173	116	1
	All	814	109	92	1
65–9	M	891	64	43	2
	F	571	288	137	4
	All	711	190	96	3
70–4	M	818	115	61	6
	F	418	398	173	12
	All	575	287	129	10
75–9	M	707	179	102	12
	F	271	474	224	31
	All	425	370	181	24
80–4	M	547	258	165	30
	F	153	481	300	66
	All	274	412	259	55
85–9	M	397	294	250	59
	F	82	427	370	120
	All	168	391	337	104
90+	M	224	301	373	103
	F	35	318	467	180
	All	83	314	443	160

Source: Institut National de Statistique, Brussels.

As long as both members of a couple remain alive and at least one of them is physically healthy, a move is not necessary. But after the age of 70, when the proportion of married persons in the population is reduced considerably, migration rates increase. As husbands are generally older than their wives, and the mortality rates of men exceed those of women, there are more widows than widowers and this explains the very marked increase in the mobility rates of

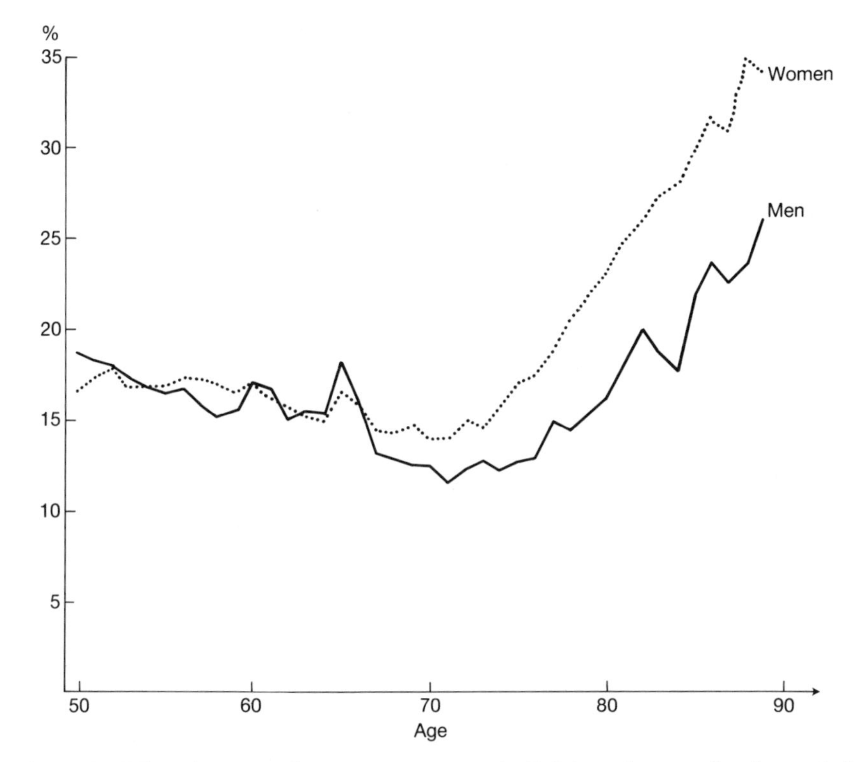

Fig. 11.2 Migration rates between communes in Belgium, by sex, for the period 1979–1982.
Source: Registre National de Population

women after that age. We would expect that mobility rates of widowed persons would exceed those of married persons of the same age, and this expectation is borne out by the figures relating to movers in 1970 tabulated by marital status in the Census of 31 December 1970. The mobility rates of widows and widowers aged 65 and over are double those of married persons of the same age, as is shown in Table 11.5. If the Belgian rates are compared with those of other countries, it is found that a similar situation exists in the Netherlands.[17] Our results which show the association between widowhood and physical or mental infirmity on one hand and higher mobility at older ages on the other have also been confirmed by Rowland for Australia.[18]

Finally, a quantitative approach of an exploratory and methodological nature could be made at local level by using the population registers of the commune of Fosses-la-Ville, a working-class village in Entre-Sambre-et-

[17] P. Drewe and H. Roosenboom, *Model Migration Schedules in the Netherlands* (Voorburg, 1983).

[18] D. T. Rowland, 'Migration during the Later Life Cycle', in *Migration in Australia* (Brisbane, (Royal Geographical Society of Australasia), 1984).

Table 11.5 Mobility rates by sex and marital status (proportions of newcomers and leavers in the *arrondissements* of Brussels and Nivelles during 1970)[a]

Age	Men		Women	
	Married	Widowed	Married	Widowed
60–4	240	276	224	310
65–9	251	341	199	246
70–4	116	314	127	248
75–9	103	334	129	235
80–4	160	323	143	262
85–9	[b]	422	[b]	325

[a] These numbers are not comparable with those in Fig. 11.2. Moreover, the effects of mortality increase with increasing age.
[b] No. of cases too small.

Meuse with about 5,000 inhabitants. The population registers are an administrative device in which all changes that occur to individuals and households in the commune are noted, so that both numbers in and structure of households can be studied.

These registers are, therefore, an extremely useful tool for the study of the dynamics of household structure and, because the data are kept on a computer, they are of great value for demographic research. By drawing a sample of one-sixth of all households in which the wife was between 40 and 80 years old on 1 January 1962, we were able to study developments in 167 households. In order to simplify the analysis and to reduce random variations arising from the small number of cases, we decided to exclude all cases of premature divorce, widowhood, and remarriage (i.e. families in which these events occurred before the wife's 45th birthday). We looked at the composition of these households on five different dates in January 1962, 1967, 1972, 1977, and 1982, and classified them as follows:

M_1: couples with unmarried children
M_0: couples without unmarried children
W_1: widows with unmarried children
W_0: widows without unmarried children
W^*_1: widowers with unmarried children
W^*_0: widowers without unmarried children

In addition we have also extracted the total number of moves and the total number of deaths which occurred during each five-year period. From these observations, which have been limited to a period of 20 years, it is possible to study changes in the life-space of families during the later stages of their lives and to include the effects of mortality. In Table 11.6 we show at five-yearly intervals what happened to couples where the wife was originally 40–5 years old. After 40 years, only three of these couples were still surviving: two without unmarried children, and one with an unmarried child. In 39 cases, the woman alone survived, and in only six cases the man. Altogether 48 family units survived.

From these figures it is possible to calculate transition probabilities which are useful for making projections. Moreover, the statistics enabled us to complete a study which we had begun in the locality previously. It is possible to calculate the average length of time spent by a family in different stages of the family life cycle, and these figures, together with the mean number of moves and the mobility rates, are shown in Table 11.7. The age-specific mobility rate is obtained by relating the total number of moves to the mean duration of time spent in each state.

Bearing in mind that the survey was limited to families with children and where there was no divorce, widowhood, or remarriage before the wife's 45th birthday, the mean lifetime of the families was 56.5 years, of which 40.1 were spent in the married state. Husbands survived their wives in 18 per cent of all cases, and the mean duration of widowerhood was 11.7 years, and of widowhood 17.2 years. In these cases the wife's mean lifetime after marriage was 57.3 years and the husband's 51.8 years. During their lifetime the family moved on average 5.5 times; the most mobile period was during the stage of family-building. The minimum level of mobility (one-tenth of that of the previous stage) occurred during the post-parental phase (M_0) when the couple had an unmarried child or children. After that stage the rate increased by one-third when the widowed partner remained with his or her married children, and by two-thirds in other cases. Altogether, one-half of all the persons who were widowed moved at least once during their period of widowhood. Twenty-one per cent moved during the year in which they were widowed, 48 per cent within five years, and 57 per cent within ten years of losing their spouse.

Summary

Information from the small number of interviews which we have carried out shows the importance of the change in geographical and social life-space which occurs during the later phases of the family life cycle. The factors responsible for these changes are the departure of children from the parental home, and later the loss of a spouse and of physical or intellectual indpendence.

Very little information is available from traditional sources about the dynamics of these changes in family relationships during the later stages of life. It is possible to obtain a theoretical figure for the number of kin available to persons of different ages by simulation methods. However, to pass from this theoretical figure to the number actually available for social relationships is difficult, because of the great variety of circumstances which can affect that number. Current population statistics are of limited value for this purpose;

Table 11.6 Distribution at five-yearly intervals of a group consisting originally of 100 couples with unmarried children, in which the wife was between 40 and 45 years old (based on observations over a period of 20 years of 167 households in Fosses-la-Ville, Belgium)

Type of Household	Wife's age								
	40–5	45–50	50–5	55–60	60–5	65–70	70–5	75–80	80–5
M_1	100	76	59	35	19	8	2	1	1
M_0	—	16	27	46	52	35	19	8	2
W_1	—	8	11	12	12	12	13	6	4
W_0	—	—	—	4	14	34	44	43	35
W_1^*	—	—	3	3	3	—	1	1	—
W_0^*	—	—	—	—	1	7	4	7	6
All households	100	100	100	100	100	96	83	66	48
Extinct households	—	—	—	—	—	4	17	34	52

Table 11.7 Average number of years spent by each family in different stages of the family life cycle[a] Fosses-la-Ville, 1982–1984

Stage of cycle	Mean length (yrs.)	Mean no. of moves	Mobility rate
Pre-parental[b]	2.3	0.86	0.375
Growing[b]	6.3	2.00	0.318
Intermediate[b]	14.1	1.14	0.081
Declining (M_1)	7.1	0.31	0.044
Post-parental (M_0)	10.3	0.34	0.033
Widowed with unmarried children	4.8	0.021	0.044
Widowed without unmarried children	11.6	0.64	0.055
TOTAL	56.5	5.50	0.097

[a] Only couples with children in which the woman neither divorced nor was widowed or remarried before her 45th birthday are included.

[b] Data from survey 3B, Duchêne and Poulain, op. cit. (n. 14).

their principal advantage lies in the completeness of coverage. Census statistics yield an instantaneous picture of the structure of households and family nuclei, but do not help with a longitudinal approach in which transition probabilities between the different stages can be calculated. Thus it is necessary to take surveys in which information about the network of relations between different individuals can be obtained, and which will characterize the individual life-spaces. Although they are a rich source of information, their value is limited for a dynamic and longitudinal approach. At older ages, recall lapse and bias introduced by mortality will affect the results of retrospective surveys when these are used to construct synthetic cohorts in order to obtain a longitudinal picture.

In the second part of this chapter we have used an exploratory approach and have tried to quantify data wherever possible. From local tabulations of information contained in population registers we have traced changes in the status of 167 households, in which the wife was between 40 and 80 years old in 1962 over a period of 20 years, at five-yearly intervals. By limiting the analysis to families with children and in which the marriage of the parents had lasted until at least the wife's 45th birthday, we were able to calculate transition probabilities and mean durations spent in different stages of the family life cycle. The value of such studies becomes apparent for household projections and particularly for the study of conditions among the old and the very old—an important subject given the high cost of social provision for people of those ages. From the interviews it was clear that mobility, which we have called 'old-age mobility', was particularly important. Aggregate data from the computerized population register for individual years of age show that mobility rates double between the 70th and 90th birthday for men and increase even more for women. Information from the Census of 1970 also makes it clear that mobility rates among the widowed are double those of married persons of the same age. This shows the importance of mobility following the loss of a spouse; nearly half of all widowed person move after the death of their spouse and thus change their life-space.

12 The Residence Patterns of the Elderly in Europe in the 1980s

RICHARD WALL

Cambridge Group for the History of Population and Social Structure

Households and Censuses

It is by no means straightforward to track developments in the composition of the European household since the end of the Second World War.[1] The authorities responsible for the censuses in different countries are less concerned with charting the evolving form of the household than with providing information required by other departments of government, local as well as central. We are therefore more likely to encounter tabulations showing the extent of migration across local authority boundaries than of movements between households; and we are likely to see more tabulations of pensioners than of the elderly. The measurement of change is additionally thwarted by the adoption on the part of the census authorities of new definitions of such basic concepts as 'household', 'household head', and 'family' in response to calls for the standardization of definitions and perceived modifications in societal norms and structure. Nevertheless, recent trends towards smaller households and more people living alone are so strong that they can be discerned in any number of tabulations of family and household produced to different definitions, with modified sub-categories and age cut-off points.[2] The greatest difficulty is caused by the formation of cohabiting or partner unions, and this has forced a number of governments to resort to sample surveys to obtain information which cannot be obtained from censuses of the whole population at all, or only at prohibitive administrative and political cost. A case in point is provided by the table which has now appeared in the *Statistical Yearbook of the Netherlands* which shows how many women of reproductive age, married or unmarried, co-reside with a male partner, and

[1] This is a revised and extended version of a paper originally presented to the IUSSP seminar in Berlin in September 1984.

[2] See e.g. the series of studies of trends in household composition in various European countries published in the journal *Population*, in particular T. Nilsson, 'Les Ménages en Suède, 1960–1980', *Population*, 1985 (2) and O. Blanc, 'Les Ménages en Suisse. Quelques aspects de leur évolution de 1960 à 1980 à travers les statistiques de recensement', *Population*, 1983 (4–5). On some of the major definitional problems, see n. 21 below, and cf. R. Wall, J. Robin, and P. Laslett (eds.), *Family Forms in Historic Europe* (Cambridge, 1983), pp. 48–9; L. Roussel, 'Les Ménages d'une personne: l'évolution récente', *Population*, 1983 (6); and H. le Bras, *Child and Family* (Paris, 1979), pp. 75–8.

in the case of the unmarried, whether they do or do no intend to marry that partner, not forgetting those who are not prepared to say, or who did not know.

Such a table may or may not be considered an adequate representation of the change in social structure, but it does at least mark a clear advance on formulations of this phase of the life cycle, which depict a swift and irreversible movement from the child in the parental household to husband or wife in an independent household. The very term 'life cycle', with its implications of universality and regularity of change, now seems anachronistic.

It is, of course, one thing to recognize that the changes to family and household patterns have rendered inappropriate the traditional conceptualization of the life cycle into distinct phases tied to marital status and parenthood, and quite another to devise a replacement that is, at the same time, both simple and all-embracing. Even cross-trabulations of individuals at a particular phase of the life cycle of the sort to which reference has already been made can become quite complex. There is a lack, too, of appropriate source material, since periodic censuses, even when they contain questions on place of residence one or five years before the census date, are ill-adapted to the study of the fluidity of movement between households. However, some progress has been made with the development of longitudinal surveys of the population,[3] and in time an improvement formulation of the individual life cycle may emerge. On the other hand, the increasing fragility of family relationships which involve co-residence poses considerable problems for the concept of a family life cycle. It would seem more sensible, as well as more feasible, simply to track adults through a series of relationships rather than to introduce such terms as 'broken family' and 'reconstituted' to describe a family, with all the necessary subdivisions that allow for the presence, absence, or permanent departure of children produced by various predecessors of the existing family.[4]

The particular phase of the life cycle with which this chapter deals is the greatly expanded section of the population aged 65 or older. It is possible to find some account of the household patterns of the elderly in the 1980s for most European countries, and although non-standard definitions and table design create difficulties, as with an overview of the household forms, the range of information provided is impressive. Unfortunately, the ingenuity that has gone into the design of sometimes very detailed tabulations has not been matched by equal attention to developments in other countries, so that appropriate comparisons are not always available for some of the more

[3] For a brief assessment of the research possibilities opening up in Britain, see M. Murphy, O. Sullivan, and A. Brown, 'Sources of Data for Modelling Household Change with Special Reference to the OPCS 1% Longitudinal Survey', paper presented to EADS/NIDI workshop on modelling household formation and dissolution, Voorburg, Netherlands, Dec. 1984.

[4] For a somewhat similar view, see Roussel, op. cit. (n. 2), p. 1012.

interesting tabulations. For example, information on the number of elderly people living alone can be assembled for 16 countries, an account of the distribution of elderly persons by marital status and type of family generational span of households for membership for only one, Ireland (see Tables 12.6 and 12.11). A further limitation of the available data is their cross-sectional nature, as exploitation of the various longitudinal surveys is still in its early stages. Where the residence patterns of the very elderly can be seen to differ from those of the 'young old', as below in Table 12.11, it is impossible to be certain what proportion of the difference is due to a cohort effect (temporal change) rather than to a life-cycle effect (ageing).

Residence Patterns of the Elderly: Lines of Enquiry

The selection of the particular aspects of the residence patterns of the elderly for detailed investigation was, therefore, governed principally by what seemed likely to become available during the course of the census round of 1980. The range of information available in the 1970s on households containing elderly persons in Britain suggested a table that showed the numbers of elderly persons living in one-family or two-family households or outside families altogether, either as solitaries or with other persons related or not related,[5] none of them, however, being members of a family,[6] as well as a simpler table showing the numbers of elderly persons in households according to the number of non-elderly persons also present. Alternatively, the major enquiries by sociologists into the residence patterns of the elderly in the 1960s suggested an approach based on frequency of co-residence with (in order of priority) spouse alone, married child, unmarried child, other relative, or non-relative.[7] In practice, however, neither proved a good guide to the range of tables provided by the various census authorities of the 1980s.[8] The ordering of residence patterns in terms of a set of predetermined priorities remains the preserve of the sociologist. The tabulations of elderly persons in households

[5] The range of sub-categories produced 52 distinct types of household for the full tabulation of the structure of English households in the Census of 1971, but these were drastically cut back in the Census of 1981.

[6] The definition of a family for this purpose is that of a married couple with or without unmarried child(ren) or lone parent with unmarried child(ren). This definition, extended to cover cohabiting couples where they can be identified, has been adopted by most European census authorities, although in Sweden and France a more restrictive definition is used under which children over the age of 25 are not considered to be family members.

[7] E. Shanas, *Old People in Three Industrial Societies* (New York and London, 1968), p. 186; see also G. Sündstrom, *Caring for the Aged in Welfare Society* (Stockholm, 1983), p. 18.

[8] I am indebted to the members of the various statistical offices for responding in such positive ways to my circular requesting information on the residence patterns of elderly persons. The present chapter is very largely based on the data they supplied, supplemented on occasion by reference to the most recent statistical yearbook of the appropriate country and a few specialist studies. A full list of the tabulations consulted is given in the appendix.

against the number of non-elderly persons was found only once outside Britain, in Cyprus, a legacy perhaps from a fading imperial past. Even in the classification of the elderly into one-family, two-family, and no-family households, Britain seems to be joined only by Ireland (see Table 12.10).

The authorities responsible for the conduct of the 1980 round of censuses, faced with a variety of options relating to the form that detailed tabulations of household structure ought to take, appear in the event to have taken a number of different directions. In all, it is possible to identify four different approaches to this problem: examination of the composition of households headed by elderly persons; examination of elderly persons in terms of the number and type of person or persons with whom they co-reside; examination of the relationship between elderly persons and the head of the household; and an examination of elderly persons on the basis of the closeness of the relationship with other people in the same household (i.e. couple, lone parent, outside a family).

The first of these options is not considered here. The partial enumeration of the elderly population results in all sorts of difficulties, through the need to determine to what extent they can be taken as representative of the residence patterns of all elderly persons.[9] The advantage from the point of view of the census authorities may simply be ease of identification, particularly if further investigations are planned into the tenure status of the household and the amenities at its disposal. At the same time, the question on whom or on how many persons the elderly reference person or household head[10] can call in the household is not without interest. The second, third, and fourth options were taken up respectively in Ireland and England (Table 12.10), Poland and Switzerland (Table 12.8), and Ireland and Finland (Table 12.9). A fifth option is to detail the generational span of households that contain elderly persons, as in West Germany in 1982. This follows a similar table in the West German Census of 1976, but appears otherwise to be unique. Indeed, identification of households with grandchildren is virtually impossible in many European censuses, because they are counted as the children of the head, if no parent is present or can be identified from among the members of the intervening generation, (this is particularly difficult when that parent is the mother of an

[9] Cf. A. Parant, 'Les Personnes âgées en France et leurs conditions d'habitat', *Population*, 1981 (3), p. 579.

[10] 'Reference person' has now replaced 'household head' as the favoured term, where one individual in the household rather than its composition needs to be identified, e.g. in an examination of the relationship between the members of the household. The term 'household head' is retained in this chapter. The important issue is not whether or not to adopt the change of nomenclature, nor even to be assured that before or after the census returns reach the census office no preference has been exercised in favour of the identification of a male rather than a female household member as the reference person in cases where a choice could be exercised. Rather, the issue is whether situations in which two or more persons share more or less equally the support of a household and the exercise of joint responsibility for its development are now so common that it has become pointless to seek to identify one person as the head or the reference person.

illegitimate child).[11] For the moment, however, it is better to leave the detailed tables on one side and concentrate on a series of more basic tables relating to the elderly in institutions, serving as household heads, or living alone.

The Elderly as Members of Institutions and as Household Heads

Space constraints unfortunately preclude an extended discussion of the 13 tables presented below, outlining the residence patterns of elderly persons during the 1980s. In Table 12.1 it is shown that the population living outside private households (i.e. in institutions of one sort or another) does not exceed 10 per cent in any European country.[12] The percentage of the elderly population in institutions is lower in southern than in western Europe, and conceivably lower still in eastern Europe and the USSR. Contrary to expectations that a communist state would intervene effectively to care for the elderly, neither the extent of institutional provision nor the quality of socio-medical services in general suggests that this has in fact occurred.[13] To some extent this may reflect the lack of resources, or a decision that any available resources should be directed towards other groups, such as the working population or children on whom the prosperity of the state, present and future, might more obviously appear to depend. It would be as well to remember, however, the long tradition, dating back to pre-industrial times, of more complex households in eastern than in western Europe and a concomitant absence of direct community support for the elderly.[14] On the other hand, within western Europe, some of the variation in the proportion of the elderly population to be found in institutions simply reflects different definitions of the institutional population. For example, the reclassification in West Germany of certain inmates of institutions according to their household of usual residence undoubtedly reduces the registered institutional population relative to that recorded for other countries, such as France, where the definition of the institutional population corresponds more closely to reality. It is also to be expected that the age structure and marital status of the elderly population would vary in different countries, and that this might have some effect on the proportion who live in institutions. In both historical and present-

[11] The Office of Population Censuses and Surveys estimate on the basis of the birth records of some of these children that approximately 50,000 households of the two-family type were misclassified for this reason in the 1981 Census of England and Wales; see OPCS, Census 1981, *Household and Family Composition* (London, 0000, pp. xi–xii.

[12] Only in Cyprus was an explicit definition of the institutional population provided. Included were persons who had been staying, or were planning to stay, in the following institutions for at least a year: old people's homes, hospitals, convents, prisons, and psychiatric clinics. The institutional population of the USSR are those resident in retirement homes. See H. Yvert-Jalu, 'Les Personnes âgées en Union Soviétique', *Population*, 1985 (6), p. 851.

[13] Ibid., p. 850.

[14] Wall, *et al.*, op. cit. (n. 2), pp. 18–34, 144–50, 526–7.

day populations, those lacking close relatives (with the unmarried at greatest risk) were and are particularly likely to find themselves in institutions. The impact, however, on the differences between the proportions of the elderly sheltering in institutions in different countries appears surprisingly slight.[15]

Table 12.1 Elderly persons not living in private households

	Date	Elderly persons outside private households (%)
Western Europe		
Belgium	1970	5
France	1982	6
Great Britain	1981	5
Ireland	1979	8
Luxemburg	1981	6
Netherlands	1971	10
Switzerland	1970	7
Federal Republic of Germany	1980	3
Scandinavia		
Denmark	1987	6
Finland	1980	7
Norway	1980	5
Sweden	1974	6
Southern Europe		
Cyprus	1982	2
Greece	1971	2
Spain	1970	2
Central and eastern Europe		
Czechoslovakia	1980	2
Poland	1978	<1
USSR	1970	1

An attempt to measure the variation in the frequency of living outside private households according to the age and sex of the individual sharply reduces the number of countries for which appropriate data are available (Table 12.2). Not surprisingly, the older the individual the greater is his or her chance of residing in an institution, the rise being steeper for women than for men. Elderly men (even those over the age of 85) are more likely to remain within the household, often cared for, no doubt, by their elderly spouse. For women, because of the different survival chances of the sexes (and differences in age at first marriage) such an option is less often available. Nevertheless, at any one time only just over one-quarter of French women aged 90 and over were not enumerated in private households in 1982.

[15] E. Grundy and T. Arie, 'Institutionalisation and the Elderly: International Comparisons', *Age and Ageing*, 13 (1984), p. 131.

Table 12.2 Elderly persons not living in private households, by age and sex (%)

Age group	Cz.	F	Fr.	GB	Ir.	L	NL	P	S	FRG
Males										
65–9	<1	2	2	2	4	2	1	<1	<1	<1
70–4	1	4	3	3	6	3	2		1	1
75–9	2		4	4	8	5				
80–4		10	7	8	11	7	14	<1	6	6
85–9	4		11	16	15	16				
⩾90			15							
Females										
65–9	1	2	2	2	5	4	1	<1	<1	1
70–4	2	4	3	3	7	5	5		1	2
75–9	3		6	6	11	9				
80–4		16	10	10	15	16	25	2	9	6
85–9	7		18	24	23	27				
⩾90			27							

Note: Cz. = Czechoslovakia; F = Finland; Fr. = France; GB = Great Britain; Ir = Ireland; L = Luxemburg; NL = Netherlands; P = Poland; S = Sweden; FRG = West Germany.

The issue of the differences in life expectancy, in marriage age, and in the chance of remarriage[16] is also raised in Table 12.3, which shows the age at which the number of widowers first exceeds that of married men and that of widows exceeds the number of married women. This very summary measure of the marital status of a population will be referred to hereafter as the age of majority widowhood. Previous research on the elderly in contemporary Europe has shown the critical importance of the elderly person's marital status in determining the number and type of co-residence,[17] and the purpose behind Table 12.3 was to discover whether differences between the relative numbers of widowed and married men and women in different European countries, might be a potential source of variations in the residence patterns of elderly people.

The principal inference to be drawn from the table is that throughout Europe it is likely that higher proportions of elderly women than of elderly men will live as solitaries (as, indeed, proves to be the case—see Table 12.6). There is also evidence of some variation in the age of majority widowhood for

[16] English data show that older men are more likely than older women to be in a second or subsequent union and that, for example, more than one-third of the married men aged 95 and over in 1981 had remarried. Nevertheless, the overall effect of remarriage on the proportion widowed was simply to postpone by a single year the point at which the number of widowers would exceed the number of married men. See R. Wall, 'Residential Isolation of the Elderly: A Comparison over Time', *Ageing and Society*, (1984), p. 485.

[17] Ibid., p. 489. See also Table 12.11 below, where the family status of elderly men and women in Ireland in 1979 is examined, distinguishing the celibate from the married and widowed.

Table 12.3 Age at which widowed persons constitute a majority of the ever married

Country	Date	Widowers	Widows
Western Europe			
Austria	1982	85	68
England and Wales	1981	86	72
France	1982	88	72
Scotland	1981	84	70
West Germany	1982	85	67
Scandinavia			
Denmark	1987	87	74
Finland	1980	85	69
Iceland	1980	87	74
Sweden	1983	87	74
Central and eastern Europe			
Czechoslovakia	1980	84	69
East Germany	1981	—	68
Hungary	1980	85	69
Poland	1978	—	68

women. In central and eastern Europe, and in West Germany, this occurs when women reach their late 60s, whereas in a number of western European countries and in much of Scandinavia the same point is reached only in the early or even the mid-70s, presumably delaying, and curtailing,[18] the period of the life cycle during which the possibility of having to reside on one's own is strong. Discussion, however, of the extent to which variations in the age of majority widowhood might account for differences between the proportions of elderly men and women living as solitaries in different countries will be reserved for later.

In Table 12.4 the focus shifts to a consideration of the headship rate—the proportions of elderly men and women heading households. Headship rates provide a measure, albeit very crude, of the extent to which the elderly retain the various responsibilities usually associated with the running of a distinct residential and consumption unit. Unfortunately, posing the questions in this way gives rise to a number of difficulties, some stemming from the inconsistencies in the definition of the household, and others from the fact that married women whose spouses are also present, together with any others whose work, however defined, might be critical for the well-being of the

[18] No curtailment would occur if widows in countries where widowhood occurred during the mid-70s survived as long as widows in countries where the age of majority widowhood occurred during the late 60s. This seems unlikely but, according to the United Nations *Demographic Yearbook*, women in Iceland and Sweden (with an age of majority widowhood of 74) might expect at age 75 to live for another 11.80 and 10.63 years respectively, whereas in those countries with an age of majority widowhood of 68 or 69, only between 11.47 and 12.80 years could be expected at age 70. UN *Demographic Yearbook 1982*, table 21.

household, are not included as household heads.[19] The latter factor should not affect interpretations of the differences between levels of the headship rate in different countries, but the significance of the conflicting definitions of the household is less clear. The lower proportions of elderly persons who are heads of households in Poland, Cyprus, and Portugal (women only in the case of Portugal) than in most west European countries are certainly in broad agreement with expectations, given greater prevalence of more complex households in eastern and southern Europe.[20] On the other hand, where the use of the 'housing' concept of the household (all persons in a dwelling are considered to form a household) is in force, as in France, Finland, and Sweden, in opposition to the 'housekeeping' concept of the household, the recorded headship rates and the proportion of elderly persons identified as solitaries in the three countries concerned may be depressed relative to the proportions in other countries.[21]

Rather fewer problems surround the interpretation of the variation in the headship rate with marital status, each country being considered separately. For men it is invariably the case that the headship rates of the married exceed those of the divorced, while those of the divorced exceed those of the widowed. The least likely to head a household are celibate men. Similarly, fewer celibate than widowed, and fewer widowed than divorced women in France, West Germany, and Cyprus head households, but the hierarchy is broken in Finland and Poland, where the headship rates of celibate women are higher relative to those of divorced and widowed women. Finally, once the married population is excluded, it is remarkable how small the differences between the headship rates of elderly men and elderly women are in a particular country.[22]

In Table 12.5 the analysis of headship rates is extended to take account of

[19] See n. 10.

[20] Wall *et al*., op. cit. (n. 2), chs. 1, 3, 17.

[21] According to the UN *Demographic Yearbook 1976*, p. 53, the housing definition of the household was in force in 1970 only in Sweden and Switzerland, but changes since the 1970s have complicated the picture. In Switzerland, the reclassification in 1980 of subtenants as independent households (Blanc, op. cit. (n. 2), p. 659) would seem to remove much of the difference between the housing and housekeeping definition of the household. Conversely in 1980 the authorities in Finland adopted the housing concept of the household, having previously favoured the housekeeping one. See Central Statistical Office of Finland, *Population and Housing Census 1980*, vol. vii, p. 44. There has also been a definitional change in the British census, with persons sharing a common living-room in 1981 being considered as forming one household, whether or not they took at least one meal together, but the impact on the measurement of household size appears to be marginal. See OPCS, Census 1981, *Definitions*, p. 3 and *General Household Survey 1982*, vol. x, p. 255. Another caveat concerns France. Le Bras (op. cit. (n. 2), p. 75) claims, *pace* the UN *Demographic Yearbook 1976*, p. 53, that the definition of the household used in the French census is not in conformity with the housekeeping concept recommended by the UN, and its wording seems rather to imply approximation to the housing concept.

[22] The difference is greatest in Cyprus but even there never exceeds 10%. There is a suggestion for England that, as recently as 1951, headship rates for men and women, particularly for the celibate, differed more markedly than is now the case. Wall (op. cit. (n. 16), p. 493), citing percentages for celibate men and women aged 60 and over in 1951 of 39% and 47%, and 73% and 76% for men and women respectively aged 65 and over in 1976.

Table 12.4 Headship rates

	Date	Married	Single	Widowed	Divorced	All
Elderly men heading households (%)						
Western Europe						
England and Wales	1981	—	—	—	—	92
France	1975	95	72	75	76	90
Ireland	1979	—	—	—	—	83
Netherlands	1981	96	54	74		88
West Germany	1982	97	77	82	85	95
Scandinavia						
Finland	1980[a]	70	62	64	68	
Southern Europe						
Cyprus	1982	92	53	61	65	85[b]
Portugal	1981	—	—	—	—	86
Central and eastern Europe						
Poland	1978	85	56	63	80	
Elderly women heading households (%)						
Western Europe						
England and Wales	1981	—	—	—	—	53
France	1975	3	70	74	78	47
Ireland	1979	—	—	—	—	47
Netherlands	1981	1	58	76	45	
West Germany	1982	2	78	86	92	59
Scandinavia						
Finland	1980[a]	3	63	60	44	
Southern Europe	1982	2	46	53	62	28[b]
Cyprus						
Portugal	1981	—	—	—	—	34
Central and eastern Europe						
Poland	1978	7	55	54	39	

[a] Subtenants not considered as forming separate households.
[b] Separated persons not separately shown but included in totals.

the variation that occurs after an individual has reached the age of 65. The bottom panel of the table shows a general rise with age in the proportion of women heading households, continued into the age group 75 and over in Germany and Cyprus. Men's headship rates, on the other hand, fall with age. The explanation lies in the increasing probability of widowhood and accompanying registration as a household head as women age, whereas the new widowers will already have been recorded as heads. Generally speaking, once marital status is controlled, headship rates fall with age, as the top half of the table shows. Both in Cyprus and in West Germany the decline with age is steeper in the case of the widowed than for the celibate. This might imply that the former are more likely than the latter to retire from the headship of the household, although, as the data represent a cross-section of age groups rather than of cohorts, an alternative explanation alleging a change in the residence patterns of recent cohorts of widowed cannot be excluded. In either case, it is interesting to note that headship rates of the widowed remain above those of the celibate even after the age of 75.

Table 12.5 Elderly persons heading households by age, sex, and marital status (per cent)

Marital status	Cyprus 1982			Ireland 1979			West Germany 1982		
	(Age group) 65–9	70–4	75+	65–9	70–4	75+	65–9	70–4	75+
Males									
Single	60	59	42	—	—	—	81	76	74
Married[a]	94	92	88	—	—	—	98	97	95
Widowed	73	65	57	—	—	—	90	87	78
Divorced	73	79	57	—	—	—	90	86	79
Separated[a]	86	76	71	—	—	—	—	—	—
All	92	88	78	87	84	77	97	95	90
Females									
Single	51	45	41	—	—	—	78	81	77
Married[a]	2	1	2	—	—	—	2	2	3
Widowed	63	59	45	—	—	—	91	89	81
Divorced	64	64	61	—	—	—	94	91	90
Separated[a]	67	55	61	—	—	—	—	—	—
All	23	28	32	18	24	23	50	58	66

[a] Separated included with married in the case of West Germany.

Elderly Persons and their Co-residents

In the remaining tables the focus changes from an examination of the numbers of the elderly living in or heading households to an evaluation of the nature of the households containing elderly people, beginning with the proportion of elderly persons now living on their own (Table 12.6). In some countries more than 40 per cent of women aged 65 and over are now in this position. Such high proportions of solitaries create a dilemma for those authorities which provide some formal care for the elderly who remain in their homes, as those in need cannot always be easily identified amongst the mass of elderly solitaries. By contrast, in Poland little more than one-quarter of elderly women live on their own, while even lower proportions were recorded in Portugal and Ireland.[23] There can be little surprise, however, given that elderly men are so much more likely than elderly women still to be married, that fewer elderly men than elderly women will be living on their own.[24] As was the case with elderly women, there is variation from country to country in the proportions residing as solitaries, with two of the three countries in which the lowest proportion of female solitaries was recorded also registering the lowest proportions of male solitaries. The exception is Ireland, where the proportions of men living on their own is little lower than the levels reached elsewhere in western Europe, in sharp contrast to the situation of elderly women. Conversely, the high solitary rate among elderly women in West Germany is not paralleled by a similarly high rate among elderly men. Both these features of the social structure require further investigation, although from Table 12.3 it is clear that, in the context of western Europe, in West Germany the number of widows first exceeds that of married women at a relatively early age. It is also in West Germany that the difference between the age at which widows outnumber married women and widowers outnumber married men is largest (18 years).

More generally, however, there would appear to be no consistent relationship between the age of majority widowhood and the proportion of the elderly population who reside as solitaries. This is interesting, as within a particular country marital status is clearly critical in determining the frequency with which persons head households and the type of household in which they reside.[25] Comparison of Tables 12.3 and 12.6 reveals, however, that in Sweden the age of majority widowhood is high and there is also a high proportion of solitaries. West Germany, on the other hand, shares the high proportion of elderly female solitaries but the age of majority widowhood is low. Admittedly, the distribution of the population by marital status is only very imperfectly captured by so crude a measure as the age of majority widowhood. The impact of marital status on differences between the living arrangements of the elderly in different countries might, therefore, be somewhat greater than appears here. An objection to this argument, however, is the fact that when a correction factor for the different age and marital-status distributions of the various countries is applied, this explains little of the variation in the proportions of the elderly populations residing in institutions.[26]

[23] Yvert-Jalu (op. cit. (n. 12), p. 848) reports that the proportion of solitaries amongst the elderly in the USSR has increased to 25% by 1980. Compared with other countries the relative proportion of solitaries in West Germany is undoubtedly overstated, because of double counting of persons who occupy more than one house and the reclassification of many residents in institutions to their households of normal residence.

[24] See Table 12.3, and Wall, op. cit. (n. 16), pp. 485–6.

[25] Table 12.4 details headship rates. Table 12.11 demonstrates for Ireland the impact of marital status on the proportion of elderly persons who are not members of a family; and see Wall, op. cit. (n. 16), p. 489.

[26] Grundy and Arie op. cit. (n. 15), p. 131.

Table 12.6 Elderly persons living alone (per cent)

	Date	Males	Females	Both
Western Europe				
Belgium	1981	17	32	26
France	1983	16	43	32
Great Britain	1983	20	45	35
Ireland	1979	14	22	18
Netherlands	1971			20
Switzerland	1980	14	39	29
Federal Republic of Germany	1982	16	53	39
Scandinavia				
Denmark	1987	—	—	39
Finland	1976	—	—	30
Norway	1980	—	—	32
Sweden[a]	1975	26	55	41
Southern Europe				
Cyprus[b]	1982	—	—	25
Portugal	1981	10	23	18
Central and eastern Europe				
Hungary	1980	—	—	20
Poland	1978	10	28	21
USSR[b]: urban	1970	5	20	—
rural	1970	5	24	—

[a] Includes inmates of institutions.
[b] % of population aged ⩾60.

Variation in the frequency of residence as a solitary, once an individual has passed the age of 65, is measured in Table 12.7. In Great Britain the rates for both men and women rise much more steeply than in either Ireland or Poland, or even in France. In Poland and Ireland, the rates stabilize or even fall back slightly after the age of 75, indicating that in these two countries there are other alternatives than that of becoming a solitary householder to cope with the increasing likelihood of widowhood in extreme old age.[27]

The nature of these alternatives can be explored through a more detailed analysis of the composition of households that contain elderly persons (Tables 12.8–12.11).[28] Table 12.8 sets out the relationships between elderly persons and the head of the household in Poland and in Switzerland. In Poland, where more than 20 per cent of elderly persons (10 per cent of men and nearly 30 per cent of women) were enumerated in 1978 as parents of the head of the household, the extended family still features prominently in the lives of the

[27] Even for England, survey data indicate that the trend in the proportions of the very elderly (aged 75 and over) living on their own falls considerably short of the rise in the proportion of the elderly lacking a spouse. See Wall, op. cit. (n. 16), p. 486.

[28] The logic underlying these tabulations has already been outlined in the section of this chapter entitled 'Residence Patterns of the Elderly', and no further comment is necessary here.

Table 12.7 Elderly persons living alone, by age and sex (per cent)

Age	Males						Females					
	(1)	(2)	(3)	(4)	(5)	(6)	(1)	(2)	(3)	(4)	(5)	(6)
65–9	12	13	13	11	9	8	32	18	37	31	30	26
70–4	19	15	17	14	12	12	42	24	46	39	40	30
75–9	25			18			53			48		
80–4	33	15	24	23	21	10	60	23	51	53	40	28
85+				29						51		

Note: (1) Great Britain 1983; (2) Ireland 1979; (3) Finland 1980; (4) France 1982; (5) Netherlands 1981; (6) Poland 1978.

elderly. In Switzerland, it is virtually non-existent as a residential group, and conversely a large number of elderly persons head their own households, more than half of these as solitaries (cf. Table 12.6).

For a breakdown of relationships of elderly persons which takes account of their ages it is necessary to turn to a different pair of countries (Finland and Ireland), and a different tabulation which measures the closeness of the relationship of the elderly person with other persons residing in the household (Table 12.9). In both countries the proportion of persons not residing in families rises steeply with age, while the proportion of couples falls. Here the influence of the changing balance during the course of old age in the numbers of married and widowed is clear. The different probabilities of being widowed for men and women are likewise reflected in the fact that fewer elderly women were married than elderly men. Of much greater interest are the differences between the two countries: the greater prominence of lone parents, particularly among the very old in Ireland, the higher proportions of elderly men in Ireland who were not members of families, and, conversely, the lower proportions of married men. Proportions of women who were not members of families in Ireland are, on the other hand, slightly lower than those in Finland. In order to account for these differences it would be necessary to investigate in some depth such factors as past rates of out-migration, and nuptiality levels of the non-migrating population in both countries, an operation that clearly falls well outside the scope of the present enquiry. Nevertheless, the fact that in Ireland many of the men who were not members of families were single[29] certainly suggests a link with the low level of men's nuptiality in the Irish past.

In the English Census of 1981 the residence patterns of the elderly were investigated on the basis of the family structure of the household in which the elderly person resided rather than on the basis of family status. These data are

[29] For example, just over three-quarters of all men aged 65–9 who were not members of families had never married. Their share in the older age groups was naturally somewhat smaller, but they still constituted more than half of non-family members aged 75–9.

Table 12.8 Elderly persons: relationship to head of household (per cent)

Relationship to household head	Poland 1978			Switzerland, 1982
	Males	Females	Both sexes	Both sexes
Heads				
solitary	10	28	21	68 (solitary and other combined)
other	71	11	34	
Spouse	5	27	18	23
Parents[a]	12	28	22	5
Other relatives[a]	2 (other relatives and inmates combined)	5 (other relatives and inmates combined)	4 (other relatives and inmates combined)	2
Inmates				1
ALL	100	100	100	100

[a] Parents-in-law included with parents for Poland; with other relatives for Switzerland.

Table 12.9 Family status of elderly persons

Age	Finland 1980 (%)				Ireland 1979 (%)			
	Not in family	Couple	Lone parent	All	Not in family	Couple	Lone parent	All
Males								
65–9	19	78	2	100	32	64	4	100
70–4	24	73	2	100	37	58	5	100
75–9	36 (ages 75–9 to 85+ combined)	59	4	100	42	52	6	100
80–4					45	45	10	100
85+					51	35	14	100
Females								
65–9	50	42	8	100	45	42	13	100
70–4	62	31	7	100	57	29	14	100
75–9	76 (ages 75–9 to 85+ combined)	15	8	100	65	19	17	100
80–4					66	11	22	100
85+					68	6	26	100

presented in Table 12.10 and show that more than three-quarters of the elderly were solitaries, or lived in households where there were no unmarried children. Fortunately, an extended version of the same tabulation was also included in the Census of Ireland in 1979. Compared with the situation in England and Wales, there is a much greater incidence both of elderly persons living in no-family households consisting of two or more persons, and of elderly persons living in households containing children. Five per cent of the Irish elderly live in two-family households compared with 1 per cent of the English and Welsh elderly.

Table 12.10(*a*) Elderly persons and their co-residents by household type (per cent)

Household type	England and Wales 1981			Ireland 1979
	M[a]	F[a]	Both	Both
No family				
Solitary	17	37	30	18
Other no family	5	7	7	14
One-family				
Couple alone	63	40	48	19
Couple + others				5
Couple + child	11	8	9	14
Couple + child + others				12
Lone parent + child	3	6	5	9
Lone parent + child + others				3
Two-family	1	1	1	5
≥ Three-family				0
ALL	100	100	100	100

Table 12.10(*b*) Marital status of elderly persons and their co-residents (per cent)

Household type	England and Wales 1981					
	Single		Married		Widowed	
	M[a]	F[a]	M[a]	F[a]	M[a]	F[a]
No family						
Solitary	54	59	1	2	67	70
Other no family	32	32	1	1	9	8
One-family						
Couple	6	3	83	83	4	3
Couple + child	3	2	13	12	7	5
Lone parent + child	4	4	0	1	12	13
Two-family	0	0	2	2	0	0
ALL	100	100	100	100	100	100

[a] These figures are for males aged 65 and over and females aged 60 and over.

For Ireland, it is also possible to measure the frequency of residence in a no-family or family household during the course of old age, and this information is presented in Table 12.11. A composite picture of the residence patterns of the Irish elderly now emerges. The low and relatively constant proportions of solitaries during the later states of the the life cycle in Ireland that were noted earlier (Table 12.7), despite the fact that low proportions of the elderly were married, can be accounted for by the frequency with which elderly persons, particularly the celibate, lived with others who were not members of families, and by the frequency with which older celibates, together with the older widowed, were accepted into family households.[30] It is noticeable, too, that once marital status and age are controlled, there is little difference between the family status of elderly men and women, as indeed proved to be the case with the headship rate (cf. Table 12.5 and Table 12.10(*b*)).

Conclusion

Accounts of the changes in the composition of European households over recent decades indicate that the movement towards smaller and less complex households, and with many people living as solitaries, is strong throughout western Europe,[31] and is visible, if less marked, in eastern and southern Europe. The focus of the present survey of the living arrangements of the elderly in the 1980s has been rather on the diversity of these arrangements in different European countries, a diversity that would undoubtedly seem all the greater if it were possible to disaggregate the patterns by region and social class.[32] Some important issues, however, remain unresolved. First, there is the question whether the differences *between countries* in the proportion of the elderly living alone or sharing with others, married or unmarried, should be considered large or small. Secondly, it needs to be established whether these differences can be identified far back in Europe's past, and have lessened in recent times. This historical perspective is unfortunately not yet available in a suitably detailed form, but it does at least suffice to show that there is both a long-standing association of complex households with eastern and southern Europe and nuclear households with north-western Europe, and no sign as yet of a convergence of European countries round a high level of one-person households.[33] The comparative perspective would indicate, therefore, that the variation across present-day Europe in the overall shape of the household is indeed significant, if not as significant or as large as that prevailing in pre-industrial times; and given the share elderly householders now contribute to

[30] Table 12.11 differs from Table 12.9 in that, for the purpose of the latter table on the *family status* of elderly persons, members of family households, not being themselves couples or lone parents, have been included in the category 'no family'. However, when these persons were members of a household that included a family, they have in Table 12.11 been counted as belonging to a family household.

[31] See e.g. Roussel, (op. cit. (n. 2), pp. 995–1013). A general survey of the changes in the European household since 1945 is provided in Wall, 'The Development of the European Household since World War II', paper presented to the EADS/NIDI workshop on modelling household formation and dissolution, Voorburg, Netherlands, Dec. 1986.

[32] Wall, 'Regional and Temporal Variations in the Structure of the British Household since 1851', in T. Barker and M. Drake (eds.), *Population and Society in England 1850–1980* (New York and London, 1982), pp. 92–7, sets out for Great Britain variation by region in the kin composition of the household and at national level the variation by social class and socio-economic group.

[33] On the historical perspectives, see Wall *et al.*, op. cit. (n. 2), chs. 1, 3. Trends in one-person households since the Second World War are surveyed by Roussel, op cit. (n. 2) and Wall, 'The Development of the European Household' (unpublished).

Table 12.11 Membership of no family and households, Ireland, 1979 (per cent)

(*a*) Single persons

Age group	Not in family households				Members of family households				All	
	Solitary		Other		Children		Others			
	M	F	M	F	M	F	M	F	M	F
65–9	37	30	47	56	1	1	15	13	100	100
70–4	37	33	46	54	0	0	17	14	100	100
75–9	37	34	44	50	0	0	19	16	100	100
80–4	33	36	43	46	0	0	24	18	100	100
85+	30	28	38	44	0	0	32	28	100	100

(*b*) Married persons

Age group	Not in family households				Members of family households						All	
	Solitary		Others		Couples		Lone parents		Others			
	M	F	M	F	M	F	M	F	M	F	M	F
65–9	1	2	1	1	97	94	1	2	0	1	100	100
70–4	2	2	1	1	96	93	1	2	1	2	100	100
75–9	2	3	1	2	95	89	1	3	1	4	100	100
80–4	1	3	1	2	94	84	2	5	2	5	100	100
85+	1	3	1	4	92	75	3	9	3	10	100	100

(*c*) Widowed persons

Age group	Not in family households				Members of family households				All	
	Solitary		Other		Lone parents		Others			
	M	F	M	F	M	F	M	F	M	F
65–9	33	33	7	10	38	35	22	21	100	100
70–4	34	35	8	11	29	28	28	26	100	100
75–9	31	30	9	10	26	28	34	31	100	100
80–4	24	23	7	10	28	31	40	36	100	100
85+	16	15	8	10	29	35	47	40	100	100

the numbers living alone, the same presumably holds specifically in regard to the living arrangements of the elderly. In addition, it could be argued that the fact that the Europe-wide differences in living arrangements have survived the strong impetus towards smaller households is itself evidence enough that such differences have to be taken seriously. Interpretation of these patterns is considerably more hazardous, as there is no information in the census on the reasons why people move into particular types of household and avoid others. Scholars who have monitored the recent changes in household forms have attempted to distinguish, not always very convincingly, changes resulting from economic, cultural, and demographic factors.[34] This might be caricatured as the attempt to measure whether there are more people able to live alone, more people wanting to live alone, or simply more people of an age where they will live alone. Clearly, there has been a change both in the willingness and in the ability of people to establish particular households, and the difficulty has been to decide which type of factor ought to be considered dominant.

The same problem arises in trying to 'explain' variations in the living arrangements of the elderly. The impact of the state is most obvious in the amount of accommodation made available to elderly people in institutions, but the state's action (or inaction) is largely determined by value judgements as to what is 'appropriate' in particular circumstances, and by the extent of its susceptibility to pressure from interested parties.[35] Table 12.1 would suggest that, viewed in relation to most other western European and Scandinavian countries, the institutionalized elderly population in Britain is relatively small. Such comparisons are bedevilled by the existence of inconsistencies in the definition of the institutional population. On the other hand, there would appear to be no peculiarity in the structure by age or marital status of the elderly population of Britain which would lead one to expect fewer institutionalized elderly.[36] Nor does it seem likely that demographic factors could account for the varying proportions of elderly people living on their own in different European countries, and this despite the clear association between an individual's age and marital status and the likelihood of solitary living.

Assessment of the impact of cultural and economic factors is considerably more difficult because much vital information is either not readily accessible or simply not available. In particular, it would be useful to be able to offer a comparative perspective on the public services available to the frail elderly who wish to maintain their own homes and on the range of housing schemes open to them, short of institutionalization, when a completely independent existence become difficult. A comparative survey of attitudes towards the care of the elderly would also be valuable in order to see, for example, whether there is any variation by country in the strength of the desire to maintain

[34] See the contrasting interpretations offered for the rise in the proportion of solitaries by K. Schwarz and F. C. Pampel. See K. Schwarz, 'Die Alleinlebenden', *Zeitschrift für Bevölkungswissenschaft*, 2 (1983) and F. C. Pampel, 'Changes in the Propensity to Live Alone: Evidence from Consecutive Cross-sectional Surveys (1960–1976)', *Demography*, 20(4) (1983).

[35] This argument has developed from Paul Johnson's account of the malaise of the Welfare State, 'Some Historical Dimensions of the Welfare State "Crisis"', *Journal of Social Policy* (1986).

[36] Grundy and Arie, op. cit. (n. 15), p. 131.

independence in old age, which might in turn be reflected in varying proportions of the elderly living alone.

It is traditional to end with a call for further research. In the present case the need is clear, but it is hoped that more has been achieved here than a redefinition of research objectives and an illustration of a variety of approaches to the analysis of household composition. Some of the recent attempts to conceptualize the new forms of the domestic group have come close to implying that Western society is rapidly fragmenting towards its basic unit, the individual. There remains, however, a considerable diversity in living arrangements across Europe, a diversity that has survived the tumultuous changes in family forms in recent years and that may, indeed, be enduring.

Appendix

A full list appears below of the sources consulted in connection with Tables 12.1–12.11. Some census authorities were prepared to fill in a table to my specification. Others forwarded published or previously prepared tabulations (as numbered in the list). In some cases, however, further computation was necessary to produce the figures in the tables, which should not be regarded as having any 'official' weight.

Austria

Statistisches Handbuch für die Republik Österreich 1983, p. 24 and Table 2.10.

Belgium

E. Grundy and T. Arie, 'Institutionalisation and the Elderly: International Comparisons', *Age and Ageing*, 13 (1984), p. 131 (population not in private households).
Annuaire Statistique de la Belgique 1984, p. 104, Table 11 (elderly persons living alone).

Cyprus

Unpublished tables received from Department of Statistics and Research, Nicosia, on the Greek-Cypriot population.

Czechoslovakia

Unpublished tables received from the International Statistics Division of the Federální Statistický Úřad, Prague, and cf. *Statistická ročenka Československé Socialistické Republiky 1982*, p. 96.

Denmark

Computation from official statistics by G. Sündstrom (population not in private households, and elderly persons living alone). Personal computation from *Danmarks Statistik* (age of majority widowhood).

Finland

Central Statistical Office of Finland, *Population and Housing Census 1980*, Vol. vii, table 1 (population not in private housholds family status of elderly persons).
Central Statistical Office of Finland, *Population 1981*, Vol. i, Table 5 (age of majority widowhood).
Unpublished table received from Central Statistical Office of Finland (headship rates).
Central Statistical Office of Finland, *Population and Housing Census 1980*, Vol vii, Tables 1 and 5 (elderly persons living alone).

France

Institut National de la Statistique et des Études Économiques, *Recensement général de la population* 1982*: Ménages–familles*, Tables P01, P03, supplemented by unpublished Table T1) received from Institut National de la Statistique et des Études Économiques (population in non-private households).
Annuaire Statistique de la France 1984, p. 46 (age of majority widowhood).
A. Parant, 'Les Personnes âgées en France et leurs conditions d'habitat', *Population*, 1981 (3) p. 581 (headship rates).
Institut National de la Statistique et des Études Économiques, *Recensement général de la population: Ménages–familles*, Table P13 (elderly persons living alone).

Germany, East

Statistisches Jahrbuch der Deutschen Demokratischen Republik 1983, p. 347.

Germany, West

Tables unnumbered, B14, 3a–b, l. 33, received from Statistisches Bundesamt, Wiesbaden (population not in private households, age of majority widowhood, headship rates, elderly persons living alone, generational span).

Great Britain

Office of Population Censuses and Surveys (hereafter OPCS), Census 1981, *Communal Establishments*, table 2 (population not in private households).
OPCS, Census 1981, *Persons of Pensionable Age*, Tables 1, 2 (age of majority widowhood), and Table 6 (elderly and non-elderly persons in household).
OPCS, Census 1981, *Household and Family Composition*, Table 7 (headship rates) and Table 9 (elderly persons and their co-residents by household type).
OPCS, *General Household Survey 1983*, table 3A (elderly persons living alone).

Greece

Statistical Yearbook 1982, Table 24.

Hungary

Table 2.6 (age of majority widowhood) and Table 1.4 (elderly persons living alone) received from Central Statistical Office, Budapest.

Iceland

Unpublished table received from Statistical Bureau of Iceland, Reykjavik.

Ireland

Central Statistics Office, Census of Population of Ireland 1979, Vol. iii, *Household Compositions and Family Units*, Pt. 3, Table 1 (population in non-private households, family status of elderly persons, membership of no family and family households), Pt. 2, Table 11 (headship rates, elderly persons living alone), Table 14 (elderly persons and their co-residents by household type).

Luxemburg

Annuaire Statistique 1983–4, pp. 27, 77.

Netherlands

Personal communication from J. T. M. van Laanen, citing Netherlands Central Bureau of Statistics, *Woningbehoeftenonderzoek 1981* (population not in private households, headship rates, elderly persons living alone).

Norway

G. Sündstrom, *Caring for the Aged in Welfare Society* (Stockholm, 1983), p. 28 (population in non-private households).

G. Sündstrom, '100 Years of Co-residence between the generations', unpublished paper in Library of Cambridge Group for the History of Population and Social Structure, Table 6, and personal communication (elderly persons living alone).

1980 census data computed from data in Daatland 1986 by G. Sündstrom.

Poland

Unpublished tables received from Central Statistical Office, Warsaw.

Portugal

Tables 4.03 (headship rate) and 4.01 (elderly living alone) received from National Statistical Institute, Lisbon. Total population aged 65 and over as in *Anuário Estatistico 1982*, pp. 16–17.

Spain

E. Grundy and T. Arie, 'Institutionalisation and the Elderly: International Comparisons', *Age and Ageing*, 13 (1984), p. 131.

Sweden

Sveriges officiella Statistik, *Folk- och bostadsräkningen 1980*, Vol. v, Table 1 (population in institutional households).

Statistical Abstract of Sweden 1984, Table 26 (age of majority widowhood).

Nilsson, 'Les Ménages en Suède, 1960–1980', *Population*, 1985 (2), p. 235 (elderly persons living alone).

Switzerland

E. Grundy and T. Arie, 'Institutionalisation and the Elderly: International Comparisons', *Age and Ageing*, 13 (1984), p. 131 (population in non-private households).

O. Blanc, 'Les Ménages en Suisse', *Population*, 1985 (4–5), p. 664 (elderly persons living alone). Total population aged 65 and over as in *Statistisches Jahrbuch der Schweiz 1984*, p. 20.

Statistisches Jahrbuch der Schweiz 1983 (relationship to household head).

USSR

H. Yvert-Jalu, 'Les Personnes âgées en Union Soviétique', *Population*, 1985 (6), pp. 848, 851 (elderly living alone, in retirement homes).

Index